# Automated Machine Learning with Microsoft Azure

Build highly accurate and scalable end-to-end AI solutions with Azure AutoML

**Dennis Michael Sawyers**

BIRMINGHAM—MUMBAI

# Automated Machine Learning with Microsoft Azure

**Group Product Manager**: Kunal Parikh

**Publishing Product Manager**: Ali Abidi

**Senior Editor**: David Sugarman

**Content Development Editor**: Tazeen Shaikh

**Technical Editor**: Sonam Pandey

**Copy Editor**: Safis Editing

**Project Coordinator**: Aparna Ravikumar Nair

**Proofreader**: Safis Editing

**Indexer**: Manju Arasan

**Production Designer**: Vijay Kamble

First published: April 2021

Production reference: 1260321

Published by Packt Publishing Ltd.

Livery Place

35 Livery Street

Birmingham

B3 2PB, UK.

ISBN 978-1-80056-531-9

www.packt.com

*To my wife, Kyoko Sawyers, who has always been by my side and supported me through many long evenings, and to my daughter, Sophia Rose, who was born halfway through the writing of this book.*

*– Dennis Sawyers*

# Contributors

## About the author

**Dennis Michael Sawyers** is a senior **cloud solutions architect (CSA)** at Microsoft, specializing in data and AI. In his role as a CSA, he helps Fortune 500 companies leverage Microsoft Azure cloud technology to build top-class machine learning and AI solutions. Prior to his role at Microsoft, he was a data scientist at Ford Motor Company in **Global Data Insight and Analytics (GDIA)** and a researcher in anomaly detection at the highly regarded Carnegie Mellon Auton Lab. He received a master's degree in data analytics from Carnegie Mellon's Heinz College and a bachelor's degree from the University of Michigan. More than anything, Dennis is passionate about democratizing AI solutions through automated machine learning technology.

*I want to thank the people who have been close to me and supported me, especially my wife, Kyoko, for encouraging me to finish this book, Rick Durham and Sam Istephan, for teaching me Azure Machine Learning, and Sabina Cartacio, Aniththa Umamahesan, and Deepti Mokkapati from the Microsoft Azure product team for helping me learn the ins and outs of AutoML.*

# About the reviewer

**Marek Chmel** is a senior CSA at Microsoft, specializing in data and AI. He is a speaker and trainer with more than 15 years' experience. He has been a Data Platform MVP since 2012. He has earned numerous certifications, including Azure Architect, Data Engineer and Scientist Associate, Certified Ethical Hacker, and several eLearnSecurity certifications. Marek earned his master's degree in business and informatics from Nottingham Trent University. He started his career as a trainer for Microsoft Server courses and later worked as SharePoint team lead and principal database administrator. He has authored two books, *Hands-On Data Science with SQL Server 2017* and *SQL Server 2017 Administrator's Guide*.

# Table of Contents

# 3
## Training Your First AutoML Model

# Section 2:
# AutoML for Regression, Classification, and Forecasting – A Step-by-Step Guide

# 4
## Building an AutoML Regression Solution

# 5
## Building an AutoML Classification Solution

# 6
## Building an AutoML Forecasting Solution

# 7
## Using the Many Models Solution Accelerator

# Section 3:
# AutoML in Production – Automating Real-Time and Batch Scoring Solutions

# 8
## Choosing Real-Time versus Batch Scoring

# 9
## Implementing a Batch Scoring Solution

# 10
# Creating End-to-End AutoML Solutions

# 11
# Implementing a Real-Time Scoring Solution

# 12
# Realizing Business Value with AutoML

# Other Books You May Enjoy

# Index

# Preface

*Automated Machine Learning with Microsoft Azure* will help you build high-performing, accurate machine learning models in record time. It allows anyone to easily harness the power of artificial intelligence and increase the productivity and profitability of their business. With a series of clicks on a **graphical user interface** (**GUI**), novices and seasoned data scientists alike can easily train and deploy machine learning solutions to production.

This book will teach you how to use Azure AutoML with both the GUI and the Azure Machine Learning Python SDK in a careful, step-by-step fashion. First, you'll learn how to prepare data, train models, and register them to your Azure Machine Learning workspace. Then, you'll learn how to take those models and use them to create both automated batch solutions using machine learning pipelines and real-time scoring solutions using **Azure Kubernetes Service** (**AKS**).

By the time you finish *Automated Machine Learning with Microsoft Azure*, you will be able to use AutoML on your own data to not only train regression, classification, and forecasting models but also use them to solve a wide variety of business problems. You'll be able to show your business partners exactly how your machine learning models make predictions through automatically generated charts and graphs, earning their trust and respect.

## Who this book is for

Data scientists, aspiring data scientists, machine learning engineers, and anyone interested in applying artificial intelligence or machine learning in their business will find this book useful. You need to have beginner-level knowledge of artificial intelligence and a technical background in computer science, statistics, or information technology before getting started with this machine learning book. Having a background in Python will help you implement this book's more advanced features, but even data analysts and SQL experts will be able to train machine learning models after finishing this book.

# What this book covers

*Chapter 1, Introducing AutoML,* begins by explaining the current state of data science and artificial intelligence in industry and why so many companies are having such a hard time extracting value from data. It explains how data scientists work, why their processes are inherently slow, and why they need to be made quicker. Finally, it introduces AutoML as the solution to achieve the return on investment required by industry.

*Chapter 2, Getting Started with Azure Machine Learning Service,* goes into depth in explaining the different artifacts of Azure Machine Learning and how they integrate to form end-to-end machine learning solutions. You'll learn about datastores, datasets, compute instances, compute clusters, environments, and experiments, and how you use them to create machine learning solutions on Azure.

*Chapter 3, Training Your First AutoML Model,* will have you create your first AutoML model using publicly available Titanic data. You will use the Azure Machine Learning Studio GUI to upload your data into your workspace, create a dataset, and run an AutoML classification job to predict Titanic survivors. Lastly, you'll use AutoML's explainability features to see which factors were most vital to predicting survival.

*Chapter 4, Building an AutoML Regression Solution,* will help you train an AutoML regression model using the Azure Machine Learning SDK in Python. You'll learn how to access Jupyter notebooks within Azure Machine Learning, use compute clusters for remote training on the cloud, and create an AutoML model that predicts a number. By the end of this chapter, you will be able to replicate this work for any regression problem you have in the future.

*Chapter 5, Building an AutoML Classification Solution,* will help you train an AutoML classification model using the Azure Machine Learning SDK in Python in two ways. First, you'll train a binary classification model to predict one of two categories. Then, you will train a multiclass classification model to predict one of three categories. By the end of this chapter, you'll be an expert in training all types of classification models with AutoML.

*Chapter 6, Building an AutoML Forecasting Solution,* looks at forecasting, one of the most common machine learning problems and one of the hardest to master. In this chapter, you'll learn how to code a forecasting solution with AutoML, making use of advanced forecasting-specific algorithms and features. You'll learn the ins and outs of forecasting and be able to avoid many of the common mistakes people make while forecasting.

*Chapter 7, Using the Many Models Solution Accelerator,* expands on how the **Many Models Solution Accelerator** (**MMSA**) is a cutting-edge Azure technology that lets companies train hundreds of thousands of models quickly and easily. Here, you will learn how to access the MMSA and adapt it to your own problems. This is a powerful code-only solution aimed at seasoned data scientists, but even novices will be able to use it by the end of this chapter.

*Chapter 8, Choosing Real-Time versus Batch Scoring,* explores how real-time solutions and batch solutions represent the two ways to score machine learning models. This chapter delves into common business scenarios and explains how you should choose which type of solution to create. The end of this chapter features a quiz that will test your ability to match business problems to the correct type of solution, saving you time and money.

*Chapter 9, Implementing a Batch Scoring Solution,* emphasizes how machine learning pipelines are Azure Machine Learning's batch scoring solution of choice. Machine learning pipelines are containerized code where, once you create them, you can easily rerun and schedule them on an automated basis. This chapter has you use the AutoML models you created in earlier chapters to create powerful batch scoring solutions that run on a schedule of your choice.

*Chapter 10, Creating End-to-End AutoML Solutions,* emphasizes how **Azure Data Factory** (**ADF**) is a code-free data orchestration tool that integrates easily with machine learning pipelines. In this chapter, you'll learn how to seamlessly move data into and out of Azure, and how to integrate that flow with your scoring pipelines. By the end of this chapter, you will understand how ADF and AMLS combine to create the ultimate data science experience.

*Chapter 11, Implementing a Real-Time Scoring Solution,* teaches you how to create real-time scoring endpoints hosted on AKS and **Azure Container Instances** (**ACI**). You'll learn how to deploy AutoML models to an endpoint with a single click from the Azure Machine Learning Studio GUI as well as through Python code in a Jupyter notebook, completing your AutoML training.

*Chapter 12, Realizing Business Value with AutoML,* focuses on how creating an end-to-end solution is just the first step in realizing business value; you'll also need to gain end user trust. This chapter focuses on how to gain this trust through architectural diagrams, model interpretability, and presenting results in an intuitive, easy-to-understand manner. You'll learn how to become and be seen as a trusted, reliable partner to your business.

# To get the most out of this book

You will need to have the following requirements:

| Software/hardware covered in the book | Operating system requirements |
|---|---|
| Microsoft Edge or Google Chrome | Windows, macOS, or Linux |

In order to use *Automated Machine Learning with Microsoft Azure*, you will need a working internet connection. We recommend either Microsoft Edge or Google Chrome to have the best experience with the Azure portal. Furthermore, you will be required to create an Azure account (at no cost) if you do not already have one.

If you are using the digital version of this book, we advise you to type the code yourself or access the code via the GitHub repository (link available in the next section). Doing so will help you avoid any potential errors related to the copying and pasting of code.

As you work through the book, please feel free to try AutoML with your own data. It helps greatly in your learning experience to solve problems that interest you. At the end of each chapter, try adapting your own datasets to the example code.

# Download the example code files

You can download the example code files for this book from GitHub at `https://github.com/PacktPublishing/Automated-Machine-Learning-with-Microsoft-Azure`. In case there's an update to the code, it will be updated on the existing GitHub repository.

We also have other code bundles from our rich catalog of books and videos available at `https://github.com/PacktPublishing/`. Check them out!

# Download the color images

We also provide a PDF file that has color images of the screenshots/diagrams used in this book. You can download it here: `https://static.packt-cdn.com/downloads/9781800565319_ColorImages.pdf`.

# Conventions used

There are a number of text conventions used throughout this book.

Code in text: Indicates code words in text, database table names, folder names, filenames, file extensions, pathnames, dummy URLs, user input, and Twitter handles. Here is an example: "You have another helper function here, get_forecasting_output."

A block of code is set as follows:

```
from azureml.core import Workspace, Dataset, Datastore
from azureml.core import Experiment
from azureml.core.compute import ComputeTarget
from azureml.train.automl import AutoMLConfig
from azureml.train.automl.run import AutoMLRun
from azureml.widgets import RunDetails
```

Any command-line input or output is written as follows:

```
from azureml.pipeline.core import PipelineRun
experiment = Experiment(ws, 'your-experiment_name')
pipeline_run = PipelineRun(experiment, 'your-pipeline-run-id')
```

**Bold**: Indicates a new term, an important word, or words that you see onscreen. For example, words in menus or dialog boxes appear in the text like this. Here is an example: "Go to **Experiments** under **Assets** in Azure Machine Learning Studio, click your experiment name, select your run ID, click the **Models** tab, select the highest-performing algorithm, and click the **Metrics** tab."

> **Tips or important notes**
> Appear like this.

# Get in touch

Feedback from our readers is always welcome.

**General feedback**: If you have questions about any aspect of this book, mention the book title in the subject of your message and email us at customercare@packtpub.com.

**Errata**: Although we have taken every care to ensure the accuracy of our content, mistakes do happen. If you have found a mistake in this book, we would be grateful if you would report this to us. Please visit www.packtpub.com/support/errata, selecting your book, clicking on the Errata Submission Form link, and entering the details.

**Piracy**: If you come across any illegal copies of our works in any form on the Internet, we would be grateful if you would provide us with the location address or website name. Please contact us at copyright@packt.com with a link to the material.

**If you are interested in becoming an author**: If there is a topic that you have expertise in and you are interested in either writing or contributing to a book, please visit authors.packtpub.com.

# Reviews

Please leave a review. Once you have read and used this book, why not leave a review on the site that you purchased it from? Potential readers can then see and use your unbiased opinion to make purchase decisions, we at Packt can understand what you think about our products, and our authors can see your feedback on their book. Thank you!

For more information about Packt, please visit packt.com.

# Section 1: AutoML Explained – Why, What, and How

In this first part, you will understand why you should use AutoML and how it solves common industry problems. You will also build an AutoML solution through a UI.

This section comprises the following chapters:

- *Chapter 1, Introducing AutoML*
- *Chapter 2, Getting Started with Azure Machine Learning Service*
- *Chapter 3, Training Your First AutoML Model*

# 1

# Introducing AutoML

AI is everywhere. From recommending products on your favorite websites to optimizing the supply chains of Fortune 500 companies to forecasting demand for shops of all sizes, AI has emerged as a dominant force. Yet, as AI becomes more and more prevalent in the workplace, a worrisome trend has emerged: most AI projects fail.

Failure occurs for a variety of technical and non-technical reasons. Sometimes, it's because the AI model performs poorly. Other times, it's due to data issues. Machine learning algorithms require reliable, accurate, timely data, and sometimes your data fails to meet those standards. When data isn't the issue and your model performs well, failure usually occurs because end users simply do not trust AI to guide their decision making.

For every worrisome trend, however, there is a promising solution. Microsoft and a host of other companies have developed **automated machine learning** (**AutoML**) to increase the success of your AI projects. In this book, you will learn how to use AutoML on Microsoft's Azure cloud platform. This book will teach you how to boost your productivity if you are a data scientist. If you are not a data scientist, this book will enable you to build machine learning models and harness the power of AI.

In this chapter, we will begin by understanding what AI and machine learning are and explain why companies have had such trouble in seeing a return on their investment in AI. Then, we will proceed into a deeper dive into how data scientists work and why that workflow is inherently slow and mistake-prone from a project success perspective. Finally, we conclude the chapter by introducing AutoML as the key to unlocking productivity in machine learning projects.

In this chapter, we will cover the following topics:

- Explaining data science's ROI problem
- Analyzing why AI projects fail slowly
- Solving the ROI problem with AutoML

# Explaining data science's ROI problem

**Data scientist** has been consistently ranked the *best job in America* by Forbes Magazine from 2016 to 2019, yet the best job in America has not produced the best results for the companies employing them. According to VentureBeat, 87% of data science projects fail to make it into production. This means that most of the work that data scientists perform does not impact their employer in any meaningful way.

By itself, this is not a problem. If data scientists were cheap and plentiful, companies would see a return on their investment. However, this is simply not the case. According to the 2020 LinkedIn Salary stats, data scientists earn a total compensation of around $111,000 across all career levels in the United States. It's also very easy for them to find jobs.

Burtch Works, a United States-based executive recruiting firm, reports that, as of 2018, data scientists stayed at their job for only 2.6 years on average, and 17.6% of all data scientists changed jobs that year. Data scientists are expensive and hard to keep.

Likewise, if data scientists worked fast, even though 87% of their projects fail to have an impact, a **return on investment** (**ROI**) is still possible. Failing fast means that many projects still make it into production and the department is successful. Failing slow means that the department fails to deliver.

Unfortunately, most data science departments fail slow. To understand why, you must first understand what machine learning is, how it differs from traditional software development, and the five steps common to all machine learning projects.

## Defining machine learning, data science, and AI

**Machine learning** is the process of training statistical models to make predictions using data. It is a category within AI. **AI** is defined as computer programs that perform cognitive tasks such as decision making that would normally be performed by a human. **Data science** is a career field that combines computer science, machine learning, and other statistical techniques to solve business problems.

Data scientists use a variety of machine learning algorithms to solve business problems. **Machine learning algorithms** are best thought of as a defined set of mathematical computations to perform on data to make predictions. Common applications of machine learning that you may experience in everyday life include predicting when your credit card was used to make a fraudulent transaction, determining how much money you should be given when applying for a loan, and figuring out which items are suggested to you when shopping online. All of these decisions, big and small, are determined mechanistically through machine learning.

There are many types of algorithms, but it's not important for you to know them all. Random Forest, XGBoost, LightGBM, deep learning, CART decision trees, multilinear regression, naïve Bayes, logistic regression, and k-nearest neighbor are all examples of machine learning algorithms. These algorithms are powerful because they work by learning patterns in data that would be too complex or subtle for any human being to detect on their own.

What is important for you to know is the difference between supervised learning and unsupervised learning. **Supervised learning** uses historical, labeled data to make future predictions.

Imagine you are a restaurant manager and you want to forecast how much money you will make next month by running an advertising campaign. To accomplish this with machine learning, you would want to collect all of your sales data from previous years, including the results of previous campaigns. Since you have past results and are using them to make predictions, this is an example of supervised learning.

**Unsupervised learning** simply groups like data points together. It's useful when you have a lot of information about your customers and would like to group them into buckets so that you can advertise to them in a more targeted fashion. Azure AutoML, however, is strictly for supervised learning tasks. Thus, you always need to have past results available in your data when creating new AutoML models.

# Machine learning versus traditional software

Traditional software development and machine learning development differ tremendously. Programmers are used to creating software that takes in input and delivers output based on explicitly defined rules. Data scientists, on the other hand, collect the desired output first before making a program. They then use this output data along with input data to create a program that learns how to predict output from input.

For example, maybe you would like to build an algorithm predicting how many car accidents would occur in a given city on a given day. First, you would begin by collecting historical data such as the number of car crashes (the desired output) and any data that you guess would be useful in predicting that number (input data). Weather data, day of the week, amount of traffic, and data related to city events can all be used as input.

Once you collect the data, your next step is to create a statistical program that finds hidden patterns between the input and output data; this is called **model training**. After you train your model, your next step is to set up an **inference program** that uses new input data to predict how many car accidents will happen that day using your trained model.

Another major difference is that, with machine learning, you never know what data you're going to need to create your solution before you try it out, and you never know what you're going to get until you build a solution. Since data scientists never know what data they need to solve any given problem, they need to ask for advice from business experts and use their intuition to identify the right data to collect.

These differences are important because successful machine learning projects look very different from successful traditional software projects; confusing the two leads to failed projects. Managers with an IT background but lacking a data science background often try to follow methods and timelines inappropriate for a machine learning project.

Frankly, it's unrealistic to assign hard timelines to a process where you don't know what data you will need or what algorithms will work, and many data science projects fail simply because they weren't given adequate time or support. There is, however, a recipe for success.

## The five steps to machine learning success

Now that we know what machine learning is and how it differs from traditional software development, the next step is to learn how a typical machine learning project is structured. There are many ways you could divide the process, but there are roughly five parts, as shown in the following diagram:

Figure 1.1 – The five steps of any machine learning project

Let's look at each of these steps in turn.

## Understanding the business problem

*Step 1*, understanding the business problem, means talking to end users about what problems they are trying to solve and translating that into a machine learning problem.

For example, a problem in the world of professional basketball may be, *we are really bad at drafting European basketball players. We would like to get better at selecting the right players for our team.* You will need to figure out what the business means by a *good player*. Along the way, you may discover that most players brought over from Europe only play a few games and are sent home, and this costs the team millions of wasted dollars.

Armed with this information, you then need to translate the problem to make it solvable by machine learning. Think about it clearly. *We will use the player's historical in-game statistics and demographic information to predict the longevity of their career in the NBA* would make a good machine learning project. Translating a business problem into an AI problem always means using data to try to predict a number (the number of games played in the NBA) or a category (whether the player would head home after a handful of games).

## Collecting and cleansing data

*Step 2*, collecting and cleansing data, involves the following steps:

1. Identifying and gaining access to data sources
2. Retrieving all of the data you want
3. Joining all of your data together
4. Removing errors in the data
5. Applying business logic to create a clean dataset even a layman could understand

This is harder than it sounds. Data is often dirty and hard to find.

With our basketball case, this would mean scraping publicly available data from the web to get each player's in-game statistics and demographic information. Errors are nearly guaranteed, so you will have to work in logic to remove or fix nonsensical numbers. No human being is 190 inches tall, for example, but centimeters and inches are often confused.

The best test for whether you have properly cleansed a dataset and made it clear is to give it to a layman and ask simple questions. *"How tall is player Y? How many NBA games did player X participate in during his career?".* If they can answer, you have succeeded.

## Transforming data for machine learning

Once you have an easily understandable, cleansed dataset, the next step is transforming data for machine learning, which is called **feature engineering**. Feature engineering is the process of altering data for machine learning algorithms. Some features are necessary for the algorithm to work, while other features make it easier for the algorithm to find patterns. Common feature engineering techniques include one-hot encoding categorical variables, scaling numeric values, removing outliers, and filling in null values.

A complication is that different algorithms require different types of feature engineering. Unlike most algorithms, XGBoost does not require you to fill in null values. Decision trees aren't affected by outliers much, but outliers throw off regression models. Going back to our basketball problem, you would likely have to replace null values, scale numeric values so that each column contains only a range of numbers from 0 to 1, and one-hot encode categorical variables.

> **Important tip**
>
> One-hot encoding categorical variables simply means taking one column with many categories and turning it into many columns with either a one or a zero. For example, if you have one column with the values *USA*, *Canada*, or *Mexico*, one-hot encoding that column would create three columns, one for each country. A row with a product from the United States would have a *1* in the *USA* column and a *0* in the *Canada* and *Mexico* columns.

## Training the machine learning model

Now that you have your data and you have it in just the right format, it's time to train a machine learning model. Although this step gets a lot of glamour and hype, training machine learning models is a process that is both quick and slow. With today's technology, most machine learning models can be trained with only a few lines of code.

**Hyperparameter tuning**, in contrast, can take a very long time. Each machine learning algorithm has settings you can control, called **hyperparameters**. Hyperparameter tuning is retraining machine learning algorithms multiple times until you find the right set of parameters.

Some algorithms such as Random Forest do not get much benefit out of hyperparameter tuning. Others, such as XGBoost or LightGBM, often improve drastically. Depending on the size of your data, the algorithm you're using, and the amount of compute you have available, hyperparameter tuning can take days to weeks to finish.

Notice how much you have to know about individual algorithms to become a successful data scientist? This is one of the reasons why the field has such a high barrier to entry. Do not be intimidated, but please keep this in mind as we introduce AutoML.

## Delivering results to end users

You have now trained your model and tuned its parameters, and you can confidently predict which European players the NBA team should draft. Maybe you have achieved 80% accuracy, maybe 90%, but your predictions will definitely help the business. Despite your results, you still have to get end users to accept your model, trust your model, and use it. Unlike traditional software, this can require a Herculean effort.

First, end users are going to want to know why the model is giving its prediction, and, if you used the wrong algorithm, this is impossible. **Black-box models** use algorithms that are inherently unknowable. Then, even if you can give the business explanations, the user may feel uncomfortable with that 80% accuracy number. *"What does that mean?"*, they will ask.

Visualizations are key to relieving some of their fears. For your basketball model, you decide to simply show the business pictures of the players they should draft, along with some simple graphs showing how many players our model accurately predicted would be NBA stars and how many European NBA stars our model failed to predict.

# Putting it all together

You now know what machine learning is, how it differs from traditional software development, and the five steps inherent to any machine learning project. Unfortunately, many people in the industry do not understand any of these things. Most businesses are new to data science. Many businesses believe that data science is much more similar to software development than it is, and this interferes with the machine learning project process.

End users are confused by data scientists' questions because they don't realize that the data scientist is trying to translate their business problem into a machine learning problem. IT is confused as to why data scientists ask for access to so much data because they don't realize that data scientists don't know what data they will need before trying it out. Management is confused as to why their data scientists spend so little time building models and so much time cleansing and transforming data.

Thus, *steps 1* and *2* of the machine learning process often take longer than expected. Business users fail to communicate their business problem to data scientists in a useful way, IT is slow to grant data scientists access to data, and data scientists struggle with understanding the data they receive. *Step 5* is also complicated because end users expect models to be perfectly explainable like a typical software program, and earning their trust takes time.

Given that misinterpretation slows down the other steps, the rest of the data science process must be fast for companies to see ROI. Transforming data and training models is the core of data science work, after all. It is exactly what they were trained to do and it should be fast. As we shall see in the next section, this is rarely the case.

# Analyzing why AI projects fail slowly

Data scientists often come from research backgrounds and approach the work of building machine learning models methodically. After obtaining a business problem and determining what an AI solution looks like, the process looks like this:

1. Gather the data.

2. Cleanse the data.

3. Transform the data.

4. Build a machine learning model.

5. Determine whether the model is acceptable.

6. Tune the hyperparameters.

7. Deploy the model.

If the model is acceptable in *step 5*, data scientists will proceed to *step 6*. If the model is unacceptable, they will return to *step 3* and try different models and transformations. This process can be seen in *Figure 1.2*:

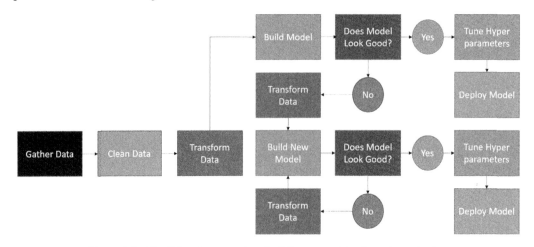

Figure 1.2 – Traditional approach to building a machine learning solution

While this process follows the five steps outlined in *Figure 1.1*, it's long and cumbersome. There are also specific drawbacks related to transforming data, building models, tuning hyperparameters, and deploying models. We will now take a closer look at the drawbacks inherent in this process that cause data science projects to fail slowly instead of quickly, greatly impacting the ROI problem:

- **Data has to be transformed differently by algorithms**. Data transformation can be a tedious process. Learning how to fill in null values, one-hot encode categorical variables, remove outliers, and scale datasets appropriately isn't easy and takes years of experience to master. It also takes a lot of code, and it's easy for novice programmers to make mistakes, especially when learning a new programming language.

  Furthermore, different data transformations are required for different algorithms. Some algorithms can handle null values while others cannot. Some can handle highly imbalanced datasets, those in which you only have a few samples of a category you're trying to predict, while other algorithms break.

  One algorithm may perform well if you remove outliers while another will be completely unaffected. Whenever you choose to try a new model, there's a high likelihood that you will need to spend time reengineering your data for your algorithm.

- **Some algorithms require hyperparameter tuning to perform well**. Unlike Random Forest, models built with algorithms such as XGBoost and LightGBM only perform well if you tune their hyperparameters, but they can perform really well.

  Thus, you have two choices: stick to models that perform decently without tuning or spend days to weeks tuning a model with high potential but no guarantee of success. Furthermore, you need a massive amount of algorithm-specific knowledge to become a successful data scientist using the traditional approach.

- **Hyperparameter tuning takes a lot of compute hours**. Days to weeks to train a single machine learning model may seem like an exaggeration, but in practice, it's common. At most companies, GPUs and CPUs are a limited resource, and datasets can be quite large. Certain companies have lines to get access to computing power, and data scientists require a lot of it.

  When hyperparameter tuning, it's common to do something called a **grid search** where every possible combination of parameters is trained over a specified numerical space. For example, say algorithm *X* has parameters *A*, *B*, and *C*, and you want to try setting *A* to *1*, *2*, and *3*, *B* to *0* and *1*, and *C* to *0.5*, *1*, and *1.5*. Tuning this model requires building 3 x 2 x 3 = 15 machine learning models to find the ideal combination.

Now, 15 models may take a few minutes or a few days to train depending on the size of the data you are using, the algorithm you wish to employ, and your computing capacity. However, 15 models is very little. Many modern machine learning algorithms require you to tune five to six parameters over a wide range of values, producing hundreds to thousands of models in search of finding the best performance.

- **Deploying models is hard and it isn't taught in school**. Even after you transform data correctly and find the perfect model with the best set of hyperparameters, you still need to deploy it to be used by the business. When new data comes in, it needs to get scored by the model and delivered somewhere. Monitoring is necessary as machine learning models do malfunction occasionally and must be retrained. Yet, data scientists are rarely trained in model deployment. It's considered more of an IT function.

  As a result of this lack of training, many companies use hacky infrastructures with an array of slapped-together technologies for machine learning deployment. A database query may be triggered by third-party software on a trigger. Data may be transformed using one computer language, stored in a file on a file share, and picked up by another process that scores the model in another language and saves it back to the file share. Fragile, ad hoc solutions are the norm, and for most data scientists, this is all on-the-job training.

- **Data scientists focus on accuracy instead of explainability**. Fundamentally, data scientists are trained to build the most accurate AI they can. Kaggle competitions are all about accuracy and new algorithms are judged based on how well they perform compared to solutions of the past.

  Businesspeople, on the other hand, often care more about the *why* behind the prediction. Forgetting to include explainability undermines the trust end users need to place in machine learning, and as a result, many models end up unused.

All in all, building machine learning models takes a lot of time, and when 87% of AI projects fail to make it to production, that's a lot of time wasted. Gathering data and cleansing data are processes that, by themselves, take a lot of time.

Transforming data for each model, tuning hyperparameters, and figuring out and implementing a deployment solution can take even longer. In such a scenario, it's easy to focus on finding the *best* model possible and overlook the most important part of the project: earning the trust of your end users and ensuring your solution gets used. Luckily, there's a solution to a lot of these problems.

# Solving the ROI problem with AutoML

Given the high failure rate of AI projects, the lack of understanding that businesses have regarding how machine learning works, and the long length of time each project takes, Microsoft and other companies have worked to develop solutions that allow faster development and a higher success rate. One such solution is AutoML.

By automating a lot of the work that data scientists do, and by harnessing the power of cloud computing, AutoML on Azure allows data scientists to work faster and allows even non-specialists to build AI solutions.

Specifically, AutoML on Azure transforms data, builds models, and tunes hyperparameters for you. Deployment is possible with a few button clicks and explainability is inherently built into the solution. Compared to the traditional machine learning process in *Figure 1.2*, the AutoML process in *Figure 1.3* is much more straightforward:

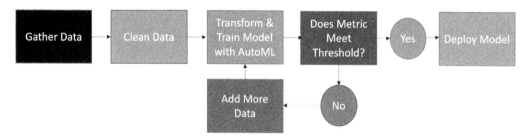

Figure 1.3 – AutoML approach to building a machine learning solution

Following the AutoML approach allows you to fail much faster and gets you to a state where you need to decide between adding more data or dropping the project. Instead of wasting time tuning models that have no chance of working, AutoML gives you a definitive answer after only a single AutoML run. Let's take a look at a more detailed description of the advantages of AutoML.

## Advantages of AutoML on Azure

Let's look at some of the advantages of AutoML:

- **AutoML transforms data automatically**: Once you have a cleansed, error-free dataset in an easy-to-understand format, you can simply load that data into AutoML. You do not need to fill in null values, one-hot encode categorical values, scale data, remove outliers, or worry about balancing datasets except in extreme cases. This is all done via AutoML's intelligent feature engineering. There are even data guardrails that automatically detect any problems in your dataset that may lead to a poorly built model.

- **AutoML trains models with the best algorithms**: After you load your data into AutoML, it will start training models using the most up-to-date algorithms. Depending on your settings and the size of your compute, AutoML will train these models in parallel using the Azure cloud. At the end of your run, AutoML will even build complex ensemble models combining the results of your highest performing models.

- **AutoML tunes hyperparameters for you**: As you use AutoML on Azure, you will notice that it will often create models using the same algorithms over and over again.

  You may notice that while early on in the run it was trying a wide range of algorithms, by the end of the run, it's focusing on only one or two. This is because it is testing out different hyperparameters. While it may not find the absolute best set of hyperparameters on any given run, it is likely to deliver a high-performing, well-tuned model.

- **AutoML has super-fast development**: Models built using AutoML on Azure can be deployed to a REST API endpoint in just a few clicks. The accompanying script details the data schema that you need to pass through to the endpoint. Once you have created the REST API, you can deploy it anywhere to easily score data and store results in a database of your choice.

- **AutoML has in-built explainability**: Recently, Microsoft has focused on responsible AI. A key element of responsible AI is being able to explain how your machine learning model is making decisions.

  AutoML-generated models come with a dashboard showing the importance of the different features used by your model. This is available for all of the models you train with AutoML unless you turn on the option to use black-box deep learning algorithms. Even individual data points can be explained, greatly helping your model to earn the trust and acceptance of business end users.

- **AutoML enables data scientists to iterate faster**: Through intelligent feature engineering, parallel model training, and automatic hyperparameter tuning, AutoML lets data scientists fail faster and succeed faster. If you cannot get decent performance with AutoML, you know that you need to add more data.

  Conversely, if you do achieve great performance with AutoML, you can either choose to deploy the model as is or use AutoML as a baseline to compare against your hand-coded models. At this point in time, it's expected that the best data scientists will be able to manually build models that outperform AutoML in some cases.

- **AutoML enables non-data scientists to do data science**: Traditional machine learning has a high barrier to entry. You have to be an expert at statistics, computer programming, and data engineering to succeed in data science, and those are just the hard skills.

  AutoML, on the other hand, can be performed by anyone who knows how to shape data. With a bit of SQL and database knowledge, you can harness the power of AI and build and deploy machine learning models that deliver business value fast.

- **AutoML is the wave of the future**: Just as AI has evolved from a buzzword to a practice, the way that machine learning solutions get created needs to evolve from research projects to well-oiled machines. AutoML is a key piece of that well-oiled machine, and AutoML on Azure has many features that will empower you to fail and succeed faster. From data transformation to deployment to end user acceptance, AutoML makes machine learning easier and more accessible than ever before.

- **AutoML is widely available**: Microsoft's AutoML is not only available on Azure but can also be used inside Power BI, ML.NET, SQL Server, Synapse, and HDInsight. As it matures further, expect it to be incorporated into more and more Azure and non-Azure Microsoft services.

# Summary

AI and machine learning may have captured the world's imagination, but there's a large gap between the pie-in-the-sky promises of AI and the reality of AI projects. Machine learning projects, in particular, fail often and slowly. Traditional managers treat data science projects like software engineering projects, and data scientists work in a manual, time-consuming manner. Luckily, AutoML has emerged as a way to speed up projects, and Microsoft has created its AutoML offering with your needs in mind.

You are now primed for *Chapter 2, Getting Started with Azure Machine Learning Service*, which will introduce you to the Microsoft Azure Machine Learning workspace. You will create an Azure Machine Learning workspace and all of the necessary components required to start an AutoML project. By the end of the chapter, you will have a firm grasp of all of the different components of Azure Machine Learning Studio and how they interact.

# 2
# Getting Started with Azure Machine Learning Service

Now that we know that the key to delivering return on investment in artificial intelligence is delivering machine learning (ML) projects at a brisk pace, we need to learn how to use **Automated Machine Learning (AutoML)** to achieve that goal. Before we can do that, however, we need to learn how to use the **Azure Machine Learning Service (AMLS)**. AMLS is Microsoft's premier ML platform on the Azure cloud.

We will begin this chapter by creating an Azure account and creating an AMLS workspace. Once you have created a workspace, you will proceed to create different types of compute to run Python code and ML jobs remotely using a cluster of machines. Next, you will learn how to work with data using the Azure dataset and datastore constructs. Finally, we will provide an overview of AutoML. This will boost your ability to create high-performing models.

In this chapter, we will cover the following topics:

- Creating your first AMLS workspace
- Building compute to run your AutoML jobs
- Working with data in AMLS
- Understanding how AutoML works on Azure

# Technical requirements

In order to complete the exercises in this chapter, you will need the following:

- Access to the internet
- A web browser, preferably Google Chrome or Microsoft Edge Chromium
- A Microsoft account

# Creating your first AMLS workspace

Navigating Microsoft Azure for the first time can be a daunting experience. With hundreds of services with similar capabilities, it's easy to get lost. Therefore, it is important for you to follow this guide step by step, beginning by creating an Azure account. If you already have an Azure account, you can skip ahead to the *Creating an AMLS workspace* section.

## Creating an Azure account

Let's begin:

1. To create an Azure account, navigate to `https://azure.microsoft.com`.

2. Click the green **Start free** button, as shown in the following screenshot. Depending on your location, this button may be located in a slightly different location. Once you've clicked this button, you will be asked to select an email address associated with your Microsoft account:

> **Note**
>
> If you use Microsoft Windows, you should have a Microsoft account. If you do
> not, then you can create a Microsoft account by following the instructions at
> `https://account.microsoft.com/account`.

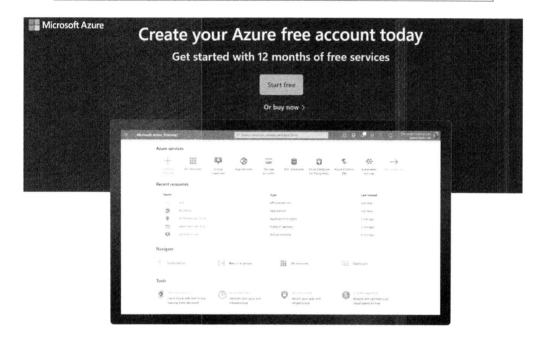

Figure 2.1 – Microsoft Azure account creation screen

Microsoft will ask you to fill in some information about your country, first name,
last name, email address, and phone number. You will then have to verify your
identity via a phone number and enter your credit card information.

Note that you will not be charged for creating an Azure account unless you upgrade.
Once you sign the agreement, you will have $200 free credit to use for your first
30 days of Azure. You will not be automatically charged at the end of the 30-day
period.

> **Important tip**
>
> If you have already signed up for a Microsoft Azure free account with an email address, you will not receive an additional $200 free credit. It can only be received once, and you will only be able to choose the pay-as-you-go option. In this case, create a new Microsoft account with a different email address and try again.

With an account in place, you can now create resources within Microsoft Azure. Hundreds of resources are available, and it can be tempting to explore them. Stay focused. Setting up AMLS is the first step you must take toward using AutoML.

## Creating an AMLS workspace

Once you have created an Azure account, you can create an **Azure Machine Learning Service (AMLS)** workspace. An AMLS workspace is a centralized resource for all your ML work on Azure. It also provides access to **AML studio**. This studio is a graphical web portal that allows easy, intuitive access to all the different components of the AMLS workspace. Let's get started:

1.  Begin by navigating to `https://portal.azure.com`.

2.  Click the **Create a resource** button, which should be in a blue cross. Resources are simply Azure services. Every Azure service, be it a virtual machine, cloud database, or ML tool, counts as a resource.

3.  After clicking the blue cross, type `Machine Learning` into the search box and press *Enter*. You will see a new screen with a large blue flask in the top-right corner. This is the AML symbol.

4.  Click **Create**. The following screenshot shows the process flow:

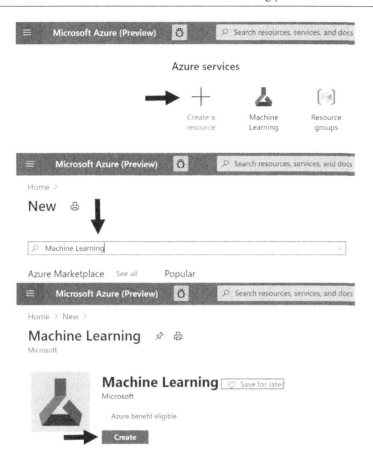

Figure 2.2 – Creating an AMLS resource

5.  You will then be presented with a screen asking you to select a subscription, fill in a resource group, create a workspace name, select a region, and select a workspace edition. If you have multiple Azure subscriptions, select the one associated with the account you would like to use. A **resource group** is simply a collection of Azure resources. Create a new one by following the naming conventions.

> **Important tip**
>
> Different Azure resources have different naming conventions. Resource groups must consist of alphanumeric characters, periods, hyphens, parentheses, and underscores, while AMLS workspaces must consist of alphanumeric characters, hyphens, and underscores. Simply follow any instructions that appear if you provide an incorrect name.

6.  Fill in the rest of the form by naming your AMLS workspace and selecting a region. Pick a region close to where you live. For example, if you live in Chicago, select North Central US or East US, but don't select North Europe. After filling out all the values, your form should look similar to what's shown in the following screenshot.

    Notice that, in addition to the AMLS workspace, you are also creating additional resources automatically. A **container registry** to hold containerized code will be automatically created for you if you require it, so do not create one:

**Basics**    Networking    Advanced    Tags    Review + create

**Project details**

Select the subscription to manage deployed resources and costs. Use resource groups like folders to organize and manage all your resources.

| | |
|---|---|
| Subscription * ⓘ | Dennis Sawyers Internal MS Learning Account ⌄ |
| └─── Resource group * ⓘ | auto-ml-example-resource-group ⌄ |
| | Create new |

**Workspace details**

Specify the name and region for the workspace.

| | |
|---|---|
| Workspace name * ⓘ | automl-example-workspace ✓ |
| Region * ⓘ | North Central US ⌄ |
| Storage account * ⓘ | (new) automlexamplew1005528502 ⌄ |
| | Create new |
| Key vault * ⓘ | (new) automlexamplew3892816466 ⌄ |
| | Create new |
| Application insights * ⓘ | (new) automlexamplew6936691182 ⌄ |
| | Create new |
| Container registry * ⓘ | None ⌄ |
| | Create new |

Figure 2.3 – Example of a filled-in AMLS workspace creation form

7.  Finish creating your AMLS workspace by clicking **Review + create**, followed by **Create**.

You will see a screen that says **Deployment is in progress**, and four different Azure resources will be created. This will include your AMLS workspace, a **Storage account** instance for storing your data, an **Azure Key Vault** instance for storing your passwords, and an **Application Insights** resource for monitoring your ML jobs. Do not delete any of these resources once they have been created.

---

**Important Tip**

Once you've created a ML pipeline or a real-time endpoint, an Azure container registry will be automatically created. Like the other automatically created resources, do not delete it.

---

# Creating an AMLS workspace with code

Alternatively, you can create an AMLS workspace by using the **Azure CLI** with either **Bash** or **PowerShell**. The **Azure command-line interface** (**Azure CLI**) is an interface you can use to create and manage Azure resources. Bash is the UNIX shell and command language, while PowerShell is a Microsoft-specific framework. The Azure CLI can be accessed via the front page of https://portal.azure.com by clicking the computer screen icon at the top left. When you hover over it, the words **Cloud Shell** will pop up.

To create an AMLS workspace, type in the following commands in the order shown here:

1.  Install the Azure CLI ML extension with the following code:

    ```
    az extension add -n azure-cli-ml
    ```

2.  Next, create a resource group. Make sure that you specify your Azure location. -n denotes the resource group's name, while -l specifies its location:

    ```
    az group create -n automl-cli-group -l eastus
    ```

3.  Instantiate your AMLS workspace. -w denotes your workspace name, while -g specifies your resource group. Make sure it matches the resource group you created in the previous step:

    ```
    az ml workspace create -w automl-ws -g automl-cli-group
    ```

You can learn more about workspace-specific commands at `https://docs.microsoft.com/en-us/azure/machine-learning/reference-azure-machine-learning-cli`.

Now that you have created an AMLS workspace, you are ready to explore its many objects. You will do this through AML studio, a GUI built on top of your AMLS workspace.

# Navigating AML studio

With your AMLS workspace created, you can now navigate to AML studio.

Either navigate to `https://ml.azure.com` or open your AMLS workspace and click **Launch Now**, which can be found in the middle of the screen. AML studio is your one-stop shop for your AMLS needs. The following screenshot shows the studio and its navigation bar:

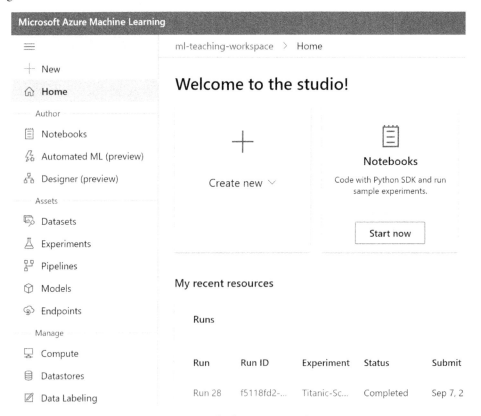

Figure 2.4 – AML studio home page and navigation

Your AML studio can be quite intimidating at first. With many tabs to navigate and a plethora of unfamiliar terms, many first-time users get lost. To make your journey easier, here's a description of each tab and what it does:

- **Home** returns you to the AML studio home page.

- **Notebooks** lets you write code using **Jupyter** or **JupyterLab**.

- **Automated ML (preview)** lets you run AutoML jobs using a guided user interface. It is currently in preview mode.

- **Designer (preview)** lets you transform data and create ML models using a guided user interface. It is currently in preview mode.

- **Datasets** are pointers to files in Azure Storage accounts or SQL queries in Azure SQL databases. You can use this tab to create new datasets or profile, update, and retrieve information on existing datasets.

- **Experiments** are records of your ML training jobs on Azure. Experiments contains the results of your runs, along with logs, charts, and graphs.

- **Pipelines** keeps track of any ML pipelines you have created. Pipelines are used for batch scoring or model training and are commonly scheduled using Azure Data Factory. Use this tab to retrieve your pipeline names and IDs.

- **Models** keeps track of any ML models you have trained and registered to your AMLS workspace. Use this tab to keep track of them.

- **Endpoints** keeps track of any real-time endpoints you have created for real-time scoring, as well as any pipeline endpoints you have created. You can also find pipeline endpoints in the **Pipelines** tab.

- **Compute** lets you create and access **compute instances** for running Jupyter, JupyterLab, and R Studio notebooks. It also lets you create **compute clusters** for running remote training jobs. We will create both in the next section.

- **Datastores** are pointers to blob containers on Azure Storage accounts or to Azure SQL databases. You can use this tab to create new datastores and retrieve information about your existing datastores.

- **Data Labeling** is useful for labeling image data. As you manually label images, you can train a machine model to make this process automatic in the future.

Throughout the rest of this chapter, we will explore the **Compute**, **Dataset**, and **Datastore** tabs. As we proceed throughout this book, we will use the **Automated ML**, **Experiment**, **Model**, **Pipeline**, and **Endpoint** tabs. We will not cover the **Notebook**, **Designer**, or **Data Labeling** tabs. To run AutoML jobs through the GUI or through code, you will first need compute, so let's start there.

# Building compute to run your AutoML jobs

The first time you open AML studio, navigate to the **Compute** tab to create a compute instance and a compute cluster. Once you open the tab, you will see four headings at the top: **Compute instances**, **Compute clusters**, **Inference clusters**, and **Attached compute**. Let's take a look at these in more detail:

- **Compute instances** are virtual machines that you can use to write and run Python code in Jupyter or JupyterLab notebooks; you can also use a compute instance to write R code using R Studio.

- **Compute clusters** are groups of virtual machines used to train ML models remotely. You can kick off jobs on a compute cluster and continue working on code in your compute instance.

- **Inference clusters** are groups of virtual machines used to score data in real time.

- **Attached compute** refers to using Databricks or HDInsight compute to run big data jobs.

Let's see them in action.

# Creating a compute instance

We'll start with a compute instance:

1.  Make sure the tab at the top is highlighted in black. Then, click the **Add New**
    button, which is the blue cross highlighted in the following screenshot:

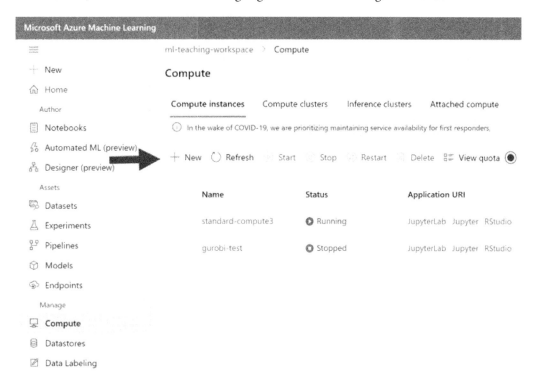

Figure 2.5 – Creating a compute instance

You will be asked to select a virtual machine type and a virtual machine size. Select
**CPU** for your virtual machine type and **Standard_DS3_v2** as your virtual machine
size. **Standard_DS3_v2** is the recommended virtual machine for most ML jobs
using small- to medium-sized datasets.

For larger datasets, you will want virtual machines with more RAM. As a rough guideline, we recommend having 20 times more RAM than the size of your data in CSV format. Once you have entered your settings, as shown in the following screenshot, click **Next**:

---

**Important Tip – CPU versus GPU**

For the majority of your AutoML and ML jobs, CPUs will be sufficient. When you are training deep learning models, however, you want to select the more expensive GPU virtual machines.

---

**Select virtual machine**

Select the virtual machine size you would like to use for your compute instance. Please note that only the creator can access the compute instance by default. Alternatively, you can assign the access to another user in the advanced settings section.

**Region** ⓘ

northcentralus

**Virtual machine type** ⓘ

◉ CPU   ○ GPU

**Virtual machine size** ⓘ

◉ Select from recommended options   ○ Select from all options

Total available quota: 600 cores ⓘ

| | Name ↑ | Category | Workload types | Av... ⓘ | Cost ⓘ |
|---|---|---|---|---|---|
| ○ | Standard_DS2_v2<br>2 cores, 7GB RAM, 14GB storage | General purpose | Development on Notebooks (or other IDE) and light weight testing | 100 c... | $0.15/hr |
| ◉ | Standard_DS3_v2<br>4 cores, 14GB RAM, 28GB storage | General purpose | Classical ML model training, AutoML runs, pipeline runs (default compute) | 100 c... | $0.29/hr |
| ○ | Standard_DS12_v2<br>4 cores, 28GB RAM, 56GB storage | Memory optimized | Training on large datasets (>1GB) parallel run steps, batch inferencing | 100 c... | $0.37/hr |
| ○ | Standard_F4s_v2<br>4 cores, 8GB RAM, 32GB storage | Compute optimized | Real-time inferencing and other latency-sensitive tasks | 100 c... | $0.17/hr |

Figure 2.6 – Compute instance settings

2.  You will then be asked to name your compute instance. Give it any name you wish or use `automl-compute-instance`, as shown in the following screenshot, and click **Create**:

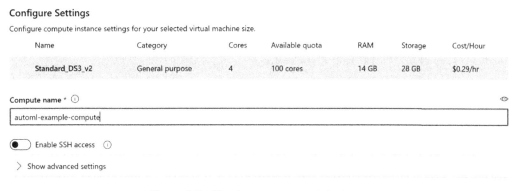

Figure 2.7 – Naming your compute instance

3.  Now that you have created a compute instance, you can start coding to complete the rest of your tasks or you can continue to use the GUI. To write in Python, simply open the link to **Jupyter**, as shown in the following screenshot:

Figure 2.8 – Opening a Jupyter notebook

4.  You can begin coding by creating a Python notebook in Jupyter. To do this, click the **New** button at the top right of the screen. From the dropdown, select the latest version of Python with AzureML, as shown in the following screenshot:

Figure 2.9 – Creating a new Python notebook

Now, you are ready to start coding!

## Creating a compute cluster

Your next step is to create a compute cluster so that you can run AutoML jobs using the visual interface. You can create a compute cluster either using code in a Jupyter notebook or through the GUI.

1.  To create a compute cluster through the GUI, click the **Compute** tab, click **Compute clusters**, and then click the **Create** button, as shown in the following screenshot:

Figure 2.10 – Creating a compute cluster

2.  There are more settings when it comes to creating a compute cluster. First, create a name by following the naming convention. Compute clusters can only have names that are 16 characters long, so think carefully. Your region is automatically selected so that it matches your workspace.

As we did previously, select **CPU** as the virtual machine's type and **Standard_DS3_v2** as the virtual machine's size. For virtual machine priority, select **Dedicated** instead of **Low priority**. Jobs running on low-priority virtual machines may be interrupted in periods of high usage. Then, click **Next**, as shown in the following screenshot:

**Select virtual machine**

Select the virtual machine size you would like to use for your compute cluster.

Region ⓘ

northcentralus

Virtual machine priority ⓘ

◉ Dedicated   ○ Low priority

Virtual machine type ⓘ

◉ CPU   ○ GPU

Virtual machine size ⓘ

◉ Select from recommended options   ○ Select from all options

Total available quota: 596 cores ⓘ

| | Name ↑ | Category | Workload types | Av... ⓘ | Cost ⓘ |
|---|---|---|---|---|---|
| ○ | Standard_DS2_v2<br>2 cores, 7GB RAM, 14GB storage | General purpose | Development on Notebooks (or other IDE) and light weight testing | 96 co... | $0.15/hr |
| ⊘ | Standard_DS3_v2<br>4 cores, 14GB RAM, 28GB storage | General purpose | Classical ML model training, AutoML runs, pipeline runs (default compute) | 96 co... | $0.29/hr |
| ○ | Standard_DS12_v2<br>4 cores, 28GB RAM, 56GB storage | Memory optimized | Training on large datasets (>1GB) parallel run steps, batch inferencing | 96 co... | $0.37/hr |
| ○ | Standard_F4s_v2<br>4 cores, 8GB RAM, 32GB storage | Compute optimized | Real-time inferencing and other latency-sensitive tasks | 100 c... | $0.17/hr |

Back   Next   Download a template for automation                    Cancel

Figure 2.11 – Compute cluster settings – part 1

3.  On the next page, begin by naming your compute cluster while following the naming convention. Compute clusters can only have names that are 16 characters long, so think carefully. Then, select the number of nodes. This is the most important difference between compute clusters and compute instances.

    With compute instances, you have a single node to run your jobs; with clusters, you can set the minimum and maximum numbers of nodes, and they will autoscale according to your job. AutoML makes use of compute clusters by training different models in parallel on separate nodes.

Set your minimum node count to 0 to minimize your costs when no jobs are running and set your maximum node count to 4. Lastly, change the number of seconds before nodes scale down to 1200 seconds, or 20 minutes, to keep your machines from shutting down while you work. Check your settings against those shown in the following screenshot and click the **Create** button:

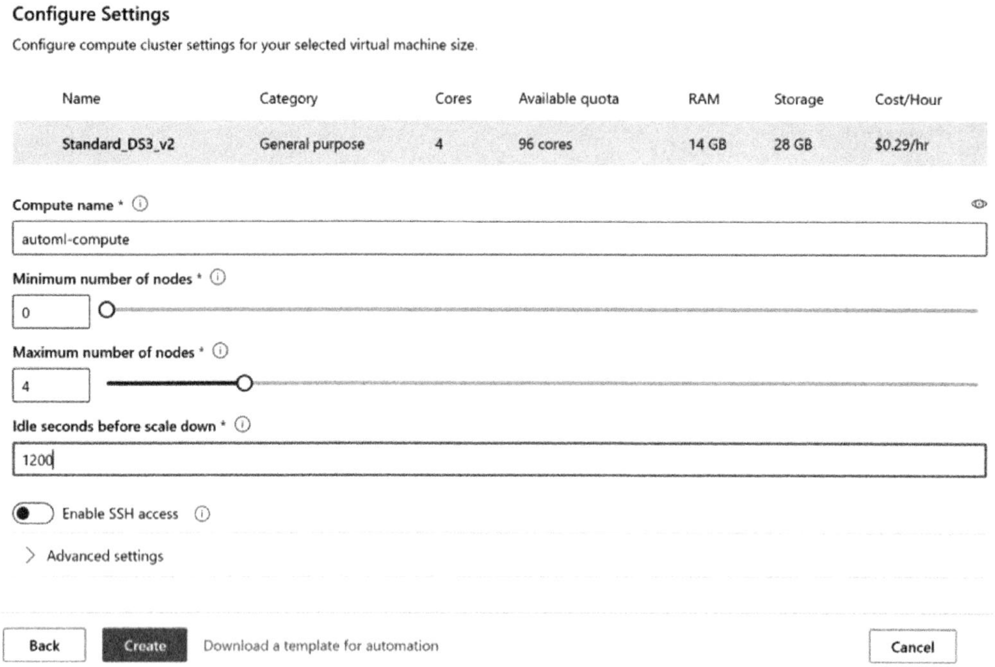

**Configure Settings**

Configure compute cluster settings for your selected virtual machine size.

| Name | Category | Cores | Available quota | RAM | Storage | Cost/Hour |
|------|----------|-------|-----------------|-----|---------|-----------|
| Standard_DS3_v2 | General purpose | 4 | 96 cores | 14 GB | 28 GB | $0.29/hr |

Compute name * ⓘ

```
automl-compute
```

Minimum number of nodes * ⓘ

```
0
```

Maximum number of nodes * ⓘ

```
4
```

Idle seconds before scale down * ⓘ

```
1200
```

( ● ) Enable SSH access  ⓘ

> Advanced settings

[ Back ]  [ Create ]   Download a template for automation                        [ Cancel ]

Figure 2.12 – Compute cluster settings – part 2

## Creating a compute cluster with code

You can also create a compute cluster using Python code in a Jupyter notebook. Let's take a look:

1.  First, import the necessary packages so that you can connect to your AMLS workspace and create your compute cluster:

```
import azureml.core
from azureml.core.workspace import Workspace
from azureml.core.compute import ComputeTarget,
AmlCompute
```

2. Now, connect to your AMLS workspace with the following code:

```
ws = Workspace.from_config()
```

3. Next, set your variables so that they match the settings you used when you created the cluster on the GUI:

```
compute_name = 'automl-cluster'
compute_min_nodes = 0
compute_max_nodes = 4
vm_size = 'Standard_DS3_v2'
idle_seconds = 1200
```

4. Once you have stored the variables, create a provisioning configuration for your compute cluster by using the following code:

```
Compute_Config = AmlCompute.provisioning_
configuration(vm_size=vm_size, min_nodes=compute_min_
nodes, max_nodes=compute_max_nodes, idle_seconds_before_
scaledown = idle_seconds)
```

5. Finally, create the compute target:

```
compute_target = ComputeTarget.create(ws, compute_name,
provisioning_config)
compute_target.wait_for_completion(show_output=True)
```

Next, we will see another way to create the compute clusters and instances.

# Creating a compute cluster and compute instance with the Azure CLI

A third way to create both compute clusters and compute instances is through the Azure CLI. To do so, open the Azure CLI by navigating to https://portal.azure.com and clicking on the computer screen icon in the top right of the screen. When you hover over the icon, it will say *Cloud Shell*. Once it's opened, do the following:

1. Create a compute instance. -n denotes the name of your compute instance, while -s specifies your virtual machine's size:

```
az ml computetarget create computeinstance -n clicompute
-s "STANDARD_DS3_V2" -v
```

2. Create a compute cluster. -n denotes the name of your compute cluster, while -s specifies your virtual machine's size. You also need to set your minimum and maximum numbers of nodes:

```
az ml computetarget create amlcompute -n clicluster -
min-nodes 0 -max-nodes 1 -s STANDARD_DS3_V2
```

You now know three ways you can create compute on AMLS: through the GUI, through Python code, and through the Azure CLI. By creating compute, you can now run all the AutoML jobs you want. Think of compute as the engine of AutoML. Like any engine, however, it requires fuel to run. If compute is the engine of AutoML, data is its fuel.

# Working with data in AMLS

Now that you've created a compute, all you need to do is create a dataset and you will be ready to run your first AutoML job. **Datasets** are simply pointers to files on your **Storage account** or pointers to SQL queries on Azure SQL databases.

A dataset is not a file itself. You can create datasets from local files, from SQL queries, or from files in your storage accounts. **Azure Open Datasets**, publicly available data curated by Microsoft, can also be registered as datasets. For this exercise, we will create a dataset using the Diabetes open dataset.

## Creating a dataset using the GUI

Let's begin:

1. Click the **Dataset** tab.

2. Click the **Create dataset** button, indicated by the blue cross, and you will be presented with a dropdown. Select **From Open Datasets**, as shown in the following screenshot.

   Note that you can also use this dropdown to create datasets from local files on your computer, from web files, or from data found in your datastores. Like datasets, **datastores** are pointers, but they point to blob containers on Azure Storage accounts or to Azure SQL databases:

**Important Tip**

Datastores can be created from Azure Blob storage, Azure File Share, Azure Data Lake Gen 1, Azure Data Lake Gen 2, Azure SQL Database, Azure PostgreSQL Database, and Azure MySQL Database.

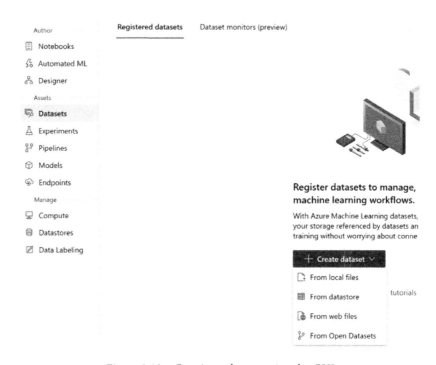

Figure 2.13 – Creating a dataset using the GUI

You will be presented with an array of datasets. Some, such as `Sample: Diabetes`, `Sample: OJ Sales Simulated Data`, and `The MNIST database of handwritten digits` are useful for demoing ML. You can use Diabetes for regression, OJ Sales for forecasting, and MNIST for deep learning image recognition.

3. Type `Diabetes` into the search bar, click the **Sample: Diabetes** box, and then click **Next**, as shown in the following screenshot:

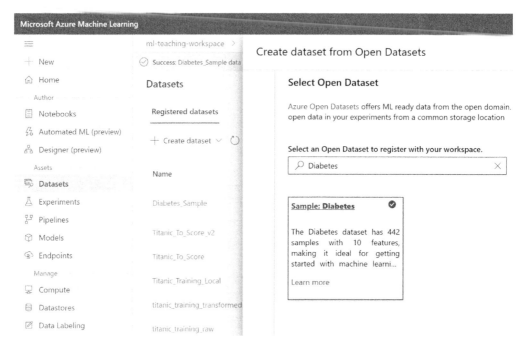

Figure 2.14 – Selecting the sample – Diabetes open dataset

4. You will now be asked to name your dataset. Dataset names must be unique in your workspace. Unlike many other Azure artifacts, dataset names may contain spaces, but they may not begin or end with a white space. Datasets also contain version numbers, beginning with 1.

Every time you update a dataset so that it points to a different file with updated data, a new version will be created. Give your dataset the name `Diabetes Sample` and click **Create**, as shown in the following screenshot:

## Dataset details

Azure Open Datasets offers ML ready data from the open domain. Registering open datasets in the workspace lets you data in your experiments from a common storage location without creating a copy of the data in your storage account.

**Register** Sample: Diabetes

| Name * | 👁 | Dataset version |
|---|---|---|
| Diabetes Sample | | 1 |

Figure 2.15 – Naming your dataset

Congratulations! Now, you have a dataset that you can use for AutoML.

# Creating a dataset using code

Like compute clusters, you can also create datasets entirely from code:

1.  Begin by loading in the following packages. `Diabetes` makes `Sample:Diabetes` available, while `Dataset` lets you create, register, and use datasets:

    ```
    from azureml.opendatasets import Diabetes
    from azureml.core import Dataset
    ```

2.  Once you have imported your packages, run the following code to pull in Diabetes data as a tabular dataset. **Tabular datasets** refer to data that contains rows and columns, whereas **file datasets** are used for non-tabular data such as image files:

    ```
    diabetes_tabular = Diabetes.get_tabular_dataset()
    ```

3.  Next, give your dataset a name and register it in your workspace. To do this, you will need the workspace code we used earlier while making a compute cluster:

    ```
    from azureml.core.workspace import Workspace
    ws = Workspace.from_config()
    diabetes = diabetes_tabular.register(workspace=ws,
    name='Diabetes Sample')
    ```

4. Once a dataset has been registered to your AMLS workspace, it's extremely easy to call it in the future. Simply navigate to the **Dataset** tab, select your dataset, and hit **Consume** to obtain the code you need to call your dataset. Click the folded page icon next to **Sample usage** to copy the code to your clipboard, as shown in the following screenshot:

Figure 2.16 – Using your dataset

You have now learned how to create a dataset using the GUI and code. Datasets are useful not only for AutoML but for all tasks within AMLS. Accessing datasets is as easy as copying automatically generated code into the studio. Try creating your own from local files using the GUI before moving on to the next section.

Your AutoML is ready to run. You built the engine in the previous section and now you have your fuel; that is, your data. Before you give AutoML a try, however, it's important to understand how it works. You wouldn't want to drive it into a ditch, after all.

# Understanding how AutoML works on Azure

Before running your first AutoML experiment, it's important to understand how AutoML works on Azure. AutoML is more than just machine learning, after all. It's also about data transformation and manipulation.

As shown in the following diagram, you can divide the stages of AutoML into roughly five parts: **Data Guardrails Check**, **Intelligent Feature Engineering**, **Iterative Data Transformation**, **Iterative ML Model Building**, and **Model Ensembling**. Only at the end of this process does AutoML produce a definitive best model:

Figure 2.17 – The Azure AutoML process

Let's take a closer look at each step in this process.

# Ensuring data quality with data guardrails

**Data guardrails** check to make sure that your data is in the correct format for AutoML, and if it is not, it will alter the data accordingly. There are currently six main checks that are performed on your data. Two of the checks – one to detect missing values and another to detect high-cardinality columns – will occur on every dataset. The other four checks are problem- or setting-dependent.

**Missing feature values imputation** will detect any null values in your dataset. **High-cardinality feature handling**, on the other hand, will identify any categorical columns with a large number of unique values. These are both important for the next step; that is, **Intelligent Feature Engineering**.

Unlike the first two checks, **validation split handling** will only occur if you set the validation configuration to **auto**. We will go over all of the different settings in *Chapters 4, 5, and 6*. This check automatically splits the data into training and test sets so that you don't have to. It's one of the many ways that AutoML speeds up the data science process.

**Class balancing detection** is specific to classification problems that are trying to predict a category, while **memory issues detection** and **frequency detection** are specific to forecasting problems that are trying to predict a future number. More on these checks will be discussed in *Chapter 5, Building an AutoML Classification Solution*, and *Chapter 6, Building an AutoML Forecasting Solution*, which cover classification and forecasting, respectively.

# Improving data with intelligent feature engineering

Once your data has passed the data guardrails check, the next step is **intelligent feature engineering**. This consists of filling in missing values, dealing with high-cardinality categorical features, generating additional features, and one-hot encoding categorical features. More advanced feature engineering techniques using k-means clustering, weight of evidence, and advanced text analytics are also applied here.

To begin, any columns consisting of all missing values, identical values, or extremely high cardinality (ID fields, GUIDs, and so on) will be automatically removed. Next, your missing numeric values will be filled in with the average (mean) of the column, while your missing categorical values will be filled with the most common value.

Following missing value imputation, additional columns will be generated for datetime features and text features. Datetime features include year, month, day, day of week, day of year, quarter, week of the year, hour, minute, and second. Text features include term frequency for groups of one, two, and three words.

> **Tip**
>
> It's sometimes better to fill in your missing values with measures other than the mean or most common value. In this case, fill in your data before it reaches AutoML.

**One-hot encoding** is then applied to all categorical columns. Simply put, this means that columns of 1s and 0s are created to represent each unique value in your original column. If your original column was *animal*, a dog will have a *1* in the newly created dog column and a *0* in all other animal columns. High-cardinality categorical columns will have grouped columns (*dog-cat*) created instead.

> **Important Note**
>
> Advanced feature engineering is also applied; these techniques require a high degree of specialized knowledge in data science and text analytics. If you would like to learn more, please check Microsoft's *Featurization in Automated ML* documentation, located at `https://docs.microsoft.com/en-us/azure/machine-learning/how-to-configure-auto-features`.

# Normalizing data for ML with iterative data transformation

ML models often perform better when you scale data. For example, if you have one column of numeric data with values between 5 and 10 and another column with values between 1 and 10 million, it's often better to normalize each column so that its minimum value is 0 and its maximum value is 1. There are many types of normalization, and luckily, AutoML performs them for you with **iterative data transformation**.

Every time AutoML trains a new model, it begins by scaling your data using one of seven methods. These seven methods are as follows:

- **StandardScaler**
- **MinMaxScaler**
- **Maximum absolute value scaler**
- **RobustScaler**
- **PCA**
- **Truncated Singular Value Decomposition**
- **SparseNormalizer**

Usually, you would have to code these yourself and try each one to determine which scaling method works best, but with AutoML, you don't even have to think about it.

# Training models quickly with iterative ML model building

The core of Azure AutoML is **iterative ML model building**. AutoML will train models in parallel based on your settings from an extensive list of algorithms. Microsoft's AutoML team has only selected the best-performing algorithms models to be included in AutoML, and before adding a new one, it undergoes extensive testing. This ensures high model performance.

As you watch AutoML train models, you will often notice that it uses the same algorithm over and over again. In this case, it's trying out different combinations of hyperparameters to achieve a higher score. Hyperparameters are simply settings you can set that are specific to an algorithm, such as **tree depth** for decision trees or **loss** in stochastic gradient descent.

Speaking of scores, each type of problem – regression, classification, and forecasting – has different metrics you can use to score. AutoML also uses a different set of algorithms for each problem type. More information on both scoring metrics and algorithms is found in *Chapters 4, 5*, and *6*, which are on regression, classification, and forecasting, respectively.

## Getting the best results with ML model ensembling

AutoML will keep training ML models until it reaches a set time limit or a set limit on the number of models. Once either of these limits is passed, it will perform **machine learning model ensembling** using a **voting ensemble** and a **stack ensemble**. Voting ensembles score data based on the weighted averages of your best models, while stack ensembles train a meta-model based on the predictions of your best models.

After training your ensemble models, AutoML will stop running and output the best model. Either the voting ensemble or stack ensemble will usually be your best-performing model. Sometimes, however, another model will slightly outperform both.

# Summary

In this chapter, you have learned about all the prerequisites that are necessary for creating AutoML solutions in Azure. You created an AMLS workspace and accessed AML studio before creating the necessary compute to run and write your AutoML jobs. You then loaded data into a datastore and registered it as a dataset to make it available for your AutoML runs.

Importantly, you should now understand the four steps of the AutoML process: a data guardrails check, intelligent feature engineering, data transformation, and iterative ML model building. Everything you have done in this chapter will enable you to create a ML model in record time.

You are now ready for *Chapter 3, Training Your First AutoML Model*, where you will build your first AutoML model through a **GUI**. This chapter will cover a range of topics, from examining data to scoring models and explaining results. By the end of that chapter, you will not only be able to train models with AutoML, but you will also be able to show and explain your results to end users in a way that's guaranteed to earn their trust.

# 3
# Training Your First AutoML Model

With an Azure account, an Azure Machine Learning workspace, a compute cluster, and a basic understanding of how AutoML works, you're now ready to train your first automated machine learning model. It will be easy and straightforward: AutoML is an equalizer that enables even novices to create advanced models in mere minutes, and you will appreciate its power by the end of this chapter regardless of your background. Practice makes perfect, and this chapter is your first step toward becoming an AutoML practitioner.

You will begin this chapter by loading data from your local machine to your **Azure Machine Learning Studio** (**AML Studio**), selecting only the columns you need for training. Then, you will proceed to train an AutoML model using the guided user interface. After training your model, you will learn how to interpret your results directly from the AMLS portal. This includes not only standard metrics such as accuracy, false positive rate, and false negative rate, but also an explainability dashboard that will wow your business end users. Lastly, there is a tips and tricks section that will assist you in future projects.

In this chapter, we will cover the following topics:

- Loading data into AMLS for AutoML
- Creating an AutoML solution
- Interpreting your AutoML results
- Explaining your AutoML model
- Obtaining better AutoML performance

# Technical requirements

To follow along with this chapter, you will require the following:

- Access to the internet
- A web browser, preferably Google Chrome or Microsoft Edge Chromium
- A Microsoft Azure account
- An Azure Machine Learning service workspace

# Loading data into AMLS for AutoML

Just as you registered the Diabetes Open dataset in *Chapter 2, Getting Started with Azure Machine Learning Service*, you will now be registering a publicly available Titanic dataset using AMLS.

Unlike the diabetes dataset, however, you will load the data directly from your desktop to the portal. The Titanic dataset holds information relating to who survived and who died aboard the infamous ill-fated voyage. You will build a model that predicts survivors based on demographic information such as age and gender, as well as ticket information, such as passenger class and ticket price:

1. First, you will need to download the Titanic data from the GitHub repository.
2. Then, you will need to open up your **Azure Machine Learning Studio** by navigating to `http://ml.azure.com`.
3. Once you are in the studio, click **Datasets** on the right-hand side of the studio under **Assets**.

4.  Then, click **Create dataset** and select **From local files** from the drop-down menu as seen in *Figure 3.1*:

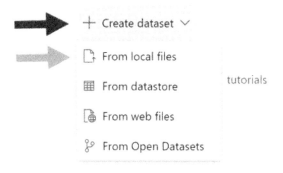

### Register datasets to manage, share, and track data in your machine learning workflows.

With Azure Machine Learning datasets, you can keep a single copy of data in your storage referenced by datasets and seamlessly access data during model training without worrying about connection strings or data paths. Learn more ☐

+  Create dataset  ∨

▢  From local files

⊞  From datastore          tutorials

▢  From web files

▫  From Open Datasets

Figure 3.1 – Creating a dataset from a local file

5.  Before loading in the Titanic data, you have to name your dataset. Write `Titanic Training Data` in the **Dataset Name** textbox. Unlike a lot of other Azure resources, you can include spaces in your dataset's name.

6.  Since the Titanic data contains columns and rows, select **Tabular** from the **Dataset type** drop-down box. Under **Dataset description**, write `Titanic data containing passenger demographic information and ticket information. We will use this data to model who survived the Titanic voyage.`

    Generally speaking, it's a good idea to include the project name and use in the dataset name, for example, *Titanic Training Data* or *Titanic Scoring Data*. In the description field, it's best practice to list the type of information found in the data, as well as which problem you are trying to solve. Please see *Figure 3.2* for reference.

7.  Click **Next** at the bottom of the screen:

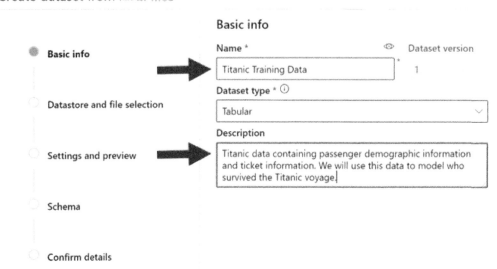

Figure 3.2 – Naming and describing your dataset

8.  Now, you will load your Titanic data onto your default datastore. Your default datastore points to the storage account that was created with your Azure Machine Learning workspace. Select your default datastore by clicking the appropriate circle, as shown in *Figure 3.3*.

9.  Click **Browse**, navigate to `titanic.csv` on your local machine, and then click **Open**. Notice that it will tell you the size of your file after it's loaded into Azure.

10. With your datastore and file selected, you can also determine the path on your datastore in which to save your file. In the empty field labeled **Upload path**, type in `/titanic/train`. This will create a directory structure with a folder called `titanic`, a subfolder called `train`, and another folder with the current date and time in UTC format. You can also use existing folders on your datastore. Please see *Figure 3.3* for reference.

11.  Click **Next** at the bottom of the screen to advance:

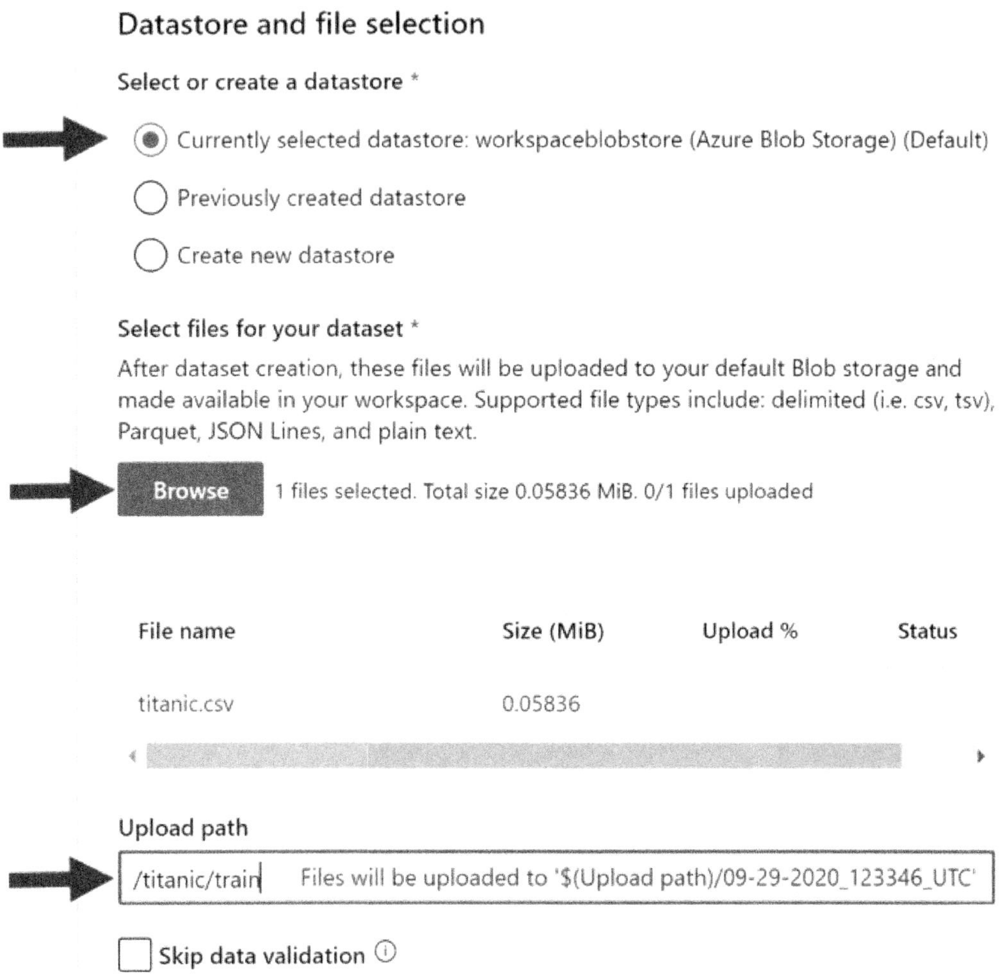

## Datastore and file selection

**Select or create a datastore** *

⊙ Currently selected datastore: workspaceblobstore (Azure Blob Storage) (Default)

○ Previously created datastore

○ Create new datastore

**Select files for your dataset** *

After dataset creation, these files will be uploaded to your default Blob storage and made available in your workspace. Supported file types include: delimited (i.e. csv, tsv), Parquet, JSON Lines, and plain text.

**Browse**    1 files selected. Total size 0.05836 MiB. 0/1 files uploaded

| File name | Size (MiB) | Upload % | Status |
|---|---|---|---|
| titanic.csv | 0.05836 | | |

**Upload path**

/titanic/train    Files will be uploaded to '$(Upload path)/09-29-2020_123346_UTC'

☐ **Skip data validation** ⓘ

Figure 3.3 – Uploading Titanic data to your datastore

12. With your data loaded onto your datastore, it's now time to set up your dataset so that the file enters your Azure Machine Learning workspace correctly. Here, there are five options:

a) From **File format**, you can select delimited files, Parquet files, text files, or JSON files. Select **Delimited** from the dropdown.

b) Then, choose the appropriate option under **Delimiter**. Since this is a CSV, a comma-separated values file, choose **comma** from the dropdown. Notice that every time you make a change, AMLS will generate a new preview of your data at the bottom of your screen.

c) You will rarely have to change **Encoding**, and it's generally best to leave it at the default setting, in this case, **UTF-8**.

d) **Column headers**, on the other hand, you will always want to specify. AMLS defaults to **No headers**, but most files you use will have them. Select **Use headers from the first file** to import your appropriate column headers.

e) **Skip rows** is a useful option when you import data with extraneous rows at the top or bottom of your file. While the Titanic data lacks these extra rows, often you will find that data contains a name, date, or organizational information on the very bottom row.

It is important to remove these extra rows or this will result in errors when you try to build a machine learning model. Please see *Figure 3.4* for an example of how your settings should look.

13. Click **Next** to select only the appropriate columns for your dataset:

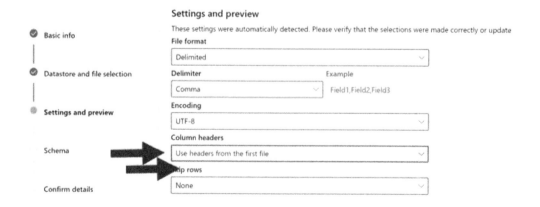

Figure 3.4 – Choosing the correct settings for your file

14. There are certain columns that are inappropriate for machine learning. While AutoML will automatically remove most of them for you, it's best practice to remove them yourself. In no order of importance, the types of columns to remove are as follows:

- Columns that contain a unique value in each row, such as *Name*, *ID*, and *Ticket*
- Columns with an excessive number of null values, such as *Cabin*
- Columns that do not contain useful information
- Columns that are derivations of your target column

15. To remove these columns from your dataset, all you need to do is move the slider to the left, as shown in *Figure 3.5*. Remove **PassengerId**, **Name**, **Ticket**, and **Cabin**:

> **Note**
> When you remove a column from your dataset, the file on the datastore is not altered. You can thereby make multiple datasets from the same file point to different columns.

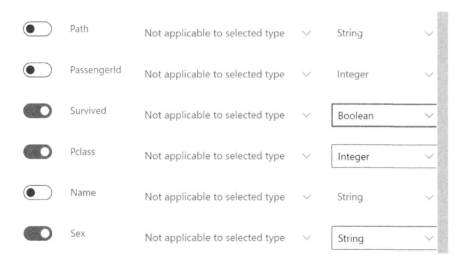

Figure 3.5 – Selecting your columns

16. From this menu, you can also specify the type of each column. There are five types: **String**, **Boolean**, **Integer**, **Decimal**, and **Date**. Booleans are for columns that have two possible values, such as 0 or 1. Change **Survived** to **Boolean**, and change **Age** to **Integer**.

17. Click **Next**.

18. You are now presented with a confirmation screen. From this screen, you can see the name you assigned to your dataset and its description, the datastore, and the path in the datastore on which the base file is located, along with the file settings. Profiling the data is also possible from this screen, as shown in *Figure 3.6*.

If you choose to profile your data, you will need to select a compute cluster. This option will give you summary statistics for each column, including the mean, min, max, standard deviation, number of missing values, number of errors, and number of unique values. Turn profiling on or off, and then click **Next** to create your dataset:

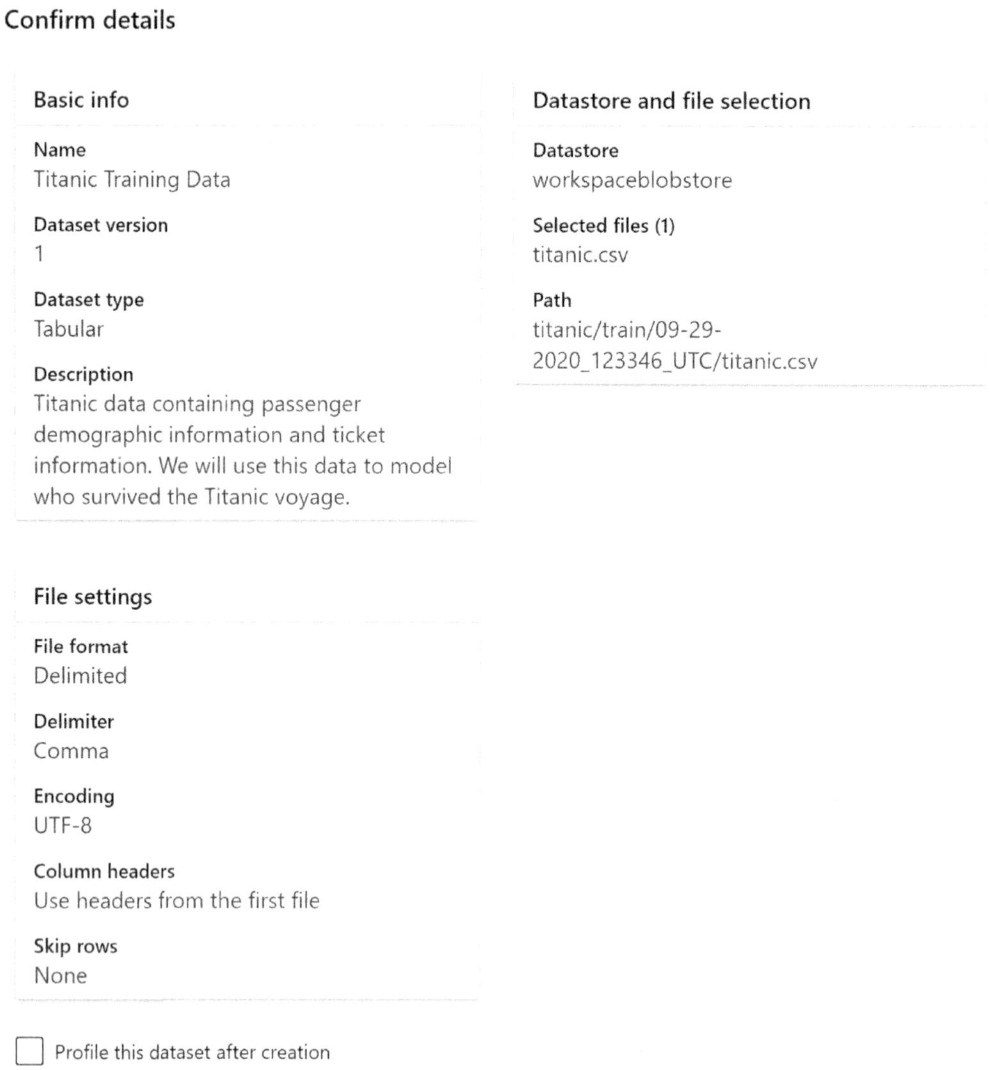

## Confirm details

### Basic info

**Name**
Titanic Training Data

**Dataset version**
1

**Dataset type**
Tabular

**Description**
Titanic data containing passenger demographic information and ticket information. We will use this data to model who survived the Titanic voyage.

### Datastore and file selection

**Datastore**
workspaceblobstore

**Selected files (1)**
titanic.csv

**Path**
titanic/train/09-29-2020_123346_UTC/titanic.csv

### File settings

**File format**
Delimited

**Delimiter**
Comma

**Encoding**
UTF-8

**Column headers**
Use headers from the first file

**Skip rows**
None

☐ Profile this dataset after creation

Figure 3.6 – Confirming your dataset details

You have now created a dataset that you can use within AMLS. With it, you will build a machine learning model that predicts which passengers survived and which passengers perished. The next step is to train a machine learning model using the AutoML guided user interface.

# Creating an AutoML solution

Now that you have loaded Titanic data into your datastore and registered it as a dataset, you are ready to train an AutoML model with a few guided clicks:

1.   To get started, click **Automated ML** from the left-hand menu under **Author**. Then, click **New Automated ML run**, marked by a blue cross, near the top left of the new page, as shown in *Figure 3.7*:

Figure 3.7 – Beginning your AutoML training run

2.   Once you have advanced to the next screen, you will be presented with all of your eligible datasets for training. Currently, only tabular datasets are supported for runs from the AutoML GUI. You can also create a new dataset from this view by clicking the **Create dataset** button. Select **Titanic Training Data**, as shown in *Figure 3.8*.

3.   Click **Next**:

Figure 3.8 – Selecting your dataset for training

After selecting your dataset, the next steps involve naming your experiment, selecting a column to predict, and selecting a compute cluster for remote training. Remember that **Experiments** records all the information related to your training run.

4.  To create a new experiment, select **Create new** and assign it the name `Titanic-Training`. You are not allowed to have spaces in your experiment names; the only special characters allowed are dashes or underscores.

5.  Next, select your **Target Column** from the drop-down menu. Your target column is the number or class you are trying to predict with your machine learning model. In this case, select **Survived**.

6.  Likewise, select a compute cluster on which AutoML will create machine learning models. Select any compute cluster you have created from the drop-down menu. AutoML will run on this compute remotely, allowing you to continue to do other work on your AMLS workspace.

7.  Please confirm your settings using *Figure 3.9* for reference and click **Next** to advance to the final screen:

---

**Important tip**

It's important to select the right size and type of compute when training an automated machine learning model. The RAM on your compute cluster should be about 20 times as large as your dataset to be on the safe side. Use GPUs when using deep learning algorithms and use CPUs for everything else. You can train AutoML models on data of up to 10 gigabytes before you should switch to a Spark-based solution.

---

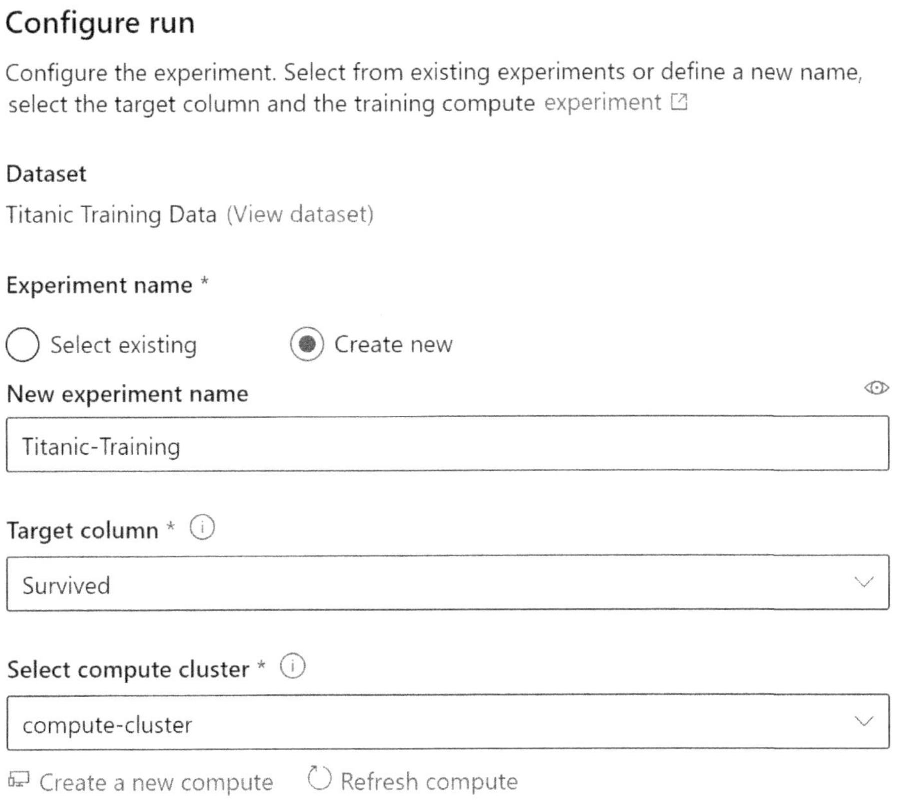

## Configure run

Configure the experiment. Select from existing experiments or define a new name, select the target column and the training compute experiment ☑

**Dataset**

Titanic Training Data (View dataset)

**Experiment name** *

◯ Select existing          ⦿ Create new

New experiment name                                                    👁

| Titanic-Training |
| --- |

**Target column** * ⓘ

| Survived | ⌄ |
| --- | --- |

**Select compute cluster** * ⓘ

| compute-cluster | ⌄ |
| --- | --- |

🖳 Create a new compute    ↻ Refresh compute

Figure 3.9 – Configuring your AutoML run

You are only a few clicks away from creating your AutoML model. There are three options in the next menu: **Classification**, **Forecasting**, and **Regression**. **Classification** is for when you are trying to predict a category, such as whether a person is likely to default on a loan or pay it back. **Regression** is for when you're trying to predict a number instead of a class, for example, trying to predict the price of a house-based feature such as its size. **Forecasting**, on the other hand, is for when you're trying to predict a number in the future.

8.  Since we are trying to predict whether or not a person survived the Titanic disaster, select **Classification**. A green checkmark will appear next to the box on the right-hand side, as seen in *Figure 3.10*:

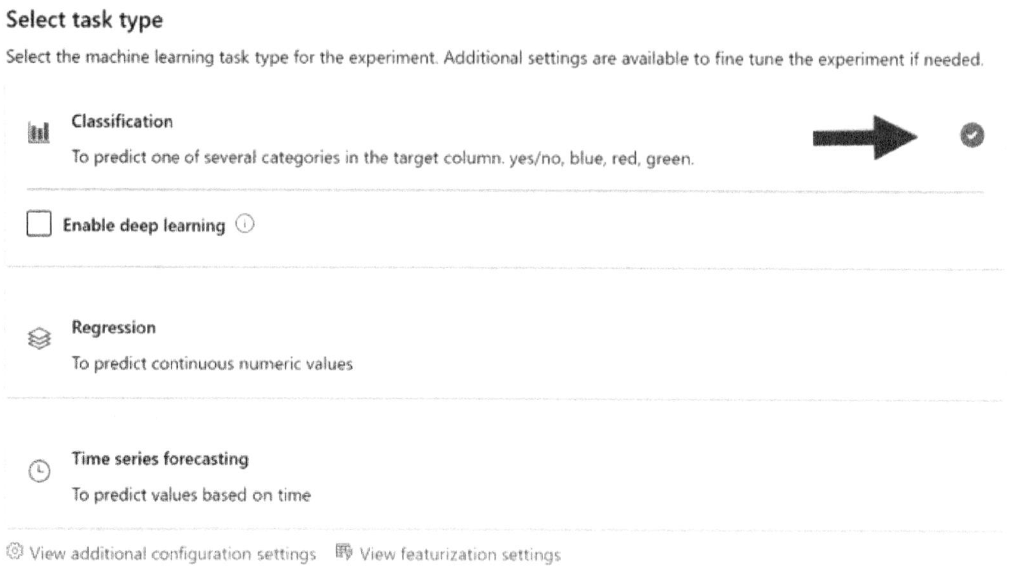

## Select task type

Select the machine learning task type for the experiment. Additional settings are available to fine tune the experiment if needed.

**Classification**
To predict one of several categories in the target column. yes/no, blue, red, green.

☐ Enable deep learning ⓘ

**Regression**
To predict continuous numeric values

**Time series forecasting**
To predict values based on time

⚙ View additional configuration settings    🖽 View featurization settings

Figure 3.10 – Selecting the right task type

There are two additional sets of settings you can configure – **additional configuration settings** and **featurization settings**. **Additional configuration settings** lets you change which metrics AutoML will use to score algorithms, enables you to block AutoML from trying certain algorithms, and lets you set the overall time when AutoML runs.

**Featurization settings** lets you deselect columns, set column types, and decide how AutoML deals with nulls for each column. More advanced data scientists are able to utilize these features for finer-grained control over how AutoML deals with missing values and how AutoML featurizes your dataset.

9.  Navigate to **View additional configuration settings**.

10. Click **Exit criterion** and set the training time to 15 minutes. Note that because training time is measured in hours, you need to set it to 0.25, as shown in *Figure 3.11*. If you accidentally set it to 15, your job will run for 15 hours before terminating:

**Important tip**

For now, stick to the default metric and default validation mechanism, **Accuracy** and **Auto**, respectively. In later chapters, we will do a deeper dive into the various metrics and validation mechanisms supported by AutoML on Azure.

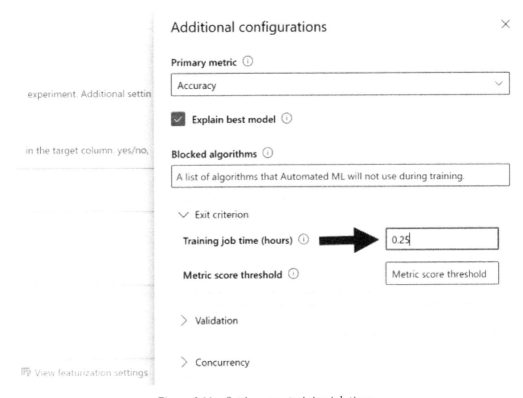

Figure 3.11 – Setting your training job time

11. Click **Save** and **Finish** and find something to do for the next 15 minutes.

You have launched your first AutoML model, and soon you will have the results.

# Interpreting your AutoML results

Your training run should have taken about 15 minutes and produced a model with around 80% accuracy. However, there is much more to your results than this simple metric. There are data guardrails that will inform you of any problems with your data. There is also a slew of different metrics for each of the three problem types and accompanying charts and graphs that can assist you in presenting your results to the business:

1. To begin, click **Automated ML** from the left-hand menu of AMLS and click the latest run from your `Titanic-Training` experiment, as seen in *Figure 3.12*:

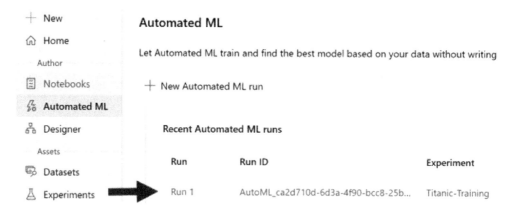

Figure 3.12 – Examining your results

You will be taken to a screen with a variety of metrics regarding your model, including the type of algorithm used to train the best-performing model, its accuracy score, the date and time it was created, and how long your AutoML run took to execute. Take advantage of the **Description** area in the bottom-right corner of your screen to write details about your run.

2. Click the pen icon and write `My first AutoML model`.

You'll notice that there are six tabs at the top of the screen: **Details**, **Data guardrails**, **Models**, **Outputs + Logs**, **Child runs**, and **Snapshot**. For the purpose of interpreting results, only **Data guardrails** and **Models** are important.

3. Click on the **Data guardrails** tab and read the results.

# Understanding data guardrails

**Data guardrails** identify and correct any problems you have in your dataset, and it's essential to know what those problems are. There are different guardrails depending on whether you are trying to solve a classification, regression, or forecasting problem. Classification problems use the following:

- **Validation split handling**: This guardrail looks at your dataset size and unique values within your columns to determine how your machine learning model should be trained and validated. For this Titanic dataset, it will choose 10-fold cross validation. Cross validation splits your data 10 ways, trains a model based on 9 of the parts, and scores the data on the remaining part. This process is repeated 10 times and the scores are averaged.

- **Class balancing detection**: This guardrail looks at your target column to determine whether there are enough samples of each of the unique values. With the Titanic data, this guardrail will pass, as there are sufficient numbers of people who survived and sufficient numbers of people who perished to build a valid model.

- **Missing features values imputation**: This guardrail will scan your data for null values, count them, and fill them automatically. With the Titanic data, you will find that there are 202 null values for the Age column, and they are filled with the mean of that column. There are also two null values for the Embarked column, and they are filled with - -, the most common value for the column.

- **High-cardinality feature detection**: This guardrail will look at your categorical columns and see whether any have too many unique values, in which case they will be binned. With the Titanic data, this guardrail is passed and the data is left unaltered.

# Understanding model metrics

After exploring data guardrails, the next step involves interpreting your model:

1. Click **Models** next to the **Data guardrails** tab. On this tab, you will see a list of AutoML-generated models ranked in order of accuracy, with the highest-scoring model on the top.

2. Click your highest-scoring model's name, as shown in *Figure 3.13*:

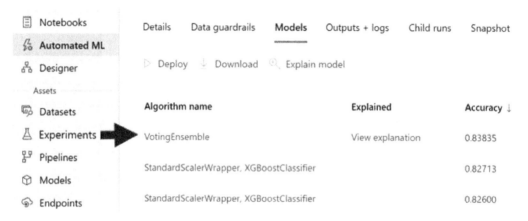

Figure 3.13 – Navigating to your model

This will take you to a similar screen with a new set of tabs at the top. **Metrics**, the fourth tab at the top, contains not only accuracy, but all of the additional metrics and graphs associated with a classification problem. You can check and deselect any you wish. There are over 20 checkboxes, but, for the purpose of this exercise, we will check three.

3. Check the **accuracy**, **confusion_matrix**, and **matthews_correlation** boxes.

**Accuracy** is a simple metric that is easy to understand, and it is what your AutoML run used to build and determine your best model. It is simply how likely your model is to be correct when making a prediction. In my case, it's 83.84%. Unlike a determinant system, machine learning models won't score exactly the same, but your best model should score similarly.

**The Matthews correlation coefficient** is a much more sophisticated metric that takes into account unbalanced classes. It's a combination of true positive, false positive, true negative, and false negative rates and ranges between -1 and 1.

A score of 1 means that your model predicts perfectly, while a score of 0 means that your model is guessing randomly. A score of -1 would mean your model is perfectly wrong every time. My score was .6541, much lower than my accuracy score, as seen in *Figure 3.14*. Your model should score similarly. This indicates that your model is probably much worse at identifying one of the two classes. As you will see next, your confusion matrix confirms this:

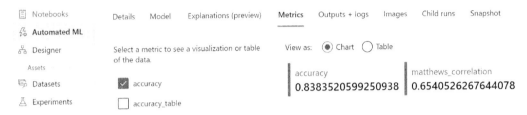

Figure 3.14 – Accuracy and Matthews correlation

**Confusion matrices** are visual representations of your classification output, focusing on true and false positives and negatives. While your accuracy was high, your Matthews correlation coefficient was low, and the confusion matrix is your perfect tool to investigate this relationship. Please see *Figure 3.15*:

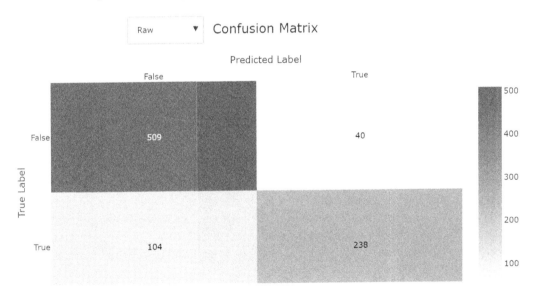

Figure 3.15 – Confusion matrix

What this output says is that my model has correctly identified 509 cases where people died on the Titanic and 238 cases where people lived. However, the model misidentified 40 people who perished as survivors and 104 people who died as having survived. *Figure 3.16* shows the relative percentages by selecting **Normalized** from the drop-down box:

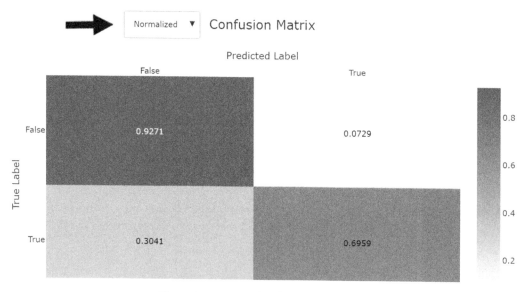

Figure 3.16 – Normalized confusion matrix

Here, we can see that the true negative rate, people who died who were correctly classified as having died, is 92.71%. The false negative rate, people who survived but were incorrectly classified, is only 7.29%. These scores are really high. However, the true positive rate, the ability of the model to predict who survives correctly, is only 69.59%. Likewise, the false positive rate is 30.41%. What we have is a model that is much better at predicting victims of the disaster than predicting survivors.

There are many other useful metrics and graphs contained under the **Metrics** tab. Try checking a few of the boxes and researching what they mean. You can also download any of the graphs directly to your computer from the next tab on your right, **Outputs + logs**. One set of useful information you will not find under the **Metrics** tab relates to what features were used to create your model. This data can be found under the **Explanations** tab, currently in preview.

# Explaining your AutoML model

Knowing your results is important, but knowing how your model derived its results is just as integral to working with machine learning. Here is where model explainability plays a key role. **Explainability** is the ability to say which features are most important in building your AutoML model. This is especially important in industries where you have to be able to legally explain your machine learning models, for example, if you built a model to determine who is approved for a loan:

1.  To begin, click the Explanations tab next to Metrics.

2.  Click the first ID under Explanation ID on the right-hand side of the screen.

3.  Click the slider button next to View previous dashboard experience.

4.  Click Global Importance.

    Immediately, you will see your columns ranked in order of importance. `Sex` is the most important column, followed by `Pclass` and `Age`, as shown in Figure 3.17. With an importance value of `1.1`, Sex is roughly twice as important as Pclass, with a score of `0.59`. All values are relative to each other. From this chart, you can say that gender was the most important feature used in creating your model.

**Select Explanation**

tabular | mimic.lightgbm | raw | classification | 4381fdb3-8165-4f04-8bcc-8e77d2e41987 | 9/29/2020, 10:39:44 PM

**Explainer:** mimic.lightgbm

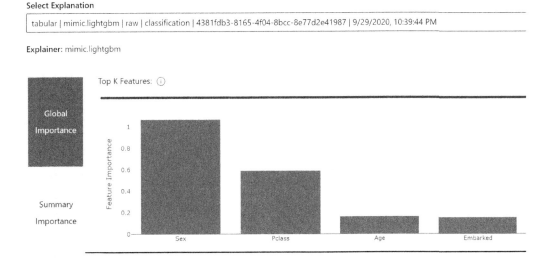

Figure 3.17 – Explainability

Now that you can explain your entire model, it's just as important to be able to explain individual points.

5.  To achieve this, click **Summary Importance** and select any individual data point.

A chart will appear below showing which features negatively or positively affected the model to predict whether the individual survived or perished. *Figure 3.18* shows the profile for a male with a first class ticket. Note that his sex negatively affects his predicted survival, while his class influences the prediction in a positive direction:

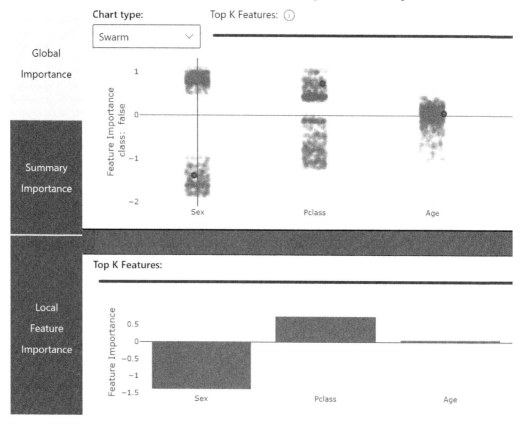

Figure 3.18 – Explainability for a male with a first-class ticket

**Explainability** can be accessed via both this dashboard interface and programmatically through Python, as we will see in later chapters. With Python, you're able to store this information in a database for safe keeping and easy retrieval. That way, you will be able to explain all of your machine learning predictions and defend any legal challenges that may arise.

Having built and understood an AutoML model, you are now ready to build many more. In order to do so more efficiently, there are many small tweaks you can make to improve performance.

# Obtaining better AutoML performance

Congratulations! You have built your first model and it performs very well. However, there are a lot of little things you can do to improve performance. You will build many more models in the future, after all, and in order to build the best models, you need to know all of the tips and tricks. Here's a list of tips and tricks to end this chapter:

- Additional **feature engineering** will often provide superior results. Feature engineering just means transforming data in ways that make it easier for machine learning algorithms to find patterns. Binning ticket prices and age into buckets in the Titanic data, for example, may provide you with superior results compared to just using prices and age as numeric columns.

- Speaking of binning, you can always bin a regression problem to turn it into a classification problem. If you're trying to predict the average lifespan of a human being, for example, you can try to predict a range of numbers instead of a straight number, such as *60-65 years,* instead of an exact number. This is a useful tactic to employ when AutoML isn't returning great results. Classification problems are easier to solve than regression problems given the same dataset, and you can often achieve similar value for your business problem.

- Enabling deep learning will often provide superior results with AutoML, but it comes at the cost of using significantly more compute power and time. Deep learning algorithms create complex neural networks to make predictions and are especially useful for AutoML when you have text data as an input feature. Instead of using a CPU-based compute cluster, use a GPU-based compute cluster for necessary power and performance.

- Forecasting in AutoML requires a carefully constructed dataset and a keen understanding of the forecasting-specific settings. Read *Chapter 6, Building an AutoML Forecasting Solution*, carefully before creating a forecasting solution with AutoML.

- Letting your AutoML job run for longer periods of time will usually mean better results, but only up to a certain point. Try letting it run for a certain amount of time and pay attention to see whether the algorithms are returning better results.

- AutoML intelligently tunes parameters of its algorithms to try to achieve a higher score. If you notice that it keeps trying the same algorithm over and over again, keep in mind that this is expected behavior and that it's trying to find the best combination of parameters for that algorithm.

- It's very likely that a voting or stack ensemble will be your best model, although it's harder to explain to people how these models work. If you have end users that need to know the math behind your models, you can **blacklist** ensemble models for your run. While you cannot presently do this through the AutoML GUI, it is possible to do this via code. Please refer to *Chapter 4, Building an AutoML Regression Solution*, for more details on blacklisting ensemble models.

- Running AutoML on compute clusters composed of small VM sizes is cheap. Feel free to experiment liberally while using low-RAM virtual machines.

# Summary

This ends Part 1 of *Automated Machine Learning with Microsoft Azure*, and you have accomplished a lot! You learned how to load in files from your local machine to your datastore and register it as a dataset. You have created your first AutoML model. You are able to not only interpret the results of your model with graphs and metrics but also explain how your model makes predictions. Lastly, you learned various tips and tricks that will allow you to fine-tune your models. You have made the first step on your journey toward mastering AutoML on Azure.

The next part of your journey will involve a lot of Python coding. In *Chapter 4, Building an AutoML Regression Solution*, you will build a regression model using the **AzureML Python Software Development Kit** (**AzureML SDK**). This SDK is a collection of commands that will allow a Python notebook to interact with your Azure workspace. You will learn how to write AutoML scripts in Python, and you will use those scripts to create powerful solutions for predicting numbers.

# Section 2: AutoML for Regression, Classification, and Forecasting – A Step-by-Step Guide

This second part focuses on training you to perform classification, regression, and forecasting **machine learning (ML)** jobs using Azure AutoML through the Azure ML Python SDK.

This section comprises the following chapters:

- *Chapter 4, Building an AutoML Regression Solution*
- *Chapter 5, Building an AutoML Classification Solution*
- *Chapter 6, Building an AutoML Forecasting Solution*
- *Chapter 7, Using the Many Models Solution Accelerator*

# 4
# Building an AutoML Regression Solution

You've taken the first step to becoming an Azure AutoML expert by building a solution with the AutoML guided user interface. Now, it's time to level up your skills by creating a solution with the **Azure Machine Learning Python Software Development Kit (AzureML Python SDK)**. Using the Diabetes dataset that we built in *Chapter 2, Getting Started with Azure Machine Learning Service,* you will build a regression solution to predict how much a person's diabetes disease has advanced over the last year.

You will begin this chapter by opening up a Jupyter notebook from your compute instance, which will let you write Python code. First, you will load in the Diabetes data. Then, you will train an AutoML model and register your trained model to your **Azure Machine Learning Service (AMLS)** workspace. You will accomplish this by using easily reusable Python scripts. After examining your model's results, you will learn how to register your model so that it can be optimized for a variety of regression-specific metrics and fine-tune your solution to improve performance.

By the end of this chapter, you will have full mastery and knowledge of Azure AutoML's regression capabilities and be able to train regression models using your own data.

In this chapter, we will cover the following topics:

- Preparing data for AutoML regression
- Training an AutoML regression model
- Registering your trained regression model
- Fine-tuning your AutoML regression model

# Technical requirements

The following are the prerequisites for this chapter:

- Access to the internet
- A web browser, preferably Google Chrome or Microsoft Edge Chromium
- A Microsoft Azure account
- An Azure Machine Learning service workspace
- The `titanic-compute-instance` compute instance from *Chapter 2, Getting Started with Azure Machine Learning Service*
- The `compute-cluster` compute cluster from *Chapter 2, Getting Started with Azure Machine Learning Service*
- The `Diabetes Sample` dataset from *Chapter 2, Getting Started with Azure Machine Learning Service*

The code for this chapter is available here: `https://github.com/PacktPublishing/Automated-Machine-Learning-with-Microsoft-Azure/blob/master/Chapter04/Chapter-4-AutoML-on-Azure.ipynb`.

# Preparing data for AutoML regression

Before you can train any model with AutoML, you must have a properly cleansed dataset. This section will walk you through how to prepare data for any AutoML regression solution. You will begin by using your compute instance to access Jupyter notebook, a code editor that will let you code in Python. Following that, you will cleanse, transform, and register your data as an Azure dataset. This will give you a dataset that's ready for training in the next section.

Some of you may be new to Python or even to coding in general, but don't worry. While scripting an AutoML solution may seem much more difficult than using the *GUI*, in reality, it's a matter of making slight changes to boilerplate code.

Using the code found in this book's GitHub repository, you only have to alter it slightly to adapt it to your own custom solution using your own custom data. Furthermore, for this exercise, you've already completed most of the prerequisites. You have your **compute instance**, **compute cluster**, and **dataset** ready, and you're only a few lines of code away from being ready to train an AutoML regression solution.

## Setting up your Jupyter environment

To write code yourself, you must open a Jupyter notebook. **Jupyter notebook** is an environment where you can write, edit, and run Python code. **Python** is a general-purpose programming language that is extremely popular among machine learning practitioners and forms the basis of the Azure Machine Learning service.

The following steps will teach you how to access a Jupyter notebook environment through your Azure compute instance. You will then learn how to create a notebook within this environment that will allow you to script your AutoML regression solution:

1.  First, open Azure Machine Learning Studio by navigating to `http://ml.azure.com`.

2.  Once you are in the studio, click **Compute** on the right-hand side of the studio, under **Manage**.

3.  If your compute instance is currently paused, check the circular checkbox next to `titanic-compute-instance` and click the **Start** button.

4.   Then, click **Jupyter** under **Application URI**, as shown in *Figure 4.1*:

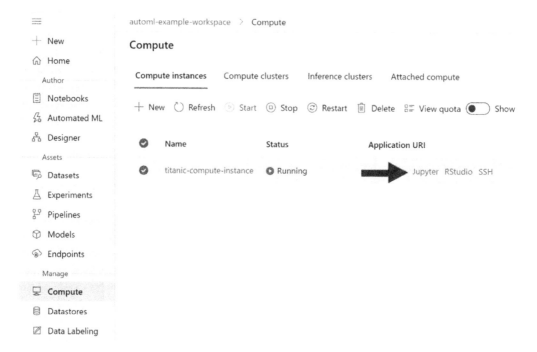

Figure 4.1 – Accessing your Jupyter environment

Once you have accessed your Jupyter environment, the next step is to create
a Jupyter notebook. You can create as many Jupyter notebooks as you like, and you
can also use this environment to upload and download files, create folder structures,
and run both Python and R scripts. **R** is another programming language that is
popular with machine learning practitioners, but we will not cover it in this book.

5.   Click **New** in the upper right-hand corner of your screen to access the
drop-down menu.

6.   Select **Python 3.6 – AzureML** from the drop-down menu, as shown in the *Figure 4.2*:

Figure 4.2 – Creating a Jupyter notebook

7.  Click the new Jupyter notebook that appears in the top-left corner of your screen;
    that is, `Untitled.ipynb`.

8.  Rename `Untitled.ipynb` to `Diabetes_Regression_AutoML` by clicking
    **Untitled** in the top-left corner of the screen, typing `Diabetes_Regression_`
    `AutoML` into the resulting textbox, and clicking **Rename**, as shown in *Figure 4.3*:

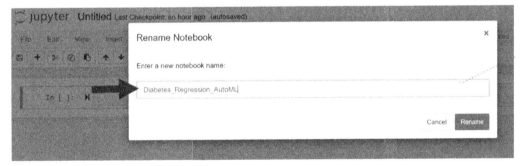

Figure 4.3 – Renaming your Jupyter notebook

By creating and renaming your Jupyter notebook, you are now ready to begin coding in
Python. This is also a step-by-step, repeatable process that consists of mostly boilerplate
code. **Boilerplate** refers to code that can be reused from project to project and requires
little to no customization. As such, you can write Azure AutoML scripts with next to no
Python experience.

# Preparing your data for AutoML

Every AutoML script begins exactly the same way. First, you load in your Python libraries. **Libraries** are simply collections of useful functions that let you complete complex tasks without having to write complicated code yourself. Then, you must set your **workspace, datastore, compute cluster,** and **dataset**. Once you've done this, manipulate your data if necessary and save it to a new dataset. If this is not necessary, simply move on to the *Training an AutoML regression model* section after loading your dataset.

In the following steps, you will load all the necessary libraries you'll need to run the entire notebook from start to finish. These libraries are sufficient to run the data preparation, model training, and model registration portions of this chapter. You will then load the Diabetes dataset you created previously in *Chapter 2, Getting Started with Azure Machine Learning Service*. After loading the data, you will make some slight data transformations before registering it as a new dataset. Let's get started:

1. Load in all the libraries you will need to run everything in this chapter by using the following code:

```
from azureml.core import Workspace, Dataset, Datastore
from azureml.core import Experiment
from azureml.core.compute import ComputeTarget
from azureml.train.automl import AutoMLConfig
from azureml.train.automl.run import AutoMLRun
from azureml.widgets import RunDetails
```

   `Workspace` lets you connect to your **Azure Machine Learning Service (AMLS)** workspace. `Dataset` and `Datastore` let you access your previously created datasets and datastores, while `Experiment` lets you log the results of your AutoML.

   `ComputeTarget` lets you use your compute cluster to run your AutoML job. On the other hand, `AutoMLConfig` enables you to configure your run, while `AutoMLRun` is necessary to train your model. Finally, `RunDetails` lets you track your job in real time.

2. Load in **pandas** and **numpy** by using the following code. These are popular Python packages that help you transform data. `pandas`, in particular, is necessary to view the data in your dataset:

```
import pandas as pd
import numpy as np
```

3.  Connect your Jupyter notebook to your AMLS workspace by using the following code:

```
ws = Workspace.from_config()
```

4.  Set your compute cluster to the one you created in *Chapter 2, Getting Started with Azure Machine Learning Service*, by using the following code:

```
compute_name = 'compute-cluster'
compute_target = ComputeTarget(ws, compute_name)
```

5.  Set your datastore by using the following code. For this exercise, we will use the **default datastore** that comes with your workspace. If you want to use a different datastore, you can replace workspaceblobstore with the name of your datastore:

```
datastore = Datastore.get_default(ws)
my_datastore_name = 'workspaceblobstore'
my_datastore = Datastore.get(ws, my_datastore_name)
```

6.  Set your dataset by using the following code. Use the Diabetes Sample dataset you created in *Chapter 2, Getting Started with Azure Machine Learning Service*, for this. You can reuse this code by replacing the name shown in the following code:

```
dataset_name = "Diabetes Sample"
dataset = Dataset.get_by_name(ws, dataset_name,
version='latest')
```

> **Important Note**
> For this code, you will always need to use the latest version of your dataset. If you wish to use an earlier version of your dataset, you can replace 'latest' with a number.

7.  View the first 10 rows of your data, as shown in the following screenshot, by using the following code:

```
dataset.take(10).to_pandas_dataframe()
```

Whenever you view your data, it's important that you make sure the data looks correct. Verify that the columns have names that match what you expect. Make sure that the values are of the correct type, numeric or string, and that the values themselves look appropriate. If you see a number higher than 120 in the AGE column, for example, you may have problems in the dataset.

If you do find any inconsistencies within your data, it is important that you fix them before training a model with AutoML. Leaving string values in columns that should be numeric will cause AutoML to treat those columns as categorical.

In some cases, this will result in inferior performance. Likewise, leaving errors in your data may result in models that fail to make accurate predictions. As the old data science saying goes, "*Garbage in, garbage out.*" Always inspect your data to make sure it's not garbage.

The output should resemble *Figure 4.4*:

```
In [28]:    # View your dataset by converting to pandas
            dataset.take(10).to_pandas_dataframe()

Out[28]:
```

|   | AGE | SEX | BMI | BP | S1 | S2 | S3 | S4 | S5 | S6 | Y |
|---|-----|-----|-----|-----|-----|-----|-----|-----|-----|-----|-----|
| 0 | 59 | 2 | 32.1 | 101.0 | 157 | 93.2 | 38.0 | 4.00 | 4.8598 | 87 | 151 |
| 1 | 48 | 1 | 21.6 | 87.0 | 183 | 103.2 | 70.0 | 3.00 | 3.8918 | 69 | 75 |
| 2 | 72 | 2 | 30.5 | 93.0 | 156 | 93.6 | 41.0 | 4.00 | 4.6728 | 85 | 141 |
| 3 | 24 | 1 | 25.3 | 84.0 | 198 | 131.4 | 40.0 | 5.00 | 4.8903 | 89 | 206 |
| 4 | 50 | 1 | 23.0 | 101.0 | 192 | 125.4 | 52.0 | 4.00 | 4.2905 | 80 | 135 |
| 5 | 23 | 1 | 22.6 | 89.0 | 139 | 64.8 | 61.0 | 2.00 | 4.1897 | 68 | 97 |
| 6 | 36 | 2 | 22.0 | 90.0 | 160 | 99.6 | 50.0 | 3.00 | 3.9512 | 82 | 138 |
| 7 | 66 | 2 | 26.2 | 114.0 | 255 | 185.0 | 56.0 | 4.55 | 4.2485 | 92 | 63 |
| 8 | 60 | 2 | 32.1 | 83.0 | 179 | 119.4 | 42.0 | 4.00 | 4.4773 | 94 | 110 |
| 9 | 29 | 1 | 30.0 | 85.0 | 180 | 93.4 | 43.0 | 4.00 | 5.3845 | 88 | 310 |

Figure 4.4 – Viewing your dataset

8.  If you wish to change anything about your data, use pandas to do so by converting your dataset into a pandas DataFrame using the following code:

```
dfRaw = dataset.to_pandas_dataframe()
```

9.  One common thing you may want to do is drop columns. You should drop any columns that are derived from the field that you are trying to predict that contain nearly all null values, or that will not be available when you're processing new data. For example, if you don't know the new patient's Sex and Age, you can use the pandas drop function, as shown in the following code:

```
df = dfRaw.drop(['AGE','SEX'], axis=1)
```

10. Reregister your altered data and give the dataset a new name; that is, Diabetes Sample Age/Sex Dropped. Using the following code, you can save your altered pandas DataFrame to your datastore:

```
Dataset.Tabular.register_pandas_dataframe(df,
datastore,
                            "Diabetes Sample Age/Sex
Dropped")
```

11. Another common transformation you may want to try is binning. **Binning** simply refers to creating categorical variables out of one or more numeric columns. For example, we can bin the Age column into three different groups: children younger than 18 years old, adults between the ages of 18 to 64, and seniors older than 64 years old. The following code illustrates this:

```
ageBins = [0, 18, 65, 200]
dfRaw['BinnedFares'] = pd.cut(titanic['Age'], ageBins)
```

12. Data scientists can also remove outliers. **Outliers** are values that fall outside of the normal range of values within one of your columns. One common way of removing outliers is to remove any value that falls three standard deviations away from the mean value of the column.

**Standard deviation** is a measure of variance for your data that is used extensively by data scientists and statisticians. Three standard deviations from the mean means that the data points fall beyond the 99.7 percentile of the distribution and can skew your data. You can use the following code to remove outliers from the Age column:

```
AgeThreeSD = np.std(dfRaw.Age)*3
AgeMean = np.mean(dfRaw.Age)
print(round(AgeThreeSD + AgeMean)) # Prints Outlier
Threshold
# Replace all values above Threshold with Threshold
```

```
Value
dfRaw['Age'] = dfRaw['Age'].mask(dfRaw.Age > AgeMean,
 AgeMean)
```

13. One last common data transformation is creating categorical columns from numeric columns based on cutoff points. Obesity is defined as having a BMI of 30 or greater. We can make a column, `Obesity_Flag`, that contains a 1 or 0 value to indicate whether an individual is obese with the following code:

```
dfRaw['BMI'] = np.where(dfRaw['BMI'] > 30, 1,0)
```

14. Once again, save your altered data to your datastore and register it as a dataset called `Diabetes Sample Full Transform` by using the following code:

```
Dataset.Tabular.register_pandas_dataframe(dfRaw,
 datastore,
                        "Diabetes Sample Full
Transform")
```

You have accomplished a lot in this section. Your libraries have been loaded in, your workspace has been set, and you have all the necessary resources coded to easily create an AutoML run. Additionally, you have multiple versions of your Diabetes data saved as different datasets that you will use to train three AutoML models in the next section.

# Training an AutoML regression model

Compared to setting up your Jupyter environment and preparing your data, training an AutoML model involves fewer steps. First, you will need to set a name for your **experiment**. Remember that experiments automatically log information about your AutoML runs. Next, you will need to set your **Target** column, which is the column you wish to predict, and a few other settings. Finally, you will use AutoML to train a model and watch the results in real time.

In this section, you will create an experiment, configure the various parameters and settings specific to AutoML regression tasks, and train three AutoML regression models using the datasets you created in the previous section. Let's get started:

1.  Set `Experiment` and give it a name by using the following code. This is where all of the logs and metrics of your run will be stored in the AML studio:

```
experiment_name = 'Diabetes-Sample-Regression'
exp = Experiment(workspace=ws, name=experiment_name)
```

2.  Set your `Target` column with the following code. AutoML will train a model that predicts the value of this column – in this case, the `Y` column:

```
target_column = 'Y'
```

3.  Create a variable for your `task` using the following code. `task` is the type of AutoML model you are trying to train, and the options for this are regression, forecasting, and classification. For predicting numeric values that do not have a time element, enter `regression`:

```
task = 'regression'
```

> **Important Note**
> If you are trying to predict data that has a time element, use *forecasting* instead of *regression*. If `date` is one of your columns or you are trying to predict future values based on the current situation, use *forecasting*.

4.  Create a variable for your primary metric. This **primary metric** is how your model will be scored. You should use **normalized root mean squared error** here. This metric, referred to as **RSME**, takes the prediction and subtracts it from the actual value for each observation, squares it, and averages the score across all observations. The lower the score, the better your model. Other options for regression include **R2 score**, **Spearman correlation**, and **normalized mean absolute error**.

    The following code creates a variable and sets it to normalized RMSE. This variable will be passed into your AutoML configuration settings later:

```
primary_metric = 'normalized_root_mean_squared_error'
```

5. Create a variable for `featurization`. You can set featurization to auto or off. If you set featurization to auto, you will have to drop high-cardinality features, impute null values, one-hot encode your data, and generate additional features yourself.

   Always set it to `auto` unless you are an expert data scientist and are comfortable doing everything yourself. The following code also creates a new variable that you will pass into your AutoML configuration settings:

   ```
   featurization = 'auto'
   ```

6. To configure your AutoML, run the following code. Here, you will pass in your task, primary metric, featurization settings, compute target, dataset, and target column. You created all of these previously.

   You must also pass in how long the experiment will run for, whether it will stop early if the model's performance does not improve, the number of cross-validations, and whether your experiment will record model explanations. **Cross-validation** refers to how many times the algorithm will split the dataset and use those splits to train new models. Set this between 5 and 20:

   ```
   config = AutoMLConfig(task=task,
                         primary_metric=primary_metric,
                         featurization=featurization,
                         compute_target=compute_target,
                         training_data=dataset,
                         label_column_name=target_column,
                         experiment_timeout_minutes=15,
                         enable_early_stopping=True,
                         n_cross_validations=5,
                         model_explainability=True)
   ```

7. Train your model and watch the results in real time. The following code trains the AutoML model with your configuration settings and logs the results of the run to the experiment you created earlier.

   As it runs, this code will allow you to track the progress of your session in real time. Here, you can watch AutoML check the validity of your data, train models iteratively, and select the best model:

   ```
   AutoML_run = exp.submit(config, show_output = True)
   RunDetails(AutoML_run).show()
   ```

If you've done everything correctly, your AutoML run will kick off and you can sit back, relax, and watch it train models. First, you will see it perform a **data guardrails** check, as shown in *Figure 4.5*:

```
********************************************************************************
DATA GUARDRAILS:

TYPE:        Missing feature values imputation
STATUS:      PASSED
DESCRIPTION: No feature missing values were detected in the training data.
             Learn more about missing value imputation: https://aka.ms/AutomatedMLFeaturization


********************************************************************************

TYPE:        High cardinality feature detection
STATUS:      PASSED
DESCRIPTION: Your inputs were analyzed, and no high cardinality features were detected.
             Learn more about high cardinality feature handling: https://aka.ms/AutomatedMLFeaturization


********************************************************************************
```

Figure 4.5 – Data guardrails check

Next, AutoML will start training your models. You will notice that AutoML will train different combinations of feature transformations and algorithms. In cases where an identical feature transformation/algorithm pair is replicated, AutoML tests different hyperparameter combinations for that algorithm. As it runs, you will be able to track how long each model took to train, how well it scored, and the score of the best-performing model, as shown in *Figure 4.6*:

```
********************************************************************************
ITERATION: The iteration being evaluated.
PIPELINE: A summary description of the pipeline being evaluated.
DURATION: Time taken for the current iteration.
METRIC: The result of computing score on the fitted pipeline.
BEST: The best observed score thus far.
********************************************************************************

ITERATION   PIPELINE                                DURATION    METRIC    BEST
        0   MaxAbsScaler LightGBM                   0:00:33     0.1808    0.1808
        1   MaxAbsScaler XGBoostRegressor           0:00:25     0.1808    0.1808
        2   MaxAbsScaler DecisionTree               0:00:30     0.2027    0.1808
        3   MinMaxScaler DecisionTree               0:00:31     0.2255    0.1808
        4   StandardScalerWrapper LassoLars         0:00:29     0.1708    0.1708
        5   RobustScaler ElasticNet                 0:00:35     0.1761    0.1708
        6   StandardScalerWrapper LassoLars         0:00:32     0.1708    0.1708
        7   RobustScaler ElasticNet                 0:00:36     0.1708    0.1708
        8   RobustScaler DecisionTree               0:00:31     0.2048    0.1708
        9   MinMaxScaler DecisionTree               0:00:30     0.2458    0.1708
       10   RobustScaler DecisionTree               0:00:31     0.1889    0.1708
       11   MinMaxScaler DecisionTree               0:00:32     0.2125    0.1708
       12   StandardScalerWrapper DecisionTree      0:00:29     0.2041    0.1708
       13   StandardScalerWrapper DecisionTree      0:02:19     0.2209    0.1708
       14   RobustScaler DecisionTree               0:00:31     0.2244    0.1708
       15                                           0:00:08     nan       0.1708
       16      VotingEnsemble                       0:00:52     0.1682    0.1682
       17      StackEnsemble                        0:00:52     0.1702    0.1682
```

Figure 4.6 – AutoML results

Notice how the AutoML trained models do not progressively get better with each run. The first model that was trained has a normalized RMSE of 0.1808. The third model trained has a score of 0.2027. With normalized RMSE, the lower your score, the better.

By the end of the experiment, the best model has a score of 0.1682. When you run the model, you should see similar, but not exact, results, depending on which models AutoML trains. While you can see which models and transformations are being used under the PIPELINE column, hyperparameters remain hidden due to their large number for some algorithms.

You can also get a visualization of these results, as shown in the following graph. Given enough time, you will notice that AutoML gets better and better. This is because it's following its own internal logic of trying different feature engineering/algorithm pairs until it can no longer find a higher-performing model, upon which AutoML will finish with two ensemble algorithms and end the run.

Generally speaking, either **Voting Ensemble** or **Stack Ensemble** will be your highest-performing algorithm. After examining these results, train another model using the Diabetes Sample Age/Sex Dropped dataset and another using the Diabetes Sample Full Transform dataset.

*Figure 4.7* provides a visualization of the results:

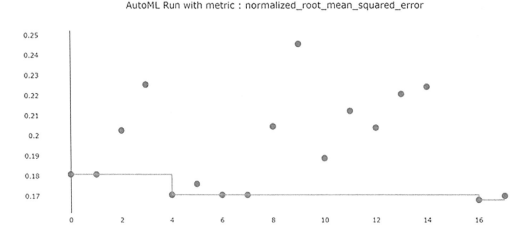

Figure 4.7 – AutoML results visualized

In addition to these two charts, both of which can be found in your Jupyter notebook, there are two more visualizations you can access via AML studio. These are the **Predicted vs True** graph and your **Residuals** histogram. *Predicted vs True* shows you how well your model performed versus an ideal model, whereas *Residuals* gives you an idea of whether your errors are normally distributed or not.

You can access these graphs by following these steps:

1.  Navigate to the front page of AML studio.
2.  Click **Models** on the left-hand panel, under **Assets**.
3.  Click `Diabetes-AllData-Regression-AutoML`. This is the name of the model you trained.
4.  Click the blue link under **Run ID**. It should begin with AutoML, followed by a long string of letters and digits. This is the ID that your experiment was logged under.
5.  Click **Metrics**.
6.  Check the boxes for **predicted_true** and **residuals**.

*Predicted vs True* shows you how well your predictions performed against a model that predicts every data point perfectly. The horizontal axis represents your true values, whereas the vertical axis represents your predicted values. Likewise, the dotted green line represents the perfect model, while the solid blue line represents your actual model. There are also light-blue boundaries around your actual model, showing you the confidence interval. Confidence intervals estimate a range of how well your model would perform in the real world. Please carefully examine *Figure 4.8*:

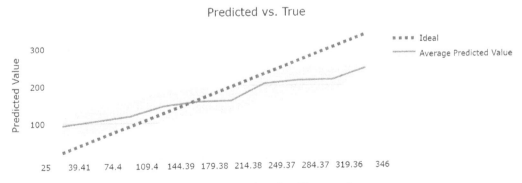

Figure 4.8 – Predicted vs. True graph

*Residuals*, on the other hand, is a histogram that bins your error values and counts the number of data points in each bin. Error is simply how far off your predicted value was from the true value. For example, in *Figure 4.9*, we can see that there about 100 data points where the error fell between -38.5 and 0, and about 115 data points where the error fell between 0 and 38.5.

When examining this chart, you should make sure that it's bell-shaped. If your chart isn't bell-shaped, this means that something is causing a pattern in your errors and that you need to investigate the cause; usually, this means you are missing an important variable:

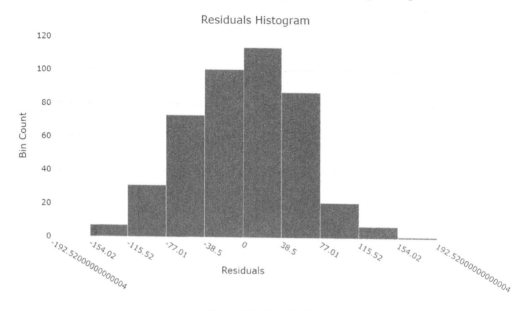

Figure 4.9 – Residuals

Although you have trained a high-performing machine learning model with AutoML, your work is not over yet. Ultimately, a machine learning model is only useful if you can use it to predict new data points. The past is the past, after all, and business value always lies in future situations.

In this case, you are trying to predict patient outcomes so that you can identify and preemptively treat patients whose disease will progress the most quickly. To do so, you must first register your model for future use. We will look at this in the next section.

# Registering your trained regression model

AutoML lets you easily register your trained models for future use. In *Chapter 9, Implementing a Batch Scoring Solution*, and *Chapter 11, Implementing a Real-Time Scoring Solution*, you will create batch execution inference pipelines and real-time scoring endpoints that will use your models. When registering your model, you can add tags and descriptions for easier tracking.

One especially useful feature is the ability to register models based on metrics other than the one you used to score your model. Thus, even though you trained a model using normalized RMSE, you can also register the model that had the best R2 score, even if that model is different.

In this section, you will write a simple description of your model, tag it, and give it a name. After that, you will register the model to your AMLS workspace. It also contains code that will let you register different models based on other metrics. Let's get started:

1.  First, give your model a name, a description, and some tags. **Tags** let you easily search for models, so think carefully as you implement them. Pay close attention to their format. You can enter as many tags as you wish and feel free to be verbose in your description:

    ```
    description = 'Best AutoML Regression Run using
    Diabetes Sample Data. This model requires the Age and
    Sex Columns.'
    tags = {'project' : "Diabetes", "creator" : "your
    name"}
    model_name = 'Diabetes-AllData-Regression-AutoML'
    ```

2.  Next, register your model to your AMLS workspace, passing in your model's name, tags, and description. Use the AutoML_run process you trained in the previous section:

    ```
    AutoML_run.register_model(model_name=model_name,
    description=description, tags=tags)
    ```

> **Important Note**
>
> If time has elapsed since the time you trained your AutoML model, you can retrieve it by finding its **run ID** in the **Experiments** section of AML studio. Simply click on **Experiments** under **Assets**, select the correct experiment name, and copy the **run ID** provided. Then, set AutoML_run using this ID, as follows:
>
> ```
> experiment_name = 'Diabetes-Sample-Regression'
>
> exp = Experiment(workspace=ws, name=experiment_
> name)
>
> AutoML_run = AutoMLRun(experiment = exp, run_id =
> 'your_run_id')
> ```

3.  Try registering a different model based on R2 score. Give it a slightly different name, add an additional tag, and use an identical description:

```
description = 'Best AutoML Regression Run using \
Diabetes Sample Data. This model requires the Age and \
Sex Columns.'
tags = {'project' : "Diabetes", "creator" : "your
name", "metric" : "R2"}
model_name = 'Diabetes-AllData-Regression-AutoML-R2'
AutoML_run.register_model(model_name=model_name,
description=description, tags=tags, metric =
'r2_score')
```

With that, your model has been registered and is ready for use. You have created a regression model that can be used to identify how diabetes is likely to progress in a patient over a 1-year period based on their gender, age, blood pressure, BMI, and six blood serum measurements. Try registering other AutoML models you've trained using the other datasets you created in this chapter. Give them appropriate tags, names, and descriptions that differentiate them.

It's important to emphasize the importance of a good tagging strategy and robust descriptions. As you are working on a machine learning project, it's not such a big deal, as you will remember which models you trained and what datasets you trained them with. However, as you move on to other projects and as time passes, your memory becomes less and less reliable. If you don't have good tags, locating your models becomes a difficult endeavor.

A proper tagging strategy will include the project name, the project creator, the metric the model was trained on, the dataset the model was trained with, and other pertinent information about the model. There is no need to include a version number, as AutoML includes one automatically. If you register a different model with the same name, a new version of the model will be registered and the old one can still be accessed by specifying its version number.

Once you've registered a few different models, try accessing one using the following code:

```
model = Model(ws,' 'Diabetes-AllData-Regression-AutoML-R2')
```

Now, you know how to register and call models that you've trained with AutoML. With this accomplished, we can move on and look at some tips and tricks that will improve your regression models as you train them more in the future.

# Fine-tuning your AutoML regression model

In this section, you will first review tips and tricks for improving your AutoML regression models and then review the algorithms used by AutoML for regression.

## Improving AutoML regression models

While AutoML will handle most of the complicated data transformations and feature engineering for you, there are a few tips you can follow to increase the accuracy of your model. Some of these tips are true across all three AutoML tasks – *regression*, *classification*, and *forecasting* – while others are regression-specific. Following them will yield higher-performing models and, more importantly, hone your understanding of machine learning techniques. I have listed a few tips and tricks here for quick reference:

- Fill in null values before passing them on to AutoML. Alternatively, drop any rows that contain a null value. Just because AutoML will automatically fill your null values does not mean that it will do a great job.

  In some situations, filling in null values with the mean of the column is appropriate. For example, if you're missing the price of an item, it's very likely that the mean price will approximate the missing value. For noisier columns, think deeply about how you should go about filling in missing values or whether you should include those datapoints at all. Here's some Python code that will fill in null values for you:

  ```
  mean_age = dfRaw.AGE.mean()
  dfRaw.AGE = dfRaw.AGE.fillna(value=meanAge)
  ```

- Become familiar with all of the different AutoML configuration options. You can find them at this link: `https://docs.microsoft.com/en-us/python/api/azureml-train-automl-client/azureml.train.automl.automlconfig.automlconfig?view=azure-ml-py`.

- Use `y_min` and `y_max` to take care of any outliers in your `Target` column. If you have values that are outliers, such as values that are 3 or more standard deviations away from the mean value of your `Target` column, setting `y_min` and `y_max` to 3 standard deviations below and above your mean, respectively, can yield better performing models. This only applies to regression models.

  The following code calculates the mean and standard deviation of the `Target` column and uses them to set `y_min` and `y_max`:

```
TargetSD = np.std(dfRaw.Y)*3
TargetMean = np.mean(dfRaw.Y)
y_min = TargetMean - TargetSD
y_max = TargetMean + TargetSD
```

- Research the four different primary metrics to understand which metrics fit your problem best. Normalized RMSE will suffice for most regression problems, but many research papers exist on the pros and cons of using other metrics.

- Use `https://docs.microsoft.com/en-us/azure/machine-learning/how-to-understand-automated-ml` to understand what a good regression model looks like. A good model will have unbiased residuals, meaning that your model over and under predicts equally. A good model will also more closely fit the ideal line in the *Predicted vs True* graph shown in *Figure 4.8*.

- Go to **Experiments** under **Assets** in AML studio, click your experiment's name, select your run ID, click the **Models** tab, select the highest-performing algorithm, and click the **Metrics** tab. This will provide you with all of the different metrics and charts necessary to evaluate your algorithm.

- You can use the `weight_column_name` configuration option to assign a weight column to your dataset. If some observations are more important to get right than others, assign a higher weight to those observations.

  For example, you can assign a weight of 2 to an important observation while assigning a weight of 1 to normal observations, thus weighing important observations twice as heavily. For example, if you're building an algorithm that predicts electricity usage of a factory, you may want to peak usage times more heavily.

- Enable longer experiment runtimes to obtain higher-performing models. Sometimes, this enables AutoML to find better hyperparameters for the models it trains. Other times, increasing the runtime doesn't help so much, but it's always worth giving it a try.

- If AutoML does not provide a satisfactory model, try adding more data. You can add either more historical data (more rows) or additional information (more columns). Be careful not to add too many columns to a very small dataset, however, as this can lead to overfitting.

    **Overfitting** is where you produce a very good model that doesn't generalize to new datapoints. If this happens to you, try adding more historical data or removing columns from your dataset.

- In the end, if, after applying all of these tips and tricks, your model is still unsatisfactory, try changing your regression problem to a classification problem. Generally, classification problems are easier to solve than regression problems. The way you achieve this is by binning your target column.

    Instead of trying to predict a specific number, your algorithm will try to predict a range of numbers instead. You have to be creative for this approach to work. For example, with the `Diabetes Sample` dataset, try binning the `Target` column using the following code:

```
ySD = np.std(dfRaw.Y)
yMean = np.mean(dfRaw.Y)
yMin = np.min(dfRaw.Y)
yMax = np.max(dfRaw.Y)
low = yMean - ySD
high = yMean + ySD
yBins = [yMin, low, yMean, high, yMax]
dfRaw['BinnedY'] = pd.cut(dfRaw['Y'], yBins)
```

Whenever you employ the trick of turning a regression problem into a classification problem, keep in mind that the resulting target column must be meaningful. In the following screenshot, we can see the values of the `Target` column indicating the extent to which the disease has progressed in patients.

If there are substantial, meaningful differences between the four different bins, then this is a valid way to approach the problem. However, if the patients in each bin do not differ from each other in terms of medical outcome, then you should bin the data to make sure patients are lumped together correctly.

In *Figure 4.10*, we can see the values of the `Target` column indicating the extent to which the disease has progressed in patients:

```
(25.0, 75.128]
(75.128, 152.133]
(152.133, 229.139]
(229.139, 346.0]
```

Figure 4.10 – Results of binning the Diabetes data

You are now familiar with many of the little techniques that data scientists employ to achieve higher-performing models and solve business problems. This list is far from exhaustive, and you will encounter more techniques as you build more models with AutoML. Anytime you find some interesting way to improve your model's performance, it is important to write it down somewhere and store the code in a repository.

Whenever you encounter a difficult problem that seems impossible to solve, reread all of the tips in this section, then search your repository. Most of the time, with the right data and the right transformations, AutoML will be able to generate a solution on par with most data scientists. Other times, it's a matter of fine-tuning settings. Sometimes, the only thing you can do is try turning your regression problem into a classification problem and try again.

One last thing that will help you use AutoML more efficiently is developing an understanding of the algorithms underlying the technology.

# Understanding AutoML regression algorithms

AutoML uses many state-of-the-art machine learning algorithms. While it isn't necessary for you to understand them in order to use AutoML, learning more about them will help you develop as a data scientist. Certain algorithms perform better in certain situations. Furthermore, you can group the algorithms into roughly five groups.

**Standard regression algorithms** are those which assign coefficients to your explanatory variables in order to predict your target column. AutoML uses two of these techniques: **Elastic net** and **LARS (least angular regression) lasso**.

Elastic net trains a regression model using both L1 and L2 regularization techniques. **L1**, also called **lasso**, reduces the coefficients on less important variables to 0, while **L2**, called **ridge**, reduces the value of coefficients of less important variables. Elastic net combines both techniques to create simpler models that are easier to explain while not dropping as many variables as lasso regression. LARS lasso is a technique for data with lots of columns that iteratively uses the most important columns, but doesn't perform well with noisy data.

**Tree algorithms** split data based on a series of if-then decision rules, resulting in a mapping that resembles a branching tree. As you go further down the tree, you eventually reach a point where the algorithm predicts a value based on the series of rules it creates. AutoML uses three of these techniques:

- **Decision tree** is a simple algorithm which is easily explainable but prone to overfitting, performing well on training data at the expense of generalizing to new data.

- **Random forest** creates an ensemble of decision trees and averages them together. Each tree is created from a random sample of the training set and columns are randomly chosen to create decision rules.

- **Extremely randomized trees** goes one step further by also randomizing the values chosen to make splits. This randomness reduces the variance of the models when generalized to new data, creating better models.

**Gradient boosting algorithms** work by combining many weak performing decision tree models, called **weak learners**, together. These algorithms start by creating a single weak leaner, looking for data points on which it doesn't perform well, and creating another weak learner on that subset of data. This process is repeated until a certain threshold is met. AutoML uses three of these algorithms: **XGBoost**, **LightGBM**, and **gradient boosting**. All three work similarly and were chosen based on their high performance, but must be carefully tuned to avoid overfitting.

**Nearest neighbor algorithms** work by looking at each row of data and calculating the mean value of similar data points, called nearest neighbors. K-nearest neighbors are the sole type of nearest neighbor algorithm used by AutoML. K refers to the number of nearest neighbors the algorithm examines when making its prediction. KNN works well when your data has a low number of columns as it tends to overfit when you use many columns to predict your target column.

**Optimization algorithms** are those that iteratively minimize an objective function to try to converge on the best prediction. AutoML uses three of these: **Stochastic gradient descent (SGD)**, **online gradient descent regressor**, and **fast linear regressor**. Each of these algorithms work by finding the slope of an objective function for each column and working down the slope until it gets as close to 0 as possible by adjusting weights.

This is a very slow process and SGD works by randomly picking datapoints along the slope to get to the minimum as fast as possible; online gradient descent regressor works similarly but with different weighting options. Fast linear regressor uses a new state-of-the-art optimization technique called **Stochastic Dual Coordinate Ascent (SDCA)** which optimizes a dual loss function instead of a single loss like the other algorithms.

A summary of the 12 algorithms is provided in Figure 4.11.

| Standard regression algorithms | Tree algorithms | Gradient boosting algorithms | Nearest neighbor algorithms | Optimization algorithms |
| --- | --- | --- | --- | --- |
| Elastic net | Decision tree | XGBoost | KNN | SGD |
| LARS Lasso | Random forest | LightGBM | | Online gradient descent regressor |
| | Extremely randomized trees | Gradient boosting | | Fast linear regressor |

Figure 4.11 – AutoML regression algorithms

In addition to the preceding 12 algorithms, AutoML also performs **model ensembling** at the end of each AutoML training run. Model ensembling is using the predictions of multiple machine learning models together to make a prediction. AutoML uses two ensembling techniques: voting and stacking.

**Voting ensembles** take a weighted average of your regression models and use that to make a prediction. **Stack ensembles**, in contrast, train an elastic net model using the output of other models. AutoML will train one voting ensemble and one stack ensemble per training run. Usually, one of these two ensemble models will be your highest performing model.

For more information on these models, please consult the AutoML documentation found at `https://docs.microsoft.com/en-us/azure/machine-learning/how-to-configure-auto-train#configure-your-experiment-settings`

# Summary

With this chapter, you have successfully constructed a regression model using the AzureML Python SDK. Regardless of whether you're a Python novice or expert, you have loaded data, transformed it extensively using pandas, and built a useful machine learning model with AutoML. You then registered your model to an AMLS workspace. You will use that same model in future chapters to create inference pipelines and real-time scoring endpoints using REST APIs.

By working through all the exercises in this chapter, you have obtained a level of mastery over Azure AutoML regression solutions. You can now take any set of data that's useful in predicting a number and use it to create a high-performing machine learning model. Furthermore, you can code all of this in Python and, if the model fails to perform, you know lots of little ways to improve performance, or, if worst comes to worst, change your regression problem to a classification problem.

In *Chapter 5, Building an AutoML Classification Solution*, you will learn how to solve these classification problems using AutoML, and then build a machine learning model that predicts a class instead of a number.

# 5
# Building an AutoML Classification Solution

After building your AutoML regression solution with Python in *Chapter 4, Building an AutoML Regression Solution*, you should be feeling confident in your coding abilities. In this chapter, you will build a classification solution. Unlike regression, **classification** is used to predict the category of the object of interest. For example, if you're trying to predict who is likely to become a homeowner in the next five years, classification is the right machine learning approach.

**Binary classification** is when you are trying to predict two classes, such as homeowner or not, while **multiclass classification** involves trying to predict three or more classes, such as homeowner, renter, or lives with family. You can utilize both of these techniques with Azure AutoML, and this chapter will teach you how to train both kinds of models using different datasets.

In this chapter, you will begin by navigating directly to the Jupyter environment as you did in *Chapter 4, Building an AutoML Regression Solution*. Then, you will load in the same Titanic data that you used to build a model in *Chapter 3, Training Your First AutoML Model*. Retraining an identical model would be boring, so you will enrich the dataset by adding a few derived columns.

Once you accomplish that, you will train, examine, and register your binary classification model. Then, you will train a multiclass classification model using the popular, publicly available Iris dataset that will predict what type of flower an individual plant is based on its dimensions. You will end this chapter by learning a few tips and tricks on how to fine-tune classification models. Pay close attention, as even seasoned data scientists fail to modify their classification models to align with the business problem at hand.

By the end of this chapter, you will be able to build all types of classification models on your own with ease, regardless of your previous machine learning experience.

In this chapter, we will cover the following topics:

- Prepping data for AutoML classification
- Training an AutoML classification model
- Registering your trained classification model
- Training an AutoML multiclass model
- Fine-tuning your AutoML classification model

# Technical requirements

For this chapter, you will be building models with Python code in Jupyter notebooks through **Azure Machine Learning** (**AML**) **studio**. Furthermore, you will be using datasets and Azure resources that you should have created in previous chapters. As such, the full list of requirements is as follows:

- Access to the internet
- A web browser, preferably Google Chrome or Microsoft Edge Chromium
- A Microsoft Azure account
- An **Azure Machine Learning** workspace

- The `titanic-compute-instance` compute instance created in *Chapter 2, Getting Started with Azure Machine Learning*
- The `compute-cluster` compute cluster created in *Chapter 2, Getting Started with Azure Machine Learning*
- The `Titanic Training Data` dataset from *Chapter 3, Training your First AutoML Model*
- An understanding of how to navigate to the Jupyter environment from an Azure compute instance as demonstrated in *Chapter 4, Building an AutoML Regression Solution*

# Prepping data for AutoML classification

Classification, or predicting the category of something based on its attributes, is one of the key techniques of machine learning. Just like regression, you first need to prep your data before training it with AutoML. In this section, you will first navigate to your Jupyter notebook, load in your data, and transform it for use with AutoML.

Just as you loaded in your `Diabetes Sample` dataset via Jupyter notebooks for regression, you will do the same with the `Titanic Training Data` dataset. However, this time around you will do much more extensive data transformation before training your AutoML model. This is to build upon your learning; classification datasets do not necessarily require more transformation than their regression counterparts. Identical to the previous chapter, you will begin by opening up a Jupyter notebook from your compute instance.

## Navigating to your Jupyter environment

Similar to *Chapter 4, Building an AutoML Regression Solution*, you will begin by creating a new Jupyter notebook for creating your classification model as follows:

1. First, open AML studio by navigating to `http://ml.azure.com`.

2. Once you are in the studio, click **Compute** on the right-hand side of the studio under **Manage**.

3. If your compute instance is currently paused, check the circular checkbox next to `titanic-compute-instance` and click the **Start** button.

4.   Then, click **Jupyter** under **Application URL** as seen in the following screenshot:

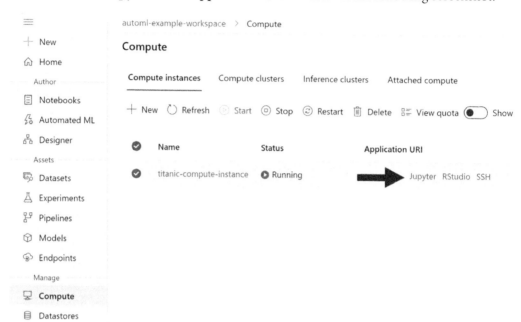

Figure 5.1 – Accessing your Jupyter environment

You should see the `Diabetes_Regression_AutoML` notebook that you previously created. Each time you create a Jupyter notebook, it will persist on your AMLS workspace even if you or other users access Jupyter from a different compute instance. Feel free to create as many notebooks as you want in this space, naming them carefully so you can easily track different projects.

5.   Click **New** in the upper right-hand corner of your screen to access the drop-down menu.

6.   Select **Python 3.6 – AzureML** from the drop-down menu.

7.   Click the new Jupyter notebook that appeared in the top-left corner of your screen, `Untitled.ipynb`.

8.  Rename Untitled.ipynb to Titanic Classification_AutoML
    by clicking **Untitled** in the top-left corner of the screen, typing Titanic_
    Classification_AutoML in the resulting textbox, and clicking **Rename** as
    shown in the following screenshot:

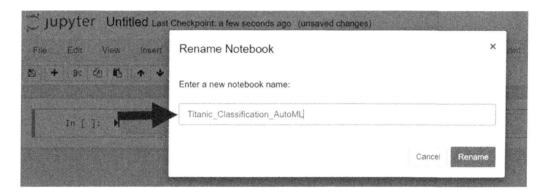

Figure 5.2 – Renaming your Jupyter notebook

With your notebook created, you are now ready to load in your Titanic data.

## Loading and transforming your data

All AutoML solutions use roughly the same boilerplate code. If you completed *Chapter 4,
Building an AutoML Regression Solution*, begin copying over your code cell by cell. After
doing so, simply follow the instructions step by step and alter your code when necessary. If
you skipped directly to this chapter, you will have to code everything from scratch.

Just as before, you will load in your Python libraries and set your workspace, datastore,
compute cluster, and dataset. You will then transform and register your enriched data
as follows:

1.  Load in all of the libraries you will need to run all of your code. Refer to
    *Chapter 4, Building an AutoML Regression Solution*, for a detailed explanation
    of all of these packages:

```
from azureml.core import Workspace, Dataset, Datastore
from azureml.core import Experiment
from azureml.core.compute import ComputeTarget
from azureml.train.automl import AutoMLConfig
from azureml.train.automl.run import AutoMLRun
from azureml.widgets import RunDetails
```

2. Load in pandas and numpy. These are popular Python packages that help you transform data. pandas, in particular, is necessary to view the data in your dataset:

```
import pandas as pd
import numpy as np
```

3. Connect your Jupyter notebook to your AMLS workspace:

```
ws = Workspace.from_config()
```

4. Set your compute cluster:

```
compute_name = 'compute-cluster'
compute_target = ComputeTarget(ws, compute_name)
```

5. Set your datastore. For this exercise, we will use the default datastore that comes with your AMLS workspace. If you want to use a different datastore, you can replace the name:

```
datastore = Datastore.get_default(ws)
my_datastore_name = 'workspaceblobstore'
my_datastore = Datastore.get(ws, my_datastore_name)
```

6. Set your dataset:

```
dataset_name = "Titanic Training Data"
dataset = Dataset.get_by_name(ws, dataset_name,
version='latest')
```

> **Note**
>
> *Step 6* is the first place where you should have altered your code. Each time you create a new classification or regression AutoML solution in Azure, use this template.

7. The following is the code to view the first 10 rows of data. Make sure that it looks correct:

```
dataset.take(10).to_pandas_dataframe()
```

The first 10 rows should appear as follows:

```
In [7]:  ▶| # View your dataset by converting to pandas
           dataset.take(10).to_pandas_dataframe()
```

```
Out[7]:
```

|   | Survived | Pclass | Sex | Age | SibSp | Parch | Fare | Embarked |
|---|----------|--------|-----|-----|-------|-------|------|----------|
| 0 | False | 3 | male | 22.0 | 1 | 0 | 7.2500 | S |
| 1 | True | 1 | female | 38.0 | 1 | 0 | 71.2833 | C |
| 2 | True | 3 | female | 26.0 | 0 | 0 | 7.9250 | S |
| 3 | True | 1 | female | 35.0 | 1 | 0 | 53.1000 | S |
| 4 | False | 3 | male | 35.0 | 0 | 0 | 8.0500 | S |
| 5 | False | 3 | male | NaN | 0 | 0 | 8.4583 | Q |
| 6 | False | 1 | male | 54.0 | 0 | 0 | 51.8625 | S |
| 7 | False | 3 | male | 2.0 | 3 | 1 | 21.0750 | S |
| 8 | True | 3 | female | 27.0 | 0 | 2 | 11.1333 | S |
| 9 | True | 2 | female | 14.0 | 1 | 0 | 30.0708 | C |

Figure 5.3 – Viewing your Titanic dataset

8.  Convert your dataset into a **pandas DataFrame**:

```
dfRaw = dataset.to_pandas_dataframe()
```

AutoML will automatically fill your null values for you, but it's not particularly savvy in its implementation. It will most often naively fill nulls based on the mean of the column. As a data scientist, you often want to be more careful with how you fill nulls to improve the accuracy of your model. The closer you can approximate the actual missing model, the better it will perform in the real world.

Notice that the Titanic data has missing values in the Age column. It's very likely that the age of the passengers will vary by other columns such as Sex. Instead of replacing these nulls with the mean value of the entire Age column, let's instead replace them with mean age by gender.

9.  Calculate the mean age of women and men in your Titanic dataset:

```
dfRaw = dataset.to_pandas_dataframe()
round(dfRaw.groupby(['Sex'])['Age'].mean())
```

This code will show you that the mean age of women is 28 years old and the mean age of men is 31 years old. You will use these numbers in the next cell.

10. Replace null values in the Age column with the appropriate number for each gender using this conditional Python code:

```
dfRaw['Age'] = dfRaw.apply(
    lambda row: 31 if np.isnan(row['Age'])\
    and row['Sex']=='male'\
    else (28 if np.isnan(row['Age'])\
        and row['Sex']=='female'\
    else row['Age']),axis=1)
```

Another common transformation is to bin numerical data. **Binning** numerical data means creating multiple categorical columns from a single numeric column, for example, splitting an age column into age ranges instead. You should bin numerical data when you suspect that the range of numbers matters more than the absolute number.

For example, if you suspect whether a person is young or old matters to whether they survived the Titanic, but not their exact age, you should bin data into groups. AutoML will not automatically bin data for you, but some algorithms, such as decision trees, do not require binning to achieve a similar effect.

11. Bin the Age column into four different age groups: Under 15, 15-35, 35-60, and over 60:

```
dfRaw['BinUnder15'] = np.where(dfRaw.Age < 15,1,0)
dfRaw['Bin15to34'] = np.where((dfRaw.Age>14)\
                              & (dfRaw.Age < 35),1,0)
dfRaw['Bin35to60'] = np.where((dfRaw.Age>34)\
                              & (dfRaw.Age < 61),1,0)
dfRaw['BinOver60'] = np.where(dfRaw.Age > 60,1,0)
```

You can try different combinations of ages if you like.

12. Now that you have binned the Age column, drop it. This will be your final DataFrame:

```
df = dfRaw.drop(['Age'],axis=1)
```

13. Reregister your altered data and give the dataset a new name, `Titanic Transformed`. This will save your transformed pandas DataFrame to your datastore, creating a new file on disk:

```
Dataset.Tabular.register_pandas_dataframe(df, datastore,
                          "Titanic Transformed")
```

You may get a warning that `register_pandas_dataframe` is an experimental method as it is a new feature of the AML SDK. You are safe to ignore this warning.

If you're new to Python, some of this code will perplex you, and that's okay. You will find great value in learning the `pandas` and `numpy` libraries, as they are two of the most popular packages for transforming data. Each time you learn a new `pandas` or `numpy` function, save an example to your personal code base for later use. Even if you never become a Python expert, however, you will still be able to use Azure AutoML to deliver a great model. Yet, Python experts will still be able to deliver the best models through careful, nuanced, and savvy data transformations.

You are now ready to train another model with your Titanic dataset. Between intelligently filling in null values and binning the `Age` column, you may expect to produce a superior model to that which you built in *Chapter 3, Training Your First AutoML Model*. Let's see if that's the case.

# Training an AutoML classification model

Training an AutoML classification model is very similar to training an AutoML regression model, but there are a few key differences. In *Chapter 4, Building an AutoML Regression Solution*, you began by setting a name for your experiment. After that, you set your target column and subsequently set your AutoML configurations. Finally, you used AutoML to train a model, performed a data guardrails check, and produced results.

All of the steps in this section are nearly the same. However, pay close attention to the data guardrails check and results, as they are substantially different when training classification models:

1. Set your `experiment` and give it a name:

```
experiment_name = 'Titanic-Transformed-Classification'
exp = Experiment(workspace=ws, name=experiment_name)
```

2.  Set your `dataset` to your transformed `Titanic` data:

```
dataset_name = "Titanic Transformed"
dataset = Dataset.get_by_name(ws, dataset_name,
version='latest')
```

3.  Set your target column, `Survived`. Capitalization matters:

```
target_column = 'Survived'
```

4.  Create a variable for your `task`: now, `task` is the type of AutoML model you are trying to train. For predicting categories, enter `classification`:

```
task = 'classification'
```

> **Important note**
>
> You can always turn a regression problem into a classification, and this is often an easier machine learning problem to solve. For example, for the diabetes problem, you can create a new column based on the `Y` column. Set a numeric threshold and assign a `1` to any patient who exceeds the threshold and a `0` to any patient below it. Then, try training a classification model with AutoML.

5.  Create a variable for your primary metric: **Primary metric** is how your model will be scored. Use **accuracy**. This metric divides the number of cases that your model accurately predicted the class (survived or not) of by the total number of cases. The higher the score, the better your model. Other options for classification include **AUC weighted**, **average precision score weighted**, **norm macro recall**, and **precision score weighted**:

```
primary_metric = 'accuracy'
```

6.  Create a variable for `featurization` and set it to `auto`:

```
featurization = 'auto'
```

You can set `featurization` to `auto` or `off`. If you set `featurization` to `off`, you will have to drop high-cardinality features, impute null values, one-hot encode your data, and generate additional features yourself.

With classification, you will also have to balance your classes, meaning that you should resample your data to have a close-to-equal number of passengers who survived and died on the Titanic. Always set it to `auto` unless you are an expert data scientist and are comfortable doing everything yourself:

7.  Set the number of classes:

```
num_classes = df[target_column].nunique()
```

This is the primary difference when training a classification model. By doing this programmatically with the following code, you will never make a mistake as you might when manually inputting the number.

> **Important note**
>
> AutoML can handle a large number of classes, but you may run into trouble if you have overly imbalanced classes. When you have 20 times the number of your largest case as your smallest case, you may want to resample your data or bin your target column to reduce the discrepancy.

8.  Configure your AutoML run: here, you will pass in your task, primary metric, featurization settings, compute target, dataset, target column, and the number of classes. All of these you have previously created. You will also pass in how long the experiment will run, whether it will stop early if the model performance does not improve, the number of cross-validations, and whether your experiment will record model explanations.

    Additionally, you will pass in whether or not you want to use **ensemble models**, models that are combinations of other models. Once again, set your cross-validation setting to between 5 and 20 splits:

```
config = AutoMLConfig(task=task,
                    primary_metric=primary_metric,
                    num_classes=num_classes,
                    featurization=featurization,
                    compute_target=compute_target,
                    training_data=dataset,
                    label_column_name=target_column,
                    experiment_timeout_minutes=15,
                    enable_early_stopping=True,
```

```
                                n_cross_validations=5,
                                model_explainability=True,
                                enable_stack_ensemble=True,
                                enable_voting_ensemble=True)
```

9.  Train your model and watch the results in real time:

```
AutoML_run = exp.submit(config, show_output = True)
RunDetails(remote_run).show()
```

Most of this code should feel familiar. Kick off your AutoML run, make yourself some coffee, come back, and watch your model run. You will then see a data guardrails check as seen in *Figure 5.4*. Notice how it has changed for classification.

First, it will check your target column to make sure that classes are balanced. Then, it will impute missing values. Here, there are two missing values in the Embarked column. Since it's a categorical column, it will be filled with the most common value. Lastly, like regression, it looks for categorical columns that have **high cardinality** or too many unique values given the dataset:

```
*******************************************************************************************
DATA GUARDRAILS:

TYPE:          Class balancing detection
STATUS:        PASSED
DESCRIPTION:   Your inputs were analyzed, and all classes are balanced in your training data.
               Learn more about imbalanced data: https://aka.ms/AutomatedMLImbalancedData

*******************************************************************************************

TYPE:          Missing feature values imputation
STATUS:        DONE
DESCRIPTION:   If the missing values are expected, let the run complete. Otherwise cancel the current run and use a script to
customize the handling of missing feature values that may be more appropriate based on the data type and business requiremen
t.
               Learn more about missing value imputation: https://aka.ms/AutomatedMLFeaturization
DETAILS:
+---------------------------------+------------------------------------+
|Column name                      |Missing value count                 |
+=================================+====================================+
|Embarked                         |2                                   |
+---------------------------------+------------------------------------+

*******************************************************************************************

TYPE:          High cardinality feature detection
STATUS:        PASSED
DESCRIPTION:   Your inputs were analyzed, and no high cardinality features were detected.
               Learn more about high cardinality feature handling: https://aka.ms/AutomatedMLFeaturization

*******************************************************************************************
```

Figure 5.4 – Data guardrails check for classification

Just as before, after completing the data guardrails check, AutoML will start training models with different combinations of feature transformations, algorithms, and hyperparameters. Some of the algorithms used will be unique to classification such as naïve Bayes, linear SVC, and **logistic regression**, while others such as **random forest**, **light GBM**, and **XGBoost** are shared with regression. Your output should resemble something similar to *Figure 5.5*:

```
********************************************************************************************
ITERATION: The iteration being evaluated.
PIPELINE: A summary description of the pipeline being evaluated.
DURATION: Time taken for the current iteration.
METRIC: The result of computing score on the fitted pipeline.
BEST: The best observed score thus far.
********************************************************************************************

ITERATION  PIPELINE                                      DURATION    METRIC      BEST
        0  MaxAbsScaler LightGBM                         0:00:33     0.8148    0.8148
        1  MaxAbsScaler XGBoostClassifier                0:00:29     0.7991    0.8148
        2  MaxAbsScaler RandomForest                     0:00:28     0.7822    0.8148
        3  MaxAbsScaler RandomForest                     0:00:30     0.7699    0.8148
        4  MaxAbsScaler SGD                              0:00:29     0.7733    0.8148
        5  MaxAbsScaler SGD                              0:00:33     0.7868    0.8148
        6  MaxAbsScaler ExtremeRandomTrees               0:00:34     0.7733    0.8148
        7  MaxAbsScaler ExtremeRandomTrees               0:00:29     0.8024    0.8148
        8  MaxAbsScaler ExtremeRandomTrees               0:00:29     0.8103    0.8148
        9  MaxAbsScaler ExtremeRandomTrees               0:00:31     0.7699    0.8148
       10  MaxAbsScaler SGD                              0:00:32     0.7856    0.8148
       11  MaxAbsScaler SGD                              0:00:33     0.7924    0.8148
       12  MaxAbsScaler RandomForest                     0:00:32     0.7878    0.8148
       13  StandardScalerWrapper ExtremeRandomTrees      0:00:31     0.7979    0.8148
       14  MaxAbsScaler RandomForest                     0:00:29     0.7228    0.8148
       15  MaxAbsScaler SGD                              0:00:32     0.7722    0.8148
       16  MaxAbsScaler RandomForest                     0:00:33     0.6868    0.8148
       17                                                0:00:08        nan    0.8148
       18   VotingEnsemble                               0:00:53     0.8148    0.8148
       19   StackEnsemble                                0:00:56     0.7968    0.8148
```

Figure 5.5 – AutoML results for classification

There are two striking things about these results: the first model trained is the best model and the algorithm you trained in *Chapter 3, Training Your First AutoML Model*, is slightly better. When models are relatively simple for machine learning to find patterns, your first model may be your best model. Our attempts to outsmart AutoML by filling in nulls ourselves and binning the Age column failed.

Despite our failure to produce a model, it's a good exercise to show the inherent power of AutoML. Often, leaving the data as is will produce an excellent model. Other times, creating new features from your existing features will produce superior models. Try experimenting to see if you can get higher-performing results with the `Titanic` dataset. See *Figure 5.6* for the visualized results, and notice that you can select other metrics from the dropdown in the top-left corner:

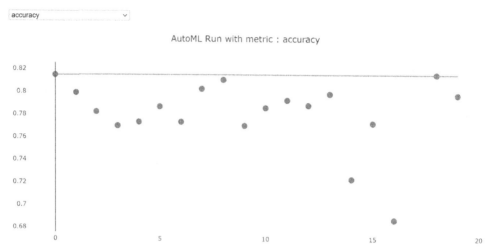

Figure 5.6 – AutoML results visualized for classification

Once you have thoroughly experimented with the `Titanic` data and have achieved the highest accuracy, you can move on to the next section to register your model. Registered models are necessary for later use in scoring new data through machine learning pipelines or real-time endpoints.

# Registering your trained classification model

The code to register classification models is identical to the code you used in *Chapter 4, Building an AutoML Regression Solution*, to register your regression model. Always register new models, as you will use them to score new data using either real-time scoring endpoints or batch execution inference pipelines depending on your use case. This will be explained in *Chapter 9, Implementing a Batch Scoring Solution*, and *Chapter 11, Implementing a Real-Time Scoring Solution*. Likewise, when registering your models, always add tags and descriptions for easier tracking:

1.  First, give your model a name, a description, and some tags:

```
description = 'Best AutoML Classification Run using
Transformed Titanic Data.'
```

```
tags = {'project' : "Titanic", "creator" : "your name"}
model_name = 'Titanic-Transformed-Classification-AutoML'
```

Tags let you easily search for models, so think carefully as you implement them.

2.  Next, register your model to your AMLS workspace, passing in your model name, tags, and description. Use the AutoML_run instance you trained in the previous section:

```
AutoML_run.register_model(model_name=model_name, \
description=description, tags=tags)
```

3.  Try registering a different model based on **normalized macro recall**. Give it a slightly different name, add an additional tag, and use an identical description:

```
description = 'Best AutoML Classification Run using \
Transformed Titanic Data.'
tags = {'project' : "Titanic", "creator" : "your name",\
  "metric" : "Norm Macro Recall"}
model_name = 'Titanic-Transformed-Classification-AutoML-
NMR'
AutoML_run.register_model(model_name=model_name, \
description=description, tags=tags, metric = 'norm_macro_
recall')
```

> **Important note**
> If time has elapsed since the last time you trained your AutoML model, you can retrieve it by finding **Run ID** in the **Experiments** section of the AML studio. Simply click on **Experiments** under **Assets**, select the correct experiment name, and copy the **Run ID** value. Set AutoML_run using this:
>
> ```
> ID.experiment_name = 'Titanic-Transformed-
> Classification-AutoML'
> exp = Experiment(workspace=ws, name=experiment_
> name)
> AutoML_run = AutoMLRun(experiment = exp, run_id =
> 'your_run_id')
> ```

You have registered your model and it is ready for use. You have created a classification model that can be used to predict who survived and who did not on the ill-fated Titanic voyage. It fell a little short of the classification model you built in *Chapter 3, Training Your First AutoML Model*, but in doing so, you learned a lot. With your lessons in mind, we can move on to tips and tricks that will improve your classification models as you train more in the future.

# Training an AutoML multiclass model

Multiclass classification involves predicting three or more classes instead of the standard binary classification. Using custom machine learning, training multiclass models is often a messy, complicated affair where you have to carefully consider the number of classes you are trying to predict, how unbalanced those classes are relative to each other, whether you should combine classes together, and how you should present your results. Luckily, AutoML takes care of all these considerations for you and makes training a multiclass model as simple as training a binary classification model.

In this section, you load in data using the publicly available Iris dataset. You will then set your AutoML classifications for multiclass classification, train and register a model, and examine your results. You will notice that much of the code is identical to the last section. By understanding the differences between binary and multiclass classification in AutoML, you will gain the confidence to tackle any type of classification problem irrespective of complexity.

1.  Download the `Iris.csv` file from the GitHub repository, `https://github.com/PacktPublishing/Automated-Machine-Learning-with-Microsoft-Azure`.

2.  Load `Iris.csv` into Azure and create a dataset called `Iris Training` following the same steps you took in *Chapter 3, Training Your First AutoML Model*.

3.  Load in all of the libraries you will need to run all of your code. Notice these libraries are identical to the ones you used for binary classification:

```
from azureml.core import Workspace, Dataset, Datastore
from azureml.core import Experiment
from azureml.core.compute import ComputeTarget
from azureml.train.automl import AutoMLConfig
from azureml.train.automl.run import AutoMLRun
from azureml.widgets import RunDetails
```

4.  Load in `pandas` and `numpy`. No matter the data you're working with, you will always find these packages useful:

```
Import pandas as pd
import numpy as np
```

5.  Connect your Jupyter notebook to your AMLS workspace:

```
ws = Workspace.from_config()
```

6.  Set your compute cluster:

```
compute_name = 'compute-cluster'
compute_target = ComputeTarget(ws, compute_name)
```

7.  Set your `datastore`:

```
datastore = Datastore.get_default(ws)
my_datastore_name = 'workspaceblobstore'
my_datastore = Datastore.get(ws, my_datastore_name)
```

8.  Set your `dataset`. Notice that this is the first piece of code that differs from binary classification, as you're using an entirely different dataset:

```
dataset_name = "Iris Training"
dataset = Dataset.get_by_name(ws, dataset_name,
version='latest')
```

9.  View the first 10 rows of your data using the following code. Make sure that it looks correct. With Iris data, you are trying to predict the `species` column:

```
dataset.take(10).to_pandas_dataframe()
```

The first 10 rows should look similar to *Figure 5.7:*

```
In [8]:    ▶ | # View your dataset by converting to pandas
              dataset.take(10).to_pandas_dataframe()
```

Out[8]:

|   | sepal_length | sepal_width | petal_length | petal_width | species |
|---|---|---|---|---|---|
| 0 | 5.1 | 3.5 | 1.4 | 0.2 | Iris-setosa |
| 1 | 4.9 | 3.0 | 1.4 | 0.2 | Iris-setosa |
| 2 | 4.7 | 3.2 | 1.3 | 0.2 | Iris-setosa |
| 3 | 4.6 | 3.1 | 1.5 | 0.2 | Iris-setosa |
| 4 | 5.0 | 3.6 | 1.4 | 0.2 | Iris-setosa |
| 5 | 5.4 | 3.9 | 1.7 | 0.4 | Iris-setosa |
| 6 | 4.6 | 3.4 | 1.4 | 0.3 | Iris-setosa |
| 7 | 5.0 | 3.4 | 1.5 | 0.2 | Iris-setosa |
| 8 | 4.4 | 2.9 | 1.4 | 0.2 | Iris-setosa |
| 9 | 4.9 | 3.1 | 1.5 | 0.1 | Iris-setosa |

Figure 5.7 – Iris data

10. Use the pandas `unique` function on the `species` column to see how many classes you need to predict. You should see three classes, *Iris-setosa*, *Iris-versicolor*, and *Iris-virginica*:

```
dataset.to_pandas_dataframe().species.unique()
```

11. Set your experiment and give it a name:

```
experiment_name = 'Iris-Multi-Classification'
exp = Experiment(workspace=ws, name=experiment_name)
```

Try to be descriptive when naming your experiments to easily track them, for example, by indicating explicitly that this training run is for multiclass classification.

12. Set your target column to `species`. Capitalization matters:

```
target_column = 'species'
```

Unlike most custom machine learning code, you do not have to convert the three different classes to integers. AutoML handles all of this on the backend.

13. Create a variable for your task: the task is the type of AutoML model you are trying to train. For predicting categories, enter `classification`:

```
task = 'classification'
```

`task` should be set to `classification` for both binary and multiclass classification problems.

14. Create a variable for your primary metric. Use `accuracy`:

```
primary metric = 'accuracy'
```

All metrics are the same for binary and multiclass classification problems, except some are calculated slightly differently by averaging the metric for each class instead of simply comparing true positives to true negatives. Accuracy, however, is calculated the same regardless of whether the problem is binary or multiclass.

15. Create a variable for `featurization` and set it to `auto`:

```
featurization = 'auto'
```

You can set `featurization` to `auto` or `off`. For multiclass problems, it is especially important to set it to `auto` so classes are properly balanced. Not doing so will impact model performance.

16. Set the number of classes to 3:

```
num_classes = 3
```

While you can do this programmatically, you can also set it to a number in cases where you already know and have confirmed the number of classes.

> **Important note**
> When training multiclass classification problems, sometimes you should hardcode in the number of classes. This ensures that your training run will fail if corrupted data enters your system and gives you an extra, unexpected class.

17. Configure your AutoML run. Nothing is different between multiclass and binary classification problems when it comes to configuring the run itself. One caveat is that multiclass classification problems often benefit from slightly higher cross validation settings. This helps ensures that the classes in each training split are more uniform. Set it to 10:

```
config = AutoMLConfig(task=task,
                      primary_metric=primary_metric,
                      num_classes=num_classes,
                      featurization=featurization,
                      compute_target=compute_target,
                      training_data=dataset,
                      label_column_name=target_column,
                      experiment_timeout_minutes=15,
                      enable_early_stopping=True,
                      n_cross_validations=10,
                      model_explainability=True,
                      enable_stack_ensemble=True,
                      enable_voting_ensemble=True)
```

18. Train your model and watch the results in real time:

```
AutoML_run = exp.submit(config, show_output = True)
RunDetails(remote_run).show()
```

19. Once your model is done training, register your model:

```
description = 'AutoML Multiclass Run using Iris Data.'
tags = {'project' : "Iris", "creator" : "your name"}
model_name = 'Iris-Multi-Classification-AutoML'
AutoML_run.register_model(model_name=model_
name,description=\
description,tags=tags)
```

As your AutoML model is running, it will perform the usual data guardrails check followed by. It is the same for binary and multiclass classification, checking for class balancing, missing features, and high cardinality. Your Iris data should pass all of these checks easily.

Once the data guardrails check is complete, AutoML will start training models as usual. Compare the models trained on multiclass Iris data versus binary class Titanic data. You should notice that most models are the same. Your output should resemble *Figure 5.8*:

```
ITERATION   PIPELINE                                 DURATION    METRIC      BEST
        0   MaxAbsScaler LightGBM                    0:00:42     0.9467     0.9467
        1   MaxAbsScaler XGBoostClassifier           0:00:49     0.9467     0.9467
        2   MinMaxScaler RandomForest                0:00:55     0.9733     0.9733
        3   MinMaxScaler RandomForest                0:00:40     0.9467     0.9733
        4   MinMaxScaler RandomForest                0:00:49     0.9400     0.9733
        5   MinMaxScaler SVM                         0:00:52     0.9467     0.9733
        6   MaxAbsScaler GradientBoosting            0:00:42     0.9533     0.9733
        7   SparseNormalizer XGBoostClassifier       0:00:43     0.9200     0.9733
        8   StandardScalerWrapper RandomForest       0:00:49     0.9533     0.9733
        9   SparseNormalizer LightGBM                0:00:45     0.9733     0.9733
       10   StandardScalerWrapper LightGBM           0:00:39     0.9400     0.9733
       11   RobustScaler ExtremeRandomTrees          0:00:39     0.9533     0.9733
       12   SparseNormalizer XGBoostClassifier       0:00:42     0.9667     0.9733
       13   SparseNormalizer XGBoostClassifier       0:00:45     0.9067     0.9733
       14   SparseNormalizer XGBoostClassifier       0:00:43     0.9133     0.9733
       15   RobustScaler KNN                         0:00:51     0.9533     0.9733
       16    VotingEnsemble                          0:00:57     0.9867     0.9867
       17    StackEnsemble                           0:01:05     0.9867     0.9867
```

Figure 5.8 – AutoML results for multiclass classification

There are excellent results. AutoML performs exceptionally well on the Iris dataset. There's also an easy way to graph your performance directly from your Jupyter notebook. Scroll down slightly past your model output until you see blue links to each of your models as seen in *Figure 5.9*. Click on your highest-performing model. For the example, it was the voting ensemble model, but it may be something different in your case:

| Iteration | Pipeline | Iteration metric | Best metric | Status | Duration | Started |
|---|---|---|---|---|---|---|
| 16 | VotingEnsemble | 0.98666667 | 0.98666667 | Completed | 0:01:07 | Jan 18, 2021 9:18 PM |
| 17 | StackEnsemble | 0.98666667 | 0.98666667 | Completed | 0:01:16 | Jan 18, 2021 9:19 PM |
| 2 | MinMaxScaler, RandomForest | 0.97333333 | 0.97333333 | Completed | 0:01:07 | Jan 18, 2021 9:04 PM |
| 9 | SparseNormalizer, LightGBM | 0.97333333 | 0.97333333 | Completed | 0:00:55 | Jan 18, 2021 9:11 PM |
| 12 | SparseNormalizer, XGBoostClassifier | 0.96666667 | 0.97333333 | Completed | 0:00:52 | Jan 18, 2021 9:14 PM |

Figure 5.9 – Model links

Clicking on this link will expose a large number of visualizations for your AutoML classification experiment. In particular, there's a **precision-recall curve**, an **ROC curve**, a **lift curve**, a **gain curve**, a **calibration curve**, and a **confusion matrix**. Business users most easily understand the confusion matrix, which shows you the number of classes that were accurately classified along with the number that were misclassified. As shown in *Figure 5.10*, AutoML only misclassified two data points out of 150 total. In both cases, the model incorrectly classified an Iris-versicolor as an Iris-virginica:

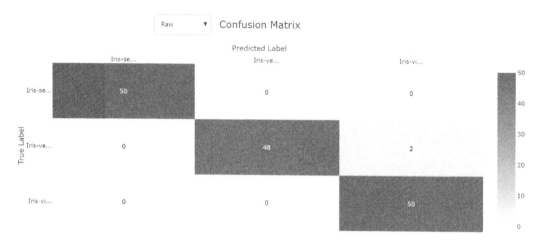

Figure 5.10 – Confusion matrix for the Iris classification model

Now that you have trained both a binary and multiclass classification model with AutoML, you can apply these techniques to your own data and business problems. If you were training custom machine learning models, you would have to memorize many little differences between binary and multiclass classification, but Azure AutoML handles all of those complexities for you. You don't even have to change your categorical column to integers.

As such, you should feel comfortable using AutoML for any classification problem you have. The final section gives you tips and tricks for achieving better model performance.

# Fine-tuning your AutoML classification model

In this section, you will first review tips and tricks for improving your AutoML classification models and then review the algorithms used by AutoML for both binary and multiclass classification.

# Improving AutoML classification models

Keeping in mind the tips and tricks from *Chapter 4, Building an AutoML Regression Solution*, here are new ones that are specific to classification:

- Unlike regression problems, nearly all classification problems in the real world require you to weigh your target column. The reason is that, for most business problems, one class is nearly always more important than the others.

  For example, imagine you are running a business and you are trying to predict which customers will stop doing business with you and leave you for a competitor. This is a common problem called customer churn or customer turnover. If you misidentify a customer as being likely to churn, all you waste is an unnecessary phone call or email. However, if your algorithm misses a customer who will churn, you lose that customer and their money.

  If you use the normal accuracy metric in AutoML, that is a poor metric for this problem. This is because it's much better to misidentify someone as *likely to switch* than it is to misidentify someone as *likely to stay*. The solution to this is to use the `weight_column_name` feature in AutoML. This allows you to create a column that weights hits and misses differently.

  For example, if your algorithm misses a customer who is likely to churn, you can penalize that miss 100 times more than if the algorithm says a customer will churn when they will not by assigning a weight of 100 to churned customers and a weight of 1 to customers who did not churn. This will train a model that excels at not missing customers who will turnover, although it will have many false positives as well.

- Become familiar with all of the different AutoML configuration options for classification. You can find them at this link: `https://docs.microsoft.com/en-us/python/api/azureml-train-automl-client/azureml.train.automl.automlconfig.automlconfig?view=azure-ml-py`.

- If your target column has a ratio of more than 20 to 1, it is a good idea to either collect more data from the smaller class or resample your data to achieve the 20 to 1 ratio.

- Research the five different primary metrics to understand which metrics fit your problem best. Classification requires a much more nuanced understanding of the business problem to make a wise metric selection.

- Use `https://docs.microsoft.com/en-us/azure/machine-learning/how-to-understand-automated-ml` to understand what a good classification model looks like. Confusion matrices are particularly valuable in determining whether your model is better at predicting one class over another. Depending on your business use case, this may or may not be a problem.

- Go to **Experiments** under **Assets** in AML studio, click your experiment name, select **Run ID**, click the **Models** tab, select the highest-performing algorithm, and click the **Metrics** tab. This will provide you with all of the different metrics and charts necessary to evaluate your algorithm.

- Explore using the `weight_column_name` configuration option to weigh your data. It is important you understand how this works. If some observations are more important to get right than others, you should always assign a higher weight to those observations.

  This is particularly important with classification models because, as mentioned before, some observations are almost always more important than others. Try assigning `0.1` to survivors and `1` to victims using the `Titanic` data and build a model. Then, try the opposite.

- **Overfitting**, where you produce a very good model that doesn't generalize to new datapoints, is as much a problem in classification as it is in regression. If this happens to you, try adding more historical data or removing columns from your dataset. If your target column has more than 2 classes, try binning it to create a simple model less prone to overfitting.

- Be on the lookout for model bias with classification problems. **Bias** can occur when your model sacrifices performance in one class for another class. The worst bias occurs when the model only predicts a single class, for example, always predicting that a Titanic passenger perished. These models can occasionally be highly accurate due to class imbalance. With the Titanic data, such a model would be 61.6% accurate.

- When dealing with large datasets, the size of your compute instance doesn't matter, but the size of your compute cluster matters a lot. This is because your compute instance is only for writing and submitting code, while the AutoML training job runs remotely on the compute cluster. It's important that you train your AutoML with appropriately sized **virtual machines** (**VMs**).

- The size of the VMs on your compute cluster should be determined by the size of your dataset used for training. Roughly speaking, the RAM of your VM should be 20 times as large as the size of the data you are training in uncompressed CSV format, or twice as large as the size of the data you are training while in a pandas DataFrame. This is because CSV files grow up to 10 times in size when converted into a DataFrame. This guarantees a smooth run.

  For example, if your base CSV file is 5 GB in size, then the RAM of each VM on your compute cluster should be at least 100 GB. In contrast, if your data is 5 GB in size after being converted into a pandas DataFrame, then you only require VMs with 10 GB of RAM.

- `AutoMLConfig` has many options that you should familiarize yourself with. One such option is `max_cores_per_iteration`. Set this to `-1` so that each model training run fully utilizes all the cores on each VM, giving you a little more processing power.

- You can train AutoML models in parallel through another `AutoMLConfig` option called `max_concurrent_iterations`. This determines how many models AutoML trains in parallel. Set this to the maximum number of nodes on your compute cluster. If you have 8 nodes on your compute cluster and set `max_concurrent_iterations` to 8, then AutoML will train 8 models at a time.

These are just a few of the many ways you can fine-tune a classification model with AutoML. You can learn more techniques by reading scientific articles on machine learning, blog posts, and how-to guides. Of course, nothing beats experience.

Try downloading as many open source classification datasets as you can find, load them into Azure, and use them to train and fine-tune AutoML models. With experience comes wisdom, and with wisdom comes the ability to solve even the toughest business problems with automated machine learning techniques. Learning the details about AutoML's classification algorithms is also important for you to develop your data science knowledge.

# Understanding AutoML classification algorithms

Many of the algorithms used by AutoML for classification are identical to the ones used by AutoML for regression. Like regression, certain algorithms perform better in certain situations. Unlike regression, AutoML uses a greater variety of algorithms for classification including neural networks.

The **tree**, **gradient boosting**, and **nearest neighbor** algorithms used by AutoML for classification are identical to the ones used for regression, and you can review them in *Chapter 4, Building an AutoML Regression Solution*. The only difference is that the classification versions predict probabilities instead of values. **Stochastic gradient descent** (**SGD**) is also used by AutoML for classification. Unique to classification are logistic regression, naïve Bayes, averaged perceptron classifier, and three different algorithms that use **support vector machines** (**SVM**).

**Logistic regression** uses a logistic function, an s-shaped sigmoid curve, to model the probability that your data belongs to a certain class. Despite its name, it is unrelated to regression. Like elastic net for regression, logistic regression uses **L1** (**lasso**) and **L2** (**ridge**) regularization to create simpler models by adjusting the coefficients of your input variables. Logistic regression is simple and easy to use, but it doesn't do well with small datasets or when your data has nonlinear relationships.

**Naïve Bayes** is another simple classification algorithm. It uses Bayes' theorem to calculate the probability of a class given each input feature in a row of your data. It then weighs each input feature equally when deciding the class. It's naïve in that it assumes that input features are independent of each other. Naïve Bayes performs well even with small data, but its chief assumption of independence is almost always violated in real life.

**Averaged perceptron classifier** is a simple type of **neural network** that uses a system of weights and linear functions to make its predictions. Like logistic regression, it's best suited to datasets with linear relationships between your input variable and target column. It's only used for binary classification.

**Support vector algorithms** classify data by drawing dividing among hyperplanes of data. Imagine visualizing your data in an n-dimensional space where n is the number of your input columns. SVM works by finding the lines that divide your data best. They work for both linear and non-linear data, even for high-dimensional data. AutoML uses three of these algorithms: **support vector classification** (**SVC**), linear SVC, and linear SVM classifier.

SVC is a standard implementation of support vector machines that works for both multiclass and binary classification problems. Linear SVC is an implementation that divides data linearly as opposed to SVC, which can divide data using nonlinear kernel functions. Linear SVM classifier, on the other hand, is similar to linear SVC but can only be used for binary classification.

A summary of the 14 algorithms is provided in the following table:

| Standard Classification Algorithms | Tree Algorithms | Gradient Boosting Algorithms | Support Vector Algorithms | Optimization Algorithms |
|---|---|---|---|---|
| Logistic regression | Decision tree | XGBoost | SVC | SGD |
| Naïve Bayes | Random forest | LightGBM | Linear SVC | Averaged perceptron classifier |
| K-nearest neighbors | Extremely randomized trees | Gradient boosting | Linear SVM classifier | |

Figure 5.11 – AutoML classification algorithms

Like regression, AutoML performs **model ensembling** at the end of each AutoML training run. **Voting ensembles** take the weighted average of predicted class probabilities and use that to predict the class of an individual row of input data. **Stack ensembles**, in contrast, train a logistic regression model using the output of other models. Usually, one of these two ensemble models will be your best model.

For more information on these models, please consult the AutoML documentation found at `https://docs.microsoft.com/en-us/azure/machine-learning/how-to-configure-auto-train#configure-your-experiment-settings`.

# Summary

You have added to your repertoire by successfully training a classification model using the AML Python SDK. You have loaded in data, heavily transformed it using pandas and Numpy, and built a toy AutoML model. You then registered that model to your AMLS workspace.

You can now start building classification models with your own data. You can easily solve both binary and multiclass classification problems, and you can present results to the business in a way they understand with confusion matrices. Many of the most common business problems, such as customer churn, are classification problems, and with the knowledge you learned in this chapter, you can solve those problems and earn trust and respect in your organization.

The next chapter, *Chapter 6, Building an AutoML Forecasting Solution*, will be vastly different from the previous two chapters. Forecasting problems have many more settings to use and understand compared to classification and regression problems, and they always require you to have a deeper understanding of your dataset. Novice data scientists also make many mistakes when training such models, and AutoML will enable you to avoid all of them.

# 6
# Building an AutoML Forecasting Solution

Having built an AutoML regression and classification solution, you are now ready to tackle a more complicated problem: **forecasting**. Forecasting is inherently a much more complex technique than either classification or regression. Those two **machine learning (ML)** problem types assume that time is irrelevant. Regardless of how much time passes, your diabetes model will always be able to accurately predict whose condition worsens over time. Your Titanic model will always be able to predict who lives and who dies. In contrast, with forecasting problems, you are always trying to predict future events based on past events; time will always be a factor in your model.

You will begin this chapter similarly to how you began *Chapter 4, Building an AutoML Regression Solution*, and *Chapter 5, Building an AutoML Classification Solution*. First, you will navigate to your Jupyter environment, load in data, train a model, and evaluate the results. You will learn two inherently different ways to train forecasting models with AutoML. One way uses only the **ARIMA** and **Prophet** algorithms; the other way uses all other available algorithms.

At the end of this chapter, you will learn tips and tricks on how to fine-tune your forecasting models by adjusting AutoML settings; there are a lot of settings specific to forecasting, so you will spend a lot of time covering their various use cases.

By the end of his chapter, you will be able to train forecasting models using AutoML without making mistakes. Relative to other techniques, forecasting problems are much easier to screw up, so this is quite an accomplishment. You will understand how to transform and arrange your data for forecasting and how to adjust AutoML settings to produce more accurate, more trustworthy models, solidifying your expertise in Azure AutoML.

In this chapter, we will cover the following topics:

- Prepping data for AutoML forecasting
- Training an AutoML forecasting model
- Registering your trained forecasting model
- Fine-tuning your AutoML forecasting model

# Technical requirements

Like *Chapter 4*, *Building an AutoML Regression Solution*, you will be creating and training models with Python code in a Jupyter notebook running on an Azure compute instance. As such, you will require a working internet connection, an **Azure Machine Learning Service (AMLS) workspace**, and a compute instance. Likewise, you will need to have a working compute cluster to train models remotely while you continue to work on your notebook. The full list of requirements is as follows:

- Access to the internet.
- A web browser, preferably Google Chrome or Microsoft Edge Chromium.
- A Microsoft Azure account.
- You should have created an AMLS workspace.
- You should have created a compute instance.
- You should have created the compute cluster in *Chapter 2*, *Getting Started with Azure Machine Learning Service*.
- You should understand how to navigate to the Jupyter environment from an Azure compute instance as demonstrated in *Chapter 4*, *Building an AutoML Regression Solution*.

The code for this chapter is available here: `https://github.com/ PacktPublishing/Automated-Machine-Learning-with-Microsoft- Azure/tree/master/Chapter06`.

# Prepping data for AutoML forecasting

Forecasting is very different from either classification or regression. ML models for regression or classification predict some output based on some input data. ML models for forecasting, on the other hand, predict a future state based on patterns found in the past. This means that there are key time-related details you need to pay attention to while shaping your data.

For this exercise, you are going to use the `OJ Sales Simulated Data` Azure Open Dataset for forecasting. Similar to the `Diabetes Sample` Azure Open Dataset you used for regression, `OJ Sales Simulated Data` is available simply by having an Azure account. You will use this data to create a model to predict future orange juice sales across different brands and stores.

There is one additional key difference; `OJ Sales Simulated Data` is a **file dataset** instead of a **tabular dataset**. While tabular datasets consist of one file containing columns and rows, file datasets consist of many files, tabular or otherwise.

Like all the other coding work you have performed in your AMLS workspace, you will begin by opening up Jupyter from your compute instance and creating a new Jupyter notebook. Then, you will load in your data, transform it into a pandas dataframe, and register it as a dataset, enabling you to use it to train an ML model with AutoML.

## Navigating to your Jupyter environment

You will begin by creating a new Jupyter notebook with the following steps:

1. First, open up your **Azure Machine Learning (AML) studio** by navigating to `http://ml.azure.com`.

2. Click **Compute** from the left-hand panel.

3. Select your compute instance. Click **Start** if it's not running.

> **Important tip**
> To save money while working on Azure, turn off your compute instance when you are not using it. Compute instances are paid for on an hourly basis.

4. Click **Jupyter** to enter your Jupyter environment.

5. Create a new Jupyter notebook by clicking **New** on the right-hand side of your screen and select **Python 3.6    AzureML**. The version of Python may be different due to updates.

6. Rename your Jupyter notebook to `OJ Forecasting_AutoML`. If you need a refresher as to how to do so, please review *Chapter 4, Building an AutoML Regression Solution*.

With your notebook created, you are now ready to load in the orange juice sales data and transform it with Python.

# Loading and transforming your data

Now it's time to work with your data, following the patterns you used in *Chapter 4, Building an AutoML Regression Solution*, and *Chapter 5, Building an AutoML Classification Solution*. The purpose of this section is to take a file dataset with many files, combine all the files together, and create a new tabular dataset. Perform the following steps:

1. Load in all of the Azure libraries you will need with the following code:

```
from azureml.core import Workspace, Dataset, Datastore
from azureml.core import Experiment
from azureml.core.compute import ComputeTarget
from azureml.train.automl import AutoMLConfig
from azureml.train.automl.run import AutoMLRun
from azureml.widgets import RunDetails
from azureml.opendatasets import OjSalesSimulated
from azureml.automl.core.forecasting_parameters import
ForecastingParameters
```

You should recognize `Workspace`, `Dataset`, `Datastore`, `Experiment`, `ComputeTarget`, `AutoMLConfig`, `AutoMLRun`, and `RunDetails` from *Chapter 4, Building an AutoML Regression Solution*.

`OjSalesSimulated` lets you directly access the `OJ Sales Simulated Data` Azure Open Dataset via the **AzureML Python SDK**. `ForecastingParameters` is necessary for AutoML forecasting tasks, as you cannot simply pass in forecasting-specific parameters to an `AutoMLConfig` object. You must first assign them to `ForecastingParameters` and then pass those parameters into your AutoML configurations.

> **Important note**
>
> If you are having trouble loading any Azure libraries, update the Azure ML
> SDK by running the `Update AzureML SDK.ipynb` notebook found here:
> https://github.com/PacktPublishing/Automated-Machine-Learning-with-
> Microsoft-Azure/blob/master/Update-AzureML-SDK.ipynb.

2.  Load in `pandas`, `numpy`, `os`, and `path` with the following code:

    ```
    import pandas as pd
    import numpy as np
    import os
    from pathlib import Path
    ```

    You should recognize `pandas` and `numpy` from *Chapter 4, Building an AutoML
    Regression Solution*. `os` and `Path` will be new to you. These packages let you create
    and manipulate files and folders in your Jupyter environment from within a Jupyter
    notebook. Moreover, they are necessary when working with file datasets such as
    `OjSimulatedSales` to turn them into tabular datasets for AutoML training.

3.  Connect your Jupyter notebook to your AMLS workspace:

    ```
    ws = Workspace.from_config()
    ```

    If you are prompted to log in, do so by following the instructions.

4.  Set your compute cluster:

    ```
    compute_name = 'compute-cluster'
    compute_target = ComputeTarget(ws, compute_name)
    ```

    You created this compute cluster in *Chapter 2, Getting Started with Azure Machine
    Learning Service*.

5.  Set your datastore. For this exercise, we will use the default datastore that comes
    with your AMLS workspace:

    ```
    datastore = Datastore.get_default(ws)
    ```

6.  Pull in a subset of 10 files from `OJ Sales Simulated Data` with this code:

    ```
    oj_sales_files = OjSalesSimulated.get_file_dataset()
    oj_sales = oj_sales_files.take(10)
    ```

> **Important tip**
>
> There are over 4,000 files in the OJ Sales Simulated Data Azure
> Open Dataset. Pulling all of them can result in extended training times.

7. Make a folder to download the files to your Jupyter environment with the following code:

```
folder_name = "OJ_Sales"
os.makedirs(folder_name, exist_ok=True)
```

In order to use file datasets, you first need to download them to your local Jupyter environment. Then, you can read them in as a pandas dataframe by concatenating the files.

8. Download the 10 files to your newly created OJ_Sales folder with the following code:

```
oj_sales.download(folder_name, overwrite=True)
```

If you navigate to the OJ Sales folder on your Jupyter environment, you should see the files there after running this code.

9. Read in the 10 files as a single pandas dataframe with the following code:

```
OJ_file_path = Path('OJ_Sales').rglob('*.csv')
OJ_files = [x for x in OJ_file_path]
df = pd.concat((pd.read_csv(f) for f in OJ_files))
```

For this, we will need to use the Path package to indicate the folder and file extension, as well as pandas to concatenate the 10 files into a single dataframe. Please note that this code will read everything in your OJ Sales folder. Do not place additional files in this folder or this will corrupt this portion of the code.

10. View the first 10 rows of your data. Make sure that it looks correct:

```
df.head(10)
```

The orange juice sales data has seven columns: WeekStarting, Store, Brand, Quantity, Advert, Price, and Revenue. Advert indicates whether there was an advertising campaign for that brand of orange juice for that week. The other columns are self-explanatory. The first 10 rows of data appear as follows:

```
In [47]:   ▶  df.head(10)
```

Out[47]:

|   | WeekStarting | Store | Brand | Quantity | Advert | Price | Revenue |
|---|---|---|---|---|---|---|---|
| 0 | 1990-06-14 | 1000 | dominicks | 12003 | 1 | 2.59 | 31087.77 |
| 1 | 1990-06-21 | 1000 | dominicks | 10239 | 1 | 2.39 | 24471.21 |
| 2 | 1990-06-28 | 1000 | dominicks | 17917 | 1 | 2.48 | 44434.16 |
| 3 | 1990-07-05 | 1000 | dominicks | 14218 | 1 | 2.33 | 33127.94 |
| 4 | 1990-07-12 | 1000 | dominicks | 15925 | 1 | 2.01 | 32009.25 |
| 5 | 1990-07-19 | 1000 | dominicks | 17850 | 1 | 2.17 | 38734.50 |
| 6 | 1990-07-26 | 1000 | dominicks | 10576 | 1 | 1.97 | 20834.72 |
| 7 | 1990-08-02 | 1000 | dominicks | 9912 | 1 | 2.26 | 22401.12 |
| 8 | 1990-08-09 | 1000 | dominicks | 9571 | 1 | 2.11 | 20194.81 |
| 9 | 1990-08-16 | 1000 | dominicks | 15748 | 1 | 2.42 | 38110.16 |

Figure 6.1 – Viewing your Orange Juice Sales dataset

11. Register your pandas dataframe as a dataset:

```
Dataset.Tabular.register_pandas_dataframe(df, datastore,
                        "OJ Sales Sample")
```

While it may seem strange to register a file dataset as a tabular dataset, tabular datasets are inherently easier to work with. File datasets are simply pointers to a folder containing a lot of files; lots of data preprocessing work must be performed on the files before you can use them. Tabular datasets, on the other hand, are formatted and ready for immediate use with AutoML.

Here, it's important to note the main differences between **time series data** and normal data. Time series data always has a time column, in this case, WeekStarting. The time column needs to be on some sort of regular cadence, for example, every day, week, month, or year. In this case, it's every week on a Thursday.

Certain algorithms, such as *Prophet* and *ARIMA*, require you to have a time column with no gaps. Other AutoML algorithms can work with gaps, but only if you do not enable certain features, such as time lags, in your target column.

> **Important tip**
>
> Gaps in your time column also prevent you from using certain features specific to forecasting, specifically lags of your target column and moving averages of those lags. These features often improve performance. Carefully study your data to remove gaps for best performance in forecasting solutions.

The other essential element of time series data are your **Grain** columns. Grain columns indicate different time series within your data. This is best illustrated by means of an example. In the orange juice data, `Store` and `Brand` are your grain columns; there are separate time series for each combination of store and brand.

If AutoML detects multiple time series on a single grain, it will automatically fail. In other words, you cannot have duplicate dates for a single grain. For this reason, carefully study your data to remove duplicate dates across the same grain when using AutoML forecasting.

With these things in mind, you are now ready to train an AutoML forecasting model. First, you will train a model without using *ARIMA* and *Prophet*. Then, you will train a model using these two algorithms.

# Training an AutoML forecasting model

Training an AutoML forecasting is most similar to training an AutoML regression model. Like regression and unlike classification, you are trying to predict a number. Unlike regression, this number is always in the future based on patterns found in the past. Also, unlike regression, you can predict a whole series of numbers into the future. For example, you can choose to predict one month out into the future or you can choose to predict 6, 12, 18, or even 24 months out.

> **Important tip**
>
> The further out you try to predict, the less accurate your forecasting model will be.

Follow the same steps you have seen in *Chapter 4, Building an AutoML Regression Solution*, and *Chapter 5, Building an AutoML Classification Solution*. First, begin by setting a name for your experiment. Then, set your target column and your AutoML configurations.

For forecasting, there is an additional step: setting your **forecasting parameters**. This is where you will set things such as your time column, grain columns, and lag settings. These settings then need to be passed into your AutoML configurations as a single forecasting parameters object. Once this is done, only then can you use AutoML to train a forecasting model.

In this section, you will repeat this process twice, first by training a model as normal using the standard algorithms available for forecasting in AutoML, and second, you will repeat this process using slightly different settings to enable ARIMA and Prophet and to compare the performance of the two AutoML models.

# Training a forecasting model with standard algorithms

To train your forecasting model using AutoML, follow these steps, continuing in the OJ Forecasting AutoML Jupyter notebook:

1.  Set your experiment and give it a name with the following code:

    ```
    experiment_name = 'OJ-Sales-Forecasting'
    exp = Experiment(workspace=ws, name=experiment_name)
    ```

    One important thing to remember is that an experiment can be a set of multiple training runs and not just a single training run. In other words, we can train multiple models with different settings under the same experiment name.

2.  Retrieve your OJ Sales Sample dataset with the following code:

    ```
    dataset_name = "OJ Sales Sample"
    dataset = Dataset.get_by_name(ws, dataset_name,
    version='latest')
    ```

3.  Set your target column to Quantity:

    ```
    target_column = 'Quantity'
    ```

    Capitalization matters with Python; keep that in mind.

4.  Create a variable for your AutoML task. task is the type of AutoML model you are trying to train. To predict future numbers, enter forecasting:

    ```
    task = 'forecasting'
    ```

---

**Important note**

It is always incorrect to train a forecasting problem as a regression problem. Even though they both nominally do the same thing, predicting a number, forecasting requires a much more careful approach to not include future values when training a model. Standard cross-validation methods that are used for regression do not apply to forecasting problems, so be sure to set `task` to `forecasting`.

---

5. Create a variable for your primary metric. **The primary metric** is how your model will be scored. Use **normalized root mean squared error** (**normalized RMSE**). This metric takes the prediction and subtracts it from the actual value for each observation, squares it, and averages the score across all observations. The lower the score, the better your model. Other options for forecasting include **R2 score**, **Spearman correlation**, and **normalized mean absolute error** (**normalized MAE**). Note that these are identical to regression metrics:

```
primary_metric = 'normalized_root_mean_squared_error'
```

6. Create a variable for `featurization`. You can set `featurization` to `auto` or `off`. Set it to `auto`:

```
featurization = 'auto'
```

If you set `featurization` to `off`, you will have to drop high cardinality features, impute null values, one-hot encode your data, and generate additional features yourself. AutoML handles these for you automatically when featurization is set to `auto`.

7. With forecasting, featurization also creates a variety of date/time features from your time column, including year, month, week, day of week, A.M./P.M., and hour of day. Always set `featurization` to `auto` unless you are an expert data scientist who can do everything yourself.

Set your forecasting parameters. There are a lot of these and we will go over them one by one as follows:

a) `country_or_region_for_holidays` determines which country to use to generate columns indicating different national holidays. You can set this parameter to either nothing, a single country, or a list of countries. Set it to US for United States. You will get a separate column for each holiday.

b) `drop_columns_names` lets you input a list of columns to drop before training your forecasting model. Drop the `Revenue` column here, as it's partially derived from your target column, `Quantity`.

> **Important note**
>
> Any time you have a column that's derived partially or wholly from your target column, drop it. This is true for all types of ML problems and is not specific to forecasting. Leaving it in will falsely give you a highly performing model. Furthermore, any time you produce an ML model that has nearly zero error, it's highly likely that you passed in a derived column.

c) `forecast_horizon` is the number of periods you want to predict into the future. It is always based on the cadence of your time column. Set this feature to 6 to predict sales 6 weeks out. If your time column was in months and not weeks, setting it to 6 would predict sales 6 months out into the future.

d) `target_rolling_window_size` creates features based on averaging lagged versions of the target column. For example, if you set it to 2, this will create a feature that is the average of the last 2 weeks' worth of data. In this case, set it to `auto` for AutoML to automatically determine how large this window should be.

e) `target_lags` creates features based on lagged versions of the target column. If you set it to 2, it will create two features, one feature for last week's sales, and another feature for sales 2 weeks previous. Set it to `auto` for AutoML to automatically determine how many lagged features you should use.

f) `feature_lags` creates features based on lagged versions of numeric columns in your dataset other than your target column. It works similarly to `target_lags`, except that it will lag every other column that is not a target column, grain column, or time column. Set it to `auto` for AutoML to automatically determine how many lagged features to use.

g) `seasonality` infers the seasonality in your time series data. It looks for repeating patterns that happen in a predictable way based on time. Set this feature to `auto` for AutoML to detect seasonal patterns in your data.

h) `short_series_handling` enables AutoML to continue running even if some of your time series are too short to model given your forecast horizon and lags. An example would be if one of your grains only had 1 time period worth of data. Set this to `true`.

> **Important tip**
> Whenever you have multiple grains in your data and new grains can enter your dataset at any time, always set `short_series_handling` to `true`. It's very likely that new grains will not have enough data to train a model, and setting this to `false` will cause your entire AutoML run to fail.

i) `use_stl` refers to **Season and Trend Decomposition using Loess**. Use this feature to generate either season or season and trend components for your time series. To generate both season and trend components, enter `season_trend`. Most forecasts do have some **seasonal component** to them, patterns that show up in the data year after year. As such, it's a good idea to set this to `season_trend`.

j) `time_column_name` indicates your time column. Specify `WeekStarting`.

k) `time_series_id_column_names` indicates your grain columns. All columns that correspond to different time series need to be included in this list. AutoML will fail if it finds duplicate dates on what it thinks should be a single grain. Specify `Store` and `Brand` to ensure that AutoML handles your data correctly.

l) `Short_series_handling_configuration` simply indicates whether or not short series should be padded. Set this to `auto` to pad short time series.

m) `validate_params` ensures that you are using acceptable forecasting parameters. Always set this to `true`.

With all of this in mind, set your forecasting parameters with the following code:

```
params=\
ForecastingParameters.from_parameters_dict(
{'country_or_region_for_holidays':'US',\
            'drop_columns_names':'Revenue',\
            'forecast_horizon': 6,\
            'target_rolling_window_size': 'auto',\
            'target_lags': 'auto',\
            'feature_lags': 'auto',\
            'seasonality': 'auto',\
            'short_series_handling': True,\
            'use_stl': 'season_trend',\
            'time_column_name':'WeekStarting',\
            'time_series_id_column_names':\
            ['Store','Brand'],\
```

```
        'short_series_handling_configuration':\
        'auto'},\
        validate_params=True)
```

> **Important note**
> There are quite a large number of parameters specific to forecasting. Take
> your time to understand these settings in depth by reading the *Azure
> AutoML ForecastingParameters* documentation here: `https://docs.`
> `microsoft.com/en-us/python/api/azureml-automl-`
> `core/azureml.automl.core.forecasting_parameters.`
> `forecastingparameters?view=azure-ml-py.`

8. Configure your AutoML run. Here, you will pass in your task, primary metric, featurization settings, compute target, dataset, target column, and forecasting parameters. All of these you have previously created. You will also pass in how long the experiment will run for, whether it will stop early if model performance does not improve, the number of cross-validations, and model explainability settings.

   Additionally, you will pass in whether or not you want to use **ensemble models**, models that are combinations of other models. For forecasting, set your cross-validation setting to 3 splits; unlike classification or regression, forecasting runs are more accurate when you set cross-validation to a lower number. This is due to the nature of how AutoML splits the data into different sets for the purpose of scoring performance:

```
config = AutoMLConfig(task=task,
                      primary_metric=primary_metric,
                      featurization=featurization,
                      compute_target=compute_target,
                      training_data=dataset,
                      label_column_name=target_column,
                      experiment_timeout_minutes=15,
                      enable_early_stopping=True,
                      n_cross_validations=3,
                      model_explainability=True,
                      enable_stack_ensemble=False,
                      enable_voting_ensemble=True,
                      forecasting_parameters=params)
```

---

**Important note**

**Stack ensembles** can lead to overfitting when used for forecasting problems. As a result, it's recommended to set it to `False`. This is not the case for regression or classification.

---

9.  Train your model and watch the results in real time:

```
AutoML_run = exp.submit(config, show_output = True)
RunDetails(AutoML_run).show()
```

As before, kick off your AutoML run, make yourself some coffee, then come back and watch your models get trained in real time. You will see a **data guardrails** check, as seen in *Figure 6.2*. Notice how it has changed for forecasting:

```
*********************************************************************************************
DATA GUARDRAILS:

TYPE:         Frequency detection
STATUS:       PASSED
DESCRIPTION:  The time series was analyzed, all data points are aligned with detected frequency.


*********************************************************************************************

TYPE:         Missing feature values imputation
STATUS:       PASSED
DESCRIPTION:  No feature missing values were detected in the training data.
              Learn more about missing value imputation: https://aka.ms/AutomatedMLFeaturization

*********************************************************************************************

TYPE:         Short series handling
STATUS:       PASSED
DESCRIPTION:  Automated ML detected enough data points for each series in the input data to continue with training.
```

Figure 6.2 – Data guardrails check for forecasting

First, data guardrails will check your time column to make sure that all data points are aligned with the correct frequency. For your `OJ Sales Sample` data, this means making sure that each data point falls on a Thursday and is separated by 1 week.

Then, data guardrails will impute missing values the same way it did for classification and regression. Here, there are no missing values in any of the columns. Lastly, it will look for time series that are too short to train with your settings. In the case that AutoML detects short series, it will create simpler models to handle these cases.

After completing the data guardrails check, AutoML will start training models with different combinations of feature transformations, algorithms, and hyperparameters. If there are no features other than the time column, grain columns, and target column, it will train ARIMA and Prophet models in addition to its standard suite of forecasting models. Your output should resemble *Figure 6.3*:

```
*********************************************************************************:
ITERATION: The iteration being evaluated.
PIPELINE: A summary description of the pipeline being evaluated.
DURATION: Time taken for the current iteration.
METRIC: The result of computing score on the fitted pipeline.
BEST: The best observed score thus far.
*********************************************************************************:
```

| ITERATION | PIPELINE | DURATION | METRIC | BEST |
|---|---|---|---|---|
| 0 | MaxAbsScaler DecisionTree | 0:00:33 | 0.0608 | 0.0608 |
| 1 | MinMaxScaler DecisionTree | 0:00:27 | 0.0761 | 0.0608 |
| 2 | StandardScalerWrapper LassoLars | 0:00:33 | 0.0244 | 0.0244 |
| 3 | RobustScaler ElasticNet | 0:00:31 | 0.1121 | 0.0244 |
| 4 | StandardScalerWrapper LassoLars | 0:00:33 | 0.0244 | 0.0244 |
| 5 | RobustScaler ElasticNet | 0:00:29 | 0.0241 | 0.0241 |
| 6 | RobustScaler DecisionTree | 0:00:33 | 0.0648 | 0.0241 |
| 7 | MinMaxScaler DecisionTree | 0:00:31 | 0.0525 | 0.0241 |
| 8 | RobustScaler DecisionTree | 0:00:36 | 0.0890 | 0.0241 |
| 9 | MinMaxScaler DecisionTree | 0:00:31 | 0.0847 | 0.0241 |
| 10 | StandardScalerWrapper DecisionTree | 0:00:34 | 0.0621 | 0.0241 |
| 11 | StandardScalerWrapper DecisionTree | 0:00:28 | 0.0395 | 0.0241 |
| 12 | RobustScaler DecisionTree | 0:00:34 | 0.0410 | 0.0241 |
| 13 | RobustScaler ElasticNet | 0:00:31 | 0.0762 | 0.0241 |
| 14 | StandardScalerWrapper DecisionTree | 0:00:37 | 0.0563 | 0.0241 |
| 15 | MinMaxScaler DecisionTree | 0:00:40 | 0.0458 | 0.0241 |
| 16 | MinMaxScaler DecisionTree | 0:00:28 | 0.0586 | 0.0241 |
| 17 | | 0:00:29 | nan | 0.0241 |
| 18 | VotingEnsemble | 0:00:41 | 0.0164 | 0.0164 |

Figure 6.3 – AutoML results for forecasting

# Training a forecasting model with Prophet and ARIMA

One important difference between forecasting and the other two types of AutoML problems are the Prophet and ARIMA algorithms. Prophet and ARIMA are inherently different from all of the other algorithms in that, in order to train them, all you need are the grain columns, the target column, and the time column. That's it. Adding any other columns will restrict AutoML from using these algorithms.

What's different about Prophet and ARIMA is that they only use patterns found in the target column to make predictions. Other variables are ignored. Sometimes, they will outperform other algorithms; other times, they will not. It's hard to know when without trying.

Because it's hard to know how well ARIMA and Prophet will perform relative to other algorithms, it's recommended to always try training them if you can. That is, if you have time series data without gaps in your time column, always train ARIMA and Prophet models first as your baseline. They take a longer time to train, so it's recommended that you increase your experiment timeout, especially with larger datasets.

To build an AutoML forecasting solution using ARIMA and Prophet, follow these steps:

1.  Copy *steps 1-6* from the previous section until you get to forecasting parameters.

2.  Within forecasting parameters, remove all of your feature columns, leaving only your time, grain, and target columns. Also, turn off all AutoML generated features, such as holidays, feature lags, and targets lags, by setting them to None, as seen in the following code block:

```
params=\
ForecastingParameters.from_parameters_dict(\
{'country_or_region_for_holidays':None,\
                    'drop_columns_names':\
                    ['Revenue','Price','Advert'],\
                    'forecast_horizon': 6,\
                    'target_rolling_window_size': None,\
                    'target_lags': None,\
                    'feature_lags': None,\
                    'seasonality': 'auto',\
                    'short_series_handling': True,\
                    'use_stl': 'season_trend',\
                    'time_column_name':'WeekStarting',\
                    'time_series_id_column_names':\
                    ['Store','Brand'],
                'short_series_handling_configuration':\
                    'auto'},\
                    validate_params=True)
```

Feature lags and target lags work by creating additional variables. This is why they need to be removed from your data in order for AutoML to run Prophet and ARIMA.

3.  Configure your AutoML run as you did in *Step 8*, passing in your updated forecasting parameters.

4.  Train your model and watch the results in real time:

```
Prophet_ARIMA_run = exp.submit(config, show_output =
True)
RunDetails(Prophet_ARIMA_run).show()
```

Once you rerun AutoML with these settings, your results should resemble *Figure 6.4*. Notice that, for this problem, ARIMA and Prophet did not return better results, and that the voting ensemble outperformed all models as usual:

| ITERATION | PIPELINE | DURATION | METRIC | BEST |
|---|---|---|---|---|
| 0 | AutoArima | 0:01:31 | 0.2910 | 0.2910 |
| 1 | ProphetModel | 0:00:58 | 0.0352 | 0.0352 |
| 2 | MaxAbsScaler DecisionTree | 0:00:31 | 0.0466 | 0.0352 |
| 3 | MinMaxScaler DecisionTree | 0:00:35 | 0.0702 | 0.0352 |
| 4 | StandardScalerWrapper LassoLars | 0:00:41 | 0.0244 | 0.0244 |
| 5 | RobustScaler ElasticNet | 0:00:33 | 0.1121 | 0.0244 |
| 6 | StandardScalerWrapper LassoLars | 0:00:33 | 0.0244 | 0.0244 |
| 7 | RobustScaler ElasticNet | 0:00:32 | 0.0241 | 0.0241 |
| 8 | RobustScaler DecisionTree | 0:00:28 | 0.0603 | 0.0241 |
| 9 | MinMaxScaler DecisionTree | 0:00:44 | 0.0415 | 0.0241 |
| 10 | RobustScaler DecisionTree | 0:00:34 | 0.0717 | 0.0241 |
| 11 | MinMaxScaler DecisionTree | 0:00:30 | 0.0716 | 0.0241 |
| 12 | StandardScalerWrapper DecisionTree | 0:00:42 | 0.0486 | 0.0241 |
| 13 | StandardScalerWrapper DecisionTree | 0:00:38 | 0.0590 | 0.0241 |
| 14 | VotingEnsemble | 0:00:49 | 0.0174 | 0.0174 |

Figure 6.4 – AutoML forecasting results with ARIMA and Prophet

You have now trained two sets of models with your OJ Sales Sample data and have achieved a pretty low normalized RMSE. You can now move on to the next section to register your model. Registered models are necessary for later use in scoring new data through ML pipelines or real-time endpoints.

# Registering your trained forecasting model

The code to register forecasting models is identical to the code you used in *Chapter 4, Building an AutoML Regression Solution*, in order to register your regression model, and in *Chapter 5, Building an AutoML Classification Solution*, in order to register your classification models. Always register new models, as you will use them in either real-time scoring endpoints or batch execution inference pipelines depending on your business scenario. Likewise, always add tags and descriptions for easier tracking:

1. First, give your model a name, a description, and some tags. **Tags** let you easily search for models, so think carefully as you implement them:

```
description = 'Best AutoML Forecasting Run using OJ Sales
Sample Data.'
tags = {'project' : "OJ Sales", "creator" : "your name"}
model_name = 'OJ-Sales-Sample-Forecasting-AutoML'
```

2.  Next, register your model to your AMLS workspace, passing in your model name, tags, and description. Use the `AutoML_run` model you trained with in the *Training an AutoML forecasting model* section:

```
AutoML_run.register_model(model_name=model_name,
description=description, tags=tags)
```

3.  Try registering a different model based on R2 score. Give it a slightly different name, add an additional tag, and use an identical description:

```
description = 'Best AutoML Forecasting Run using OJ Sales
Sample Data.'
tags = {'project' : "OJ Sales", "creator" : "your name",
"metric" : "R2 Score"}
model_name = 'OJ-Sales-Sample-Forecasting-AutoML-R2'
AutoML_run.register_model(model_name=model_name,
description=description, tags=tags, metric = 'r2_score')
```

In some situations, you will perform an AutoML training run, but you will forget to register the model. Do not fret. You can retrieve AutoML training runs using the experiment name and run ID and register the model from there. Use the following code:

```
experiment_name = 'OJ-Sales-Forecasting'
exp = Experiment(workspace=ws, name=experiment_name)
AutoML_run = AutoMLRun(experiment = exp, run_id = 'your_run_
id')
description = 'Retrieved AutoML Forecasting Run for OJ Sales
Data.'
tags = {'project' : "OJ Sales", "creator" : "your name"}
model_name = 'OJ-Sales-Sample-Forecasting-AutoML-Retrieved'
AutoML_run.register_model(model_name=model_name,
description=description, tags=tags)
```

You have now registered your forecasting model and it is ready for use. You can use it to predict the demand for orange juice across a variety of stores and brands over the next 6 weeks. You can modify it in numerous ways too, such as predicting 3 weeks', 12 weeks', or simply next weeks' sales.

Forecasting is an art, much more so than classification or regression, and that makes the next section much more important: tips and tricks for fine-tuning AutoML forecasting models.

# Fine-tuning your AutoML forecasting model

In this section, you will first review tips and tricks for improving your AutoML forecasting models and then review the algorithms used by AutoML for forecasting.

## Improving AutoML forecasting models

Forecasting is very easy to get wrong. It's easy to produce a model that seems to work in development, but fails to make accurate predictions once deployed to production. Many data scientists, even experienced ones, make mistakes. While AutoML will help you avoid some of the common mistakes, there are others that require you to exercise caution. In order to sidestep these pitfalls and make the best models possible, follow these tips and tricks:

- Any feature column that you train with has to be available in the future when you make a prediction. With `OJ Sales Sample`, this means that, if you want to predict the quantity of sales 6 weeks out and include price as an input variable, you need to know the price of each product 6 weeks out.

  Please confirm with your business partners and IT staff to see which data you will have available to make predictions. If you are not able to know the value of a feature column in the time frame over which you are trying to predict, drop that column from your training dataset.

- Standard cross-validation techniques do not work with forecasting. AutoML uses **rolling forward validation**. This technique takes the first $X$ data points of your dataset in order of the time column and uses them to predict the next $Y$ data points. Then, it takes another set of $X$ data points further into the future and uses those to make predictions, repeating the process until all data points are used.

  Cross-validation, on the other hand, ignores the time component and splits your data randomly. This is why you must always set the `task` to `forecasting` if you are trying to make future-state predictions. Setting it to regression may give you results, but they will be meaningless since they ignore the time component.

- Become familiar with all of the different AutoML configuration options for forecasting. You can find them at this link: `https://docs.microsoft.com/en-us/python/api/azureml-train-automl-client/azureml.train.automl.automlconfig.automlconfig?view=azure-ml-py`.

- Always try building a forecasting model using only ARIMA and Prophet first. These two models provide a good baseline as they only use your time column and target column to build an ML model. If models using additional features do not outperform ARIMA and Prophet, you know those additional features aren't relevant to your business problem. Drop these features from your dataset.

- Think carefully when deciding your forecast horizon. Usually, forecasting algorithms perform better when forecasting short horizons, either the next one or two time periods. When forecasting longer horizons, expect less accuracy the further out you go. Knowing this, please push back against your business partners when they ask you to forecast many time periods out.

  Generally speaking, people always want to know the future, and the further out you can predict, the happier they will be. Please explain that they should put more trust in short-term forecasts than they should in longer-term forecasts.

- Forecasting the future works best when the present situation resembles the past. Shock events will often disrupt even well-performing forecast models. When this happens, try training a model using only recent data points. This is an iterative process, as it's often difficult to tell which training points are still relevant.

  In some cases, the best thing you can do is start training models using data only from the onset of the shock event. For example, many stores experienced wildly different product demand during the coronavirus pandemic compared to pre-pandemic conditions.

- When shock events pass and things return to normal, try training forecasting models using the weighted column feature in AutoML. Set time periods during the shock event to 0.

  Remember that AutoML forecasting models should not be trained with gaps in the time column. However, data points that occurred during shock events are not relevant to normal situations. By using the weighted column and setting weights to 0 and 1, you can train a forecasting model that effectively ignores shock events without violating the no gap rule.

- Likewise, use the weight column to weight the recent past more heavily than the further past. For many problems, recent data is more relevant than past data. Interview your business partners to find key dates when your industry changed.

- Furthermore, more data only helps forecasting models if the past situation resembles the present situation. Forecasting models often produce better results when you train models using only recent, relevant data. Do not be afraid to drop data points that are too far in the past to help predict the current situation.

Once again, interview business partners to find key dates when your industry underwent massive change. Dropping data that occurred prior to the massive change will often produce superior models.

- Forecasting is finicky, much more finicky than regression or classification problems. This is because the types of things companies like to forecast are driven by market demand and what people want often changes. What's popular in the marketplace can change quickly with little warning, and, as a result, forecast models need to be retrained all of the time whenever you get the latest data.

- When you make predictions using an AutoML-trained forecasting model, it always starts by predicting values for the next time period out. Because of this, when you score data, your data must begin with that next time period. For example, if you trained a daily forecasting model on data that ends on January 5, your scoring data must begin on January 6.

- If your time column is on a monthly cadence that ends with February and you are predicting two time periods out, AutoML will make predictions for March and April. You cannot use that model to make predictions for May or June. In order to do so, you must retrain the model with training data that ends at a later date. As a result, you need to keep retraining AutoML forecasting models to make sure your predictions are up-to-date.

- To determine seasonality, plot your target column to look for any recurring seasonal patterns before using AutoML. This will let you know if you should use seasonality features or not.

- When you're trying to make forecasts on a global basis, be sure to include all countries when generating holiday features. Holidays tend to be very important when forecasting demand and market trends. Think of how Christmas affects sales in the United States of America or how the Chinese New Year affects travel patterns in China.

This ends the list of tips and tricks. It is by no means complete; you should only think of it as a start. Forecasting is a rich and interesting field with many caveats. Still, keeping these things in mind will enable you to produce accurate, reliable forecasts and avoid many of the mistakes made by novice data scientists.

More than anything, remember that forecasting is its own art, separate from other types of ML problems, and approach it as such. Lastly, you will learn which algorithms AutoML uses to forecast.

# Understanding AutoML forecasting algorithms

AutoML forecasting algorithms are nearly identical to AutoML regression algorithms. Forecasting uses all the same **tree**, **standard regression**, **gradient boosting**, and **nearest neighbor** algorithms as regression, and also uses **stochastic gradient descent**. For reference, please refer to *Chapter 4*, *Building an AutoML Regression Solution*.

In addition to these algorithms, there are three forecasting-specific algorithms: Auto-ARIMA, Prophet, and ForecastTCN. You learned about certain key differences that make ARIMA and Prophet different from the other algorithms earlier in this chapter. ForecastTCN is a **temporal convolutional network**, a type of neural network.

**Auto-ARIMA** (**Auto-Regressive Integrated Moving Average**) uses moving averages of the target column to make predictions. Unlike standard ARIMA, Auto-ARIMA optimizes ARIMA parameters to create the best model possible. It performs extremely well with univariate time series where you only have reliable information about your target column.

**Prophet** is similar to Auto-ARIMA in that it is specialized for univariate time series. Moreover, it performs extremely well when your data has strong seasonal patterns. Unlike many forecasting algorithms, Prophet is robust to outliers and wild swings in your dataset. Like Auto-ARIMA, you should always use Prophet to establish a baseline model at the onset of any forecasting project.

**ForecastTCN** is a deep learning neural network algorithm. Enable it by setting `enable_dnn` to `True` in your AutoML forecasting parameters. This algorithm is great for the most complex forecasting tasks as it can capture extremely complex nonlinear trends in your data. Deep learning is a complex topic and would be difficult to explain in even a single chapter, and is thus outside the scope of this book. ForecastTCN, like other deep learning models, performs best when trained with very large amounts of data.

A summary of these 13 algorithms is provided in *Figure 6.5*:

| Standard regression algorithms | Tree algorithms | Gradient boosting algorithms | Other algorithms shared with regression | Forecasting-specific algorithms |
| --- | --- | --- | --- | --- |
| Elastic Net<br><br>LARS Lasso | Decision Tree<br><br>Random Forest<br><br>Extremely Randomized Trees | XGBoost<br><br>LightGBM<br><br>Gradient Boosting | Stochastic Gradient Descent (SGD)<br><br>KNN | Prophet<br><br>ARIMA<br><br>ForecastTCN |

Figure 6.5 – AutoML forecasting algorithms

Like regression, AutoML performs **model ensembling** at the end of each AutoML training run. **Voting ensembles** take a weighted average of your forecasting models and use that to make a prediction. **Stack ensembles**, in contrast, train an elastic net model using the output of other models. There is a danger of overfitting when using a stack ensemble with forecasting; for that reason, it's recommended to turn it off.

For more information on these models, please consult the AutoML documentation found at `https://docs.microsoft.com/en-us/azure/machine-learning/how-to-configure-auto-train#configure-your-experiment-settings`.

# Summary

You have now successfully trained all three types of AutoML models – classification, regression, and forecasting. Not only can you train a simple forecasting model, but you also know how to improve models with the various forecasting parameters and how to build high-performing baseline models with ARIMA and Prophet.

Moreover, you've acquired a lot of knowledge regarding how forecasting differs from other problems and how to avoid common pitfalls. By utilizing the forecast horizon feature wisely, you can forecast days, months or years into the future, and now it's time to add a powerful tool to your repertoire.

In *Chapter 7, Using the Many Models Solution Accelerator*, you will be able to build individual models for each time series grain. Instead of building one forecasting model, you can build thousands of models all at the same time and score them as if they were one model. You will find that this approach can vastly enhance your model's performance and it is possible only with cloud-native technology.

# 7
# Using the Many Models Solution Accelerator

Now that you have experienced building regression, classification, and forecasting models with AutoML, it's time for you to learn how to deploy and utilize those models in actual business scenarios. Before you tackle this, however, we will first introduce you to a new, very powerful solution, that is, the **Many Models Solution Accelerator** (**MMSA**).

The MMSA lets you build hundreds to thousands of **machine learning** (**ML**) models at once and easily scales to hundreds of thousands of models. It's an advanced technology at the cutting edge of ML. Not only can you build hundreds of thousands of models, but you can also use the MMSA to easily deploy them into production.

In this chapter, you will begin by installing the accelerator and understanding the various use cases to which it applies. You will then run the three sections of the accelerator notebook-by-notebook: prepping data, training models, and forecasting new data.

In each section, you will use both sample data found within the accelerator as well as sample data that you generate with Python code. This will give you examples of using the MMSA with both file and tabular datasets. Finally, you will go over tips and tricks to maximize performance using the accelerator and you will be introduced to concepts such as **hierarchical forecasting**.

By the end of this chapter, you will have mastered using the MMSA with AutoML. You will be able to bring your own data into the MMSA, get it into the right shape, and train thousands of models. This solution is ideal for scenarios in which you wish to train similar models over a large number of products or stores, for example, building a separate forecasting model for each combination of product and store. Large companies all over the USA use it, and, by the end of this chapter, you will be able to use it too.

In this chapter, we will cover the following topics:

- Installing the many models solution accelerator
- Prepping data for many models
- Training many models simultaneously
- Scoring new data for many models
- Improving your many models results

# Technical requirements

Within this chapter, you will log in to your **Azure Machine Learning studio** (**AMLS**), open up a Jupyter notebook on a compute instance, and install the MMSA from its location on GitHub. You will then run all three pieces of the MMSA sequentially, prepping the data, training the models remotely, and forecasting the data. As such, you need to have an Azure account, a compute instance for writing Python code, and a compute cluster for remote training. The full list of requirements is as follows:

- Access to the internet.
- A web browser, preferably Google Chrome or Microsoft Edge Chromium.
- A Microsoft Azure account.
- You should have created an AMLS workspace.
- You should have created a compute instance in *Chapter 2, Getting Started with Azure Machine Learning Service.*
- You should have created the compute cluster in *Chapter 2, Getting Started with Azure Machine Learning Service.*
- You should understand how to navigate to the Jupyter environment from an AMLS compute instance, as demonstrated in *Chapter 4, Building an AutoML Regression Solution.*

The code for this chapter is available here: `https://github.com/PacktPublishing/Automated-Machine-Learning-with-Microsoft-Azure/tree/master/Chapter07`.

# Installing the many models solution accelerator

The MMSA was built by Microsoft in 2019 to address the needs of a growing number of customers who wanted to train hundreds of thousands of similar ML models simultaneously. This is particularly important for product demand forecasting, where you are trying to make forecasts for many different products at many different locations.

The impetus for the accelerator is **model accuracy**. While you could train a single model to predict product demand across all of your product lines and all of your stores, you will find that training individual models for each combination of product and store tends to yield superior performance. This is because a multitude of factors are dependent on both your algorithm and your data. It can be very difficult for some algorithms to find meaningful patterns when you're dealing with hundreds of thousands of different products distributed across the globe.

Additionally, the same columns can have different or even opposite relationships with the target column you are trying to predict. Imagine weather and product sales. When it snows outside, it's very likely that certain products, such as winter hats, gloves, or boots, will experience a spike in sales. Other products, such as ice cream, will very likely experience a decline in sales. While some algorithms can handle these opposite relationships across product lines, many cannot, and using the MMSA to build a separate model for each product will often result in better metrics.

Other common use cases besides forecasting product demand for the MMSA include predictive maintenance across thousands of devices and machines on factory plant floors, workforce optimization models across hundreds of stores, text analytics use cases and legal document search models per state in the United States, and many other similar scenarios. Still, forecasting is the most common use case. Chain stores, in particular, find the MMSA attractive.

Technically speaking, the key factor in determining whether to use the MMSA or not is the presence of one or more columns in your data, which you can use to split the data into multiple files. Columns such as store, product, and region are prime targets to split. If no such columns exist in your data, there's no reason to use the MMSA.

Likewise, if you expect that patterns in your data should be relatively stable across columns such as product, group, and region, you should train a single ML model with AutoML as you would for any other problem.

In this section, you will install the MMSA on your Jupyter environment. First, you will create a new Jupyter notebook used only for the installation. Then, you will install the MMSA on your Jupyter environment. This will create a series of files and folders. Lastly, you will be able to confirm that the MMSA has been successfully installed and identify the notebooks you will use for the remainder of this chapter.

## Creating a new notebook in your Jupyter environment

Perform the following steps to create a new Jupyter notebook on your compute instance:

1.  First, open up your AML studio instance by navigating to `http://ml.azure.com`.

2.  Click **Compute**, start up a compute instance, and open a Jupyter environment.

3.  Create a new Jupyter notebook and name it `Accelerator_Installation`. If you need a refresher, please review *Chapter 4, Building an AutoML Regression Solution.*

With your notebook created, you are now ready to install the accelerator from GitHub.

## Installing the MMSA from GitHub

The MMSA is a publicly available solution developed by Microsoft hosted on a GitHub repository. Use the following code to install the MMSA on your Jupyter environment:

1.  Clone the MMSA repo into your Jupyter notebook filesystem using the following code:

```
!git clone https://github.com/microsoft/solution-
accelerator-many-models
```

2.  All of the files have now been loaded into a new folder named `solution-accelerator-many-models`. Click the Jupyter graphic at the top of your screen to navigate to your file directory, as shown in *Figure 7.1*:

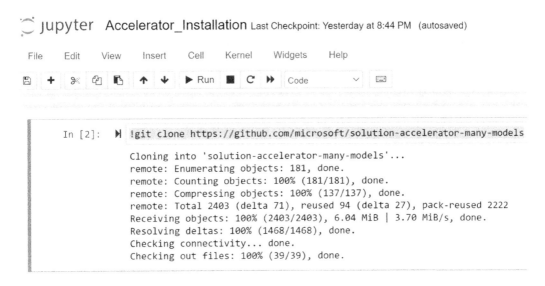

Figure 7.1 – Navigating to your file directory

3.  Open the `solution-accelerator-many-models` folder by clicking it.

4.  Upon opening the folder, you will find many files and folders. The first file you will use in the *Prepping data for many models* section is `01_Data_Preparation.ipynb`. If you wish to set up a new compute cluster for the MMSA, you should first run `00_Setup_AML_Workspace.ipynb`. Make a note of these.

5.  Moving on, open the `Automated_ML` folder. This folder contains two subfolders, called `02_AutoML_Training_Pipeline` and `03_AutoML_Forecasting_Pipeline`.

6.  Open each of the AutoML pipelines. Each one contains a Jupyter notebook with the same name as the folder. Make a note of these.

For the rest of this chapter, these will be the only three Jupyter notebooks you will interact with, `01_Data_Preparation.ipynb`, `02_AutoML_Training_Pipeline`, and `03_AutoML_Forecasting_Pipeline`. In each case, first you will run the notebook as is, running with a default sample dataset. Then, you will make another notebook and use similar code to train a different dataset. This will teach you how to use both file and tabular datasets with the MMSA, and how to work with your own data. You will begin by prepping data.

# Prepping data for many models

While training thousands of ML models simultaneously sounds complicated, the MMSA makes it easy. The example included in the notebooks uses the OJ Sales data you used in *Chapter 6, Building an AutoML Forecasting Solution*. You will prepare the data simply by opening and running 01_Data_Preparation.ipynb. By reading the instructions carefully step by step and working through the notebook slowly, you will be able to understand what each section is about.

Once you're able to understand what each section is doing and you have the OJ Sales data loaded, you will be able to load the new dataset into your Jupyter notebook. This way, by the end of this section, you will be able to load your own data into Azure, modify it for the MMSA, and master the ability to use this powerful solution.

## Prepping the sample OJ dataset

To understand how the first notebook works, follow these instructions in order:

1. Open 01_Data_Preparation.ipynb.

2. Run all of the cells in section 1.0 of the notebook. These cells create a folder called oj_sales_data in your file directory and download the OJ Sales data there. After running section 1.0, examine the files in your new folder; oj_sales_data will be located in the same directory level as 01_Data_Preparation.ipynb.

3. Run the single cell in section 2.0 of the notebook. This cell splits the data into training data and inference data based on a date. It creates two folders in the oj_sales_data folder, one called upload_train_data, and another called upload_inference_data. Look inside each of these folders after you run the cell. You should see files with names such as Store1000_dominicks.csv. Click one of the files to see what the data looks like.

4. Run all of the cells in section 3.0 of the notebook. These cells copy the data from your file directory on your compute instance to a file directory on your datastore. This copies the file structure and you end up with the oj_sales_data folder as well as your upload_train_data and upload_inference data subfolders on your datastore. If you'd like to, open up your Azure storage account and try to locate these folders. Remember that they will be in the container beginning with azureml-blobstore.

5.  Run the single cell in `section 4.0` of the notebook. This cell creates two file datasets, one named `oj_data_small_train` and the other called `oj_data_small_inference`. These are the datasets you will use in `02_AutoML_Training_Pipeline` and `03_AutoML_Forecasting_Pipeline`, respectively.

6.  Run all of the cells in `section 5.0` of the notebook to view your data.

> **Important note**
>
> If you run the notebook as is, you will train a small number of models using 10 files. You can set `dataset_maxfiles` to `11793` to train a much larger number of models in `section 1.0` of the notebook. In this case, your datasets will be called `oj_data_inference` and `oj_data_train`.

You now have the `OJ Sales` data prepped for the accelerator. In order to bring your own data into the accelerator, there are a few important caveats you need to follow. Most importantly, the `OJ Sales` data comes presplit based on store and orange juice brand. You will need to mimic this structure using your own data in a new Jupyter notebook.

## Prepping a pandas dataframe

Bringing your own data into the MMSA is unclear. `OJ Sales`, after all, is a file dataset consisting of 11,793 files. You are much more likely to use data that consists of a single file or comes from a single table within a database. Moreover, you are most likely to read it in via pandas, the most common Python package. To learn how to use pandas dataframes with the MMSA, perform the following steps:

1.  Download the `ManyModelsSampleData.csv` file from the *Automated-Machine-Learning-on-Microsoft-Azure* GitHub repository.

2.  Navigate to your Jupyter environment.

3.  Open the `solution-accelerator-many-models` folder.

4.  Click the **Upload** button in the top-left corner of your screen. Upload the `ManyModelsSampleData.csv` file to your Jupyter environment.

5.  Create a new Jupyter notebook and open it. Rename it `01_Data_PreparationMy-Data.ipynb`.

6. To load in all of the libraries, you will require the following code:

```
import pandas as pd
import numpy as np
import os
import datetime as dt
from azureml.core import Workspace, Dataset, Datastore
from scripts.helper import split_data
```

You should recognize `pandas`, `numpy`, `Workspace`, `Dataset`, and `Datastore` from *Chapter 4, Building an AutoML Regression Solution.* You've also used `os` in *Chapter 6, Building an AutoML Forecasting Solution.*

New to this script is `split_data`, which is a **helper function**. Helper functions are reusable functions written for a program to reduce complexity. The MMSA has a few helper functions and split data is used to divide data into training and inference data based on a date you pass in.

Another new package is `datetime`, which lets you convert string objects into proper Python datetime objects. This is a requirement since `split_data` requires datetime objects to function properly.

7. Read the `ManyModelsSampleData.csv` file into a pandas dataframe with the following code:

```
ManyModelsSample =\
pd.read_csv('ManyModelsSampleData.csv', header = 0)
```

Setting headers to 0 will use the first row of your CSV file for column names.

8. Create a folder called `MMSA_Sample_Folder` with the following code:

```
target_path = 'MMSA_Sample_Folder'
os.makedirs(target_path, exist_ok=True)
```

9. View your dataset:

```
ManyModelsSample
```

You will find that this dataset has three columns: `Date`, `Store`, and `Sales`. It's about as simple a forecasting dataset as you can get. There are four stores and each store has a time series that extends from January 1, 2020 until March 31, 2021. You want to forecast sales into the future.

10. Convert your `Date` column into a `datetime` object with the following code:

```
ManyModelsSample['Date'] =\
ManyModelsSample['Date'].apply(lambda x:\
dt.datetime.strptime(x, '%m/%d/%Y'))
```

This code takes your `Date` column and applies a function to it using the `datetime` package to convert it from a string into a `datetime` object.

11. Split your pandas dataframe into four separate CSV files, one for each store, and place each of them in the MMSA sample folder with the following code:

```
for x, y in ManyModelsSample.groupby('Store'):
    y.to_csv('MMSA_Sample_Folder/{}.csv'.format(x),\
  header=True, index_label=False)
```

Understand that `x` is an individual store within your `ManyModelsSample` dataframe and that `y` is a pandas dataframe with only values for that store. This code loops through all four stores and, one by one, creates a CSV file with headers inside `MMSA_Sample_Folder`. Each file will be the name of the store. In this case, the stores are named after the cities in which they are located: New York, Washington DC, San Francisco, and Seattle.

> **Important tip**
>
> The time column that you use to split your data must absolutely be a datetime object, not a string. Leaving your time column as a string will result in failed forecasting runs later on.

12. Set variables for your time column as well as the cutoff for when you are training and scoring data:

```
timestamp_column = 'Date'
split_date = '2021-03-01'
```

The MMSA documentation refers to scoring data as inference data. **Inferencing** is just another word for scoring; it's widely used in academic settings or within research-focused companies.

When you specify `split_date`, remember that the date you specify and every date after it will be used for scoring, while all dates prior to it will be used for training. Your `split_date` function must be in the format used here.

13. Split the data into training and inference files with the following code:

```
train_path, inference_path = split_data(target_path, \
timestamp_column, split_date)
```

This code uses your `split_data` helper function. Within the `MMSA_Sample_Folder`, two new folders will be created holding four sets each of training and scoring files.

14. Connect your Jupyter notebook to your AMLS workspace:

```
ws = Workspace.from_config()
```

If you are prompted to log in, do so by following the instructions.

15. Set your datastore to the default datastore that comes with your AMLS workspace:

```
datastore = ws.get_default_datastore()
```

This code is slightly different than the one you used in *Chapter 4, Building an AutoML Regression Solution*. In the AzureML SDK, there are often functions with identical uses.

16. Upload your training data to your default datastore with the following code:

```
ds_train_path = target_path + '_train'
datastore.upload(src_dir=train_path, \
target_path=ds_train_path, overwrite=True)
```

This code will write your training files to a folder called `MMSA_Sample_Folder_train` on your default datastore.

17. Upload your scoring data to your default datastore with the following code:

```
ds_inference_path = target_path + '_inference'
datastore.upload(src_dir=inference_path, \
target_path=ds_inference_path, overwrite=True)
```

This code will write your training files to a folder called `MMSA_Sample_Folder_inference` on your default datastore.

18. Create file datasets for your training and scoring data with the following code:

```
ds_train = \
Dataset.File.from_files(path=\
datastore.path(ds_train_path), validate=False)
ds_inference = Dataset.File.from_files(path=\
datastore.path(ds_inference_path), validate=False)
```

The MMSA requires file datasets to work. As such, you need to register the folders on your default datastore as file datasets. This will register the entire folder and all of its contents.

19. Create variables for the names for when you register the datasets:

```
dataset_name = 'MMSA_Sample'
train_dataset_name = dataset_name + '_train'
inference_dataset_name = dataset_name + '_inference'
```

Using this code will ensure that you register your datasets with the names `MMSA_Sample_train` and `MMSA_Sample_inference`.

20. Register your file datasets with the following code:

```
ds_train.register(ws, train_dataset_name, create_new_
version=True)
ds_inference.register(ws, inference_dataset_name, create_
new_version=True)
```

You should now have two additional datasets in your AML studio. Check by clicking **Datasets** on the left-hand panel.

Make sure you save your notebook, as this code will come in very handy in the future when you wish to use the MMSA with your own data. You have now prepped both the `OJ Sales` data as well the simple sample data and saved them as separate training and scoring file datasets. This is step number one in using the accelerator. Now that you have prepped your data, it's time for you to train a lot of models.

# Training many models simultaneously

Like prepping data for many models, training many models is simply a matter of navigating to the correct notebook and running the cells. There's no custom code required, and you are simply required to change a few settings.

Like prepping data, you will first run the notebook step by step to carefully understand how it works. Once you have that understanding, you will then create a new notebook with code that uses the datasets you made from the sample data. This will benefit you tremendously, as you will understand exactly which parts of the code you need to change to facilitate your own projects.

# Training the sample OJ dataset

To train many models using the OJ data and to understand the underlying process, follow these instructions step by step:

1. From the `solution-accelerator-many-models` folder, click on the `Automated_ML` folder.

2. From the `Automated_ML` folder, click on the `02_AutoML_Training_ Pipeline` folder.

3. Open `02_AutoML_Training_Pipeline.ipynb`.

4. Run all of the cells in `section 1.0`. This sets your datastore and your workspace and also assigns a name to your many models experiment. Notice that this code also outputs a nice table listing your AMLS workspace details along with the name of your datastore. You can add this table to all of your code if you wish or you can use the templates in this book for a more direct, spartan approach to coding.

> **Tip**
>
> If you are having trouble loading any Azure libraries, update the Azure MLSDK by running the Update `AzureML SDK.ipynb` notebook foundhere: https://github.com/PacktPublishing/Automated-Machine-Learning-with-Microsoft-Azure/blob/master/Update-AzureML-SDK.ipynb.

5. Run the single cell in `section 2.0`. This retrieves your training dataset, `oj_ data_small_train`. Notice that the dataset gets set twice here, first as a typical dataset, and then as **named input**. Named input is simply an Azure artifact that certain ML pipelines use to work with datasets. Underlying the MMSA is a **parallel run ML pipeline**. This ML pipeline lets you run different types of jobs in parallel.

> **Important tip**
>
> The MMSA often uses **AzureML contributor packages**. These are packages that are under development. You may have to uncomment out cells and install the packages in this section depending on your version of the AzureML SDK. Any packages you need to install will always be in the code.

6. Run all of the cells in `section 3.0`. These cells create a compute cluster to train all of your models, set your AutoML forecasting settings, and set your many models **parallel run** settings. Parallel run refers to how many model training runs you would like to perform at once. Currently, the limit is 320 although it is subject to increase in the future.

The key change to forecasting settings is the addition of **partition columns**. These are the columns on which different models are trained, in this case, Store and Brand. If your Azure subscription isn't able to use the STANDARD_D16S_V3 **virtual machines** (**VMs**) that the notebook uses, simply change them to STANDARD_DS3_V2.

> **Important note**
> The *node count* for your parallel run settings should be set to the number of nodes in your compute cluster. Your *process count per node* should not exceed the number of cores on each node. If you're using a Standard_DS3_v2 VM, for example, the process count per node should not exceed 4.

7.  Run both cells in section 4.0. These cells train all of your models.

8.  Run the cell in section 6.0 to get a list of your AutoML runs and the tags they were registered with. This is how you keep track of all of the different models you have registered. The MMSA automatically generates tags for your partition columns.

9.  Publish your many models training pipeline by uncommenting the first cell and running it. Do not run the second cell, as this will schedule your pipeline to automatically run on a cadence. Although this feature is useful in a production setting, it does rack up costs.

Within 15 to 30 minutes, you should have all 10 models trained and registered. Unlike normal AutoML runs, the MMSA automatically registers the best model for each grouping (in this case, orange juice brand and store) you train. This feature scales exceptionally well and some Microsoft customers are using it to train and retrain hundreds of thousands of models on an ongoing basis.

You can check the run in the portal by clicking the blue link, which will take you to the pipeline visualization seen in the following screenshot:

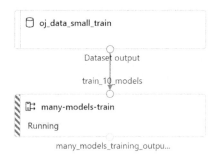

Figure 7.2 – The MMSA in action

Next, you will create a new notebook and train many models with the sample data
you loaded in as a pandas dataframe. You will substantially simplify the code in the
second notebook to achieve an identical solution. This will help you easily adapt the
MMSA to your own problems in the future.

## Training your sample dataset with the MMSA

Just as you modified the first notebook, you need to modify the second notebook to use
your own code. All the steps will be the same, but the code will be less busy and easier to
read. Begin with the following steps:

1. Open the `solution-accelerator-many-models` folder.

2. Open the `Automated_ML` folder.

3. Open the `02_AutoML_Training_Pipeline` folder.

4. Create a new Jupyter notebook and open it. Rename it `02_AutoML_Training_
   Pipeline-My-Data.ipynb`.

5. Load in all of the familiar libraries you will need with the following code:

   ```
   from azureml.core import Workspace, Datastore, Dataset
   from azureml.core import Experiment
   from azureml.core.compute import ComputeTarget
   import pandas as pd
   import os
   ```

   You should be familiar with most of these packages from the *Prepping data for
   many models* section. `ComputeTarget` is used to set a compute cluster for remote
   training and was covered in *Chapter 4, Building an AutoML Regression Solution*.

6. Load in the new libraries you will need to train your MMSA solution with the
   following code:

   ```
   from azureml.contrib.automl.pipeline.steps import
   AutoMLPipelineBuilder
   from azureml.pipeline.core import Pipeline
   from scripts.helper import get_training_output
   import logging
   ```

`AzureMLPipelineBuilder` lets you build out your many models training runs and is a contributor package. Make sure you use pip to install it here if you haven't already using the code that is commented out in the original MMSA training notebook. `Pipeline` lets you build ML pipelines, which are necessary for running the MMSA under the hood.

Finally, `get_training_output` is another helper function that lets you retrieve information about the models you trained and `logging` enables more detailed logs to be collected regarding your training run.

7. Connect your Jupyter notebook to your AMLS workspace:

```
ws = Workspace.from_config()
```

If you are prompted to log in, do so by following the instructions.

8. Set your datastore to the default datastore that comes with your AMLS workspace:

```
dstore = ws.get_default_datastore()
```

Be careful, as the datastore variable name is different from other Jupyter notebooks.

9. Set your experiment and give it a name using the following code:

```
experiment = Experiment(ws, 'manymodels-training-
pipeline-pandas-data')
```

10. Specify your training dataset with the following code:

```
filedst_10_models = Dataset.get_by_name(ws, name = 'MMSA_
Sample_train')
filedst_10_models_input =\
filedst_10_models.as_named_input('MMSA_Sample_train')
```

It doesn't matter what name you give to your named input. The important thing is the underlying dataset. The MMSA will find the correct dataset regardless.

11. Set your compute cluster, which will be used for remote training, with the following code:

```
compute = "compute-cluster"
```

If you created a different compute cluster for many models training, use that one instead.

12. Set your partition column names:

```
partition_column_names = ['Store']
```

You can have as many partition columns as necessary for your business problem. OJ Sales has two. The sample data has one.

13. Adjust your AutoML settings as needed. Specifically, set label_column_name to Sales. This is the column you are trying to predict. Change the name of debug_ log to separate it from the training run with OJ Sales. Set time_column_ name to Date. Set grain_column_names to Store.

One confusing thing about the MMSA is that you should always pass in your partition columns to grain_column_names too. For more information about these settings, refer to *Chapter 6, Building an AutoML Forecasting Solution*:

```
automl_settings = {
    "task" : 'forecasting',
    "primary_metric" : \
    'normalized_root_mean_squared_error',
    "iteration_timeout_minutes" : 10,
    "iterations" : 15,
    "experiment_timeout_hours" : 1,
    "label_column_name" : 'Sales',
    "n_cross_validations" : 3,
    "verbosity" : logging.INFO,
    "debug_log": 'automl_pandas_debug.txt',
    "time_column_name": 'Date',
    "max_horizon" : 31,
    "track_child_runs": False,
    "partition_column_names": partition_column_names,
    "grain_column_names": ['Store'],
    "pipeline_fetch_max_batch_size": 15
}
```

> **Important tip**
>
> The MMSA can be used for regression and classification of AutoML problems too. In that case, make sure you pass in the relevant settings specific to each problem type.

14. Pass in your MMSA configurations. Make sure you adjust `node_count` and `process_count_per_node` to match the number of nodes on your compute cluster and the number of cores on a single VM, respectively, with the following code:

```
train_steps =\
AutoMLPipelineBuilder.get_many_models_train_steps(
experiment=experiment,
                      automl_settings=automl_settings,
                      train_data=filedst_10_models_input,
                      compute_target=compute,
                      partition_column_names=\
                      partition_column_names,
                      node_count=4,
                      process_count_per_node=4,
                      run_invocation_timeout=3700,
                      output_datastore=dstore)
```

15. Submit your MMSA training run with the following code:

```
pipeline = Pipeline(workspace=ws, steps=train_steps)
run = experiment.submit(pipeline)
```

16. Get additional details about your MMSA training run with the following code:

```
run.wait_for_completion(show_output=True)
```

17. Publish your MMSA pipeline with the following code:

```
published_pipeline = pipeline.publish(name = \
'MMSA_pandas', description = 'MMSA Solution using a
pandas dataframe', \
version = '1', continue_on_step_failure = False)
```

This code will publish your pipeline so you can schedule it later at your leisure. Setting `continue_on_step_failure` to `False` will prevent this code from publishing a pipeline that errors out.

18. If you would like, you can copy code over from the original MMSA training notebook to schedule your MMSA pipeline to run on a cadence. You can also copy over code to look at the results of the overall run; this is very good for debugging errors.

You have now successfully trained many models using both the OJ Sales data and a sample file read in as a pandas dataframe. Instead of modifying the MMSA code from scratch, you also have a simplified notebook on hand that you can easily use to build your own solution with the MMSA. Next, you will learn how to score new data with models trained using the accelerator. This will complete your introduction to the MMSA using AutoML.

# Scoring new data for many models

Scoring new data with the MMSA is a fairly straightforward task. Once you have your models trained, simply navigate to the correct notebook, change your variables to match your training notebook, and click the run button. As there are very few settings to alter compared to the training notebook, it's even easier to use with your own code.

In this section, like the others, first you will run the out-of-the-box scoring notebook with OJ Sales. Then, you will create a new notebook to score the sample data.

## Scoring OJ sales data with the MMSA

To score OJ Sales data with the multiple models you've trained, follow these steps:

1. From the solution-accelerator-many-models folder, open the Automated_ML folder.

2. From the Automated_ML folder, open the 03_AutoML_Forecasting_Pipeline folder.

3. Open 03_AutoML_Forecasting_Pipeline.ipynb.

4. Run all of the cells in section 1.0. These cells set up your AMLS workspace, compute cluster, datastore, and experiment. Like the training notebook before it, the forecasting notebook is also an ML pipeline. Information regarding your ML pipeline runs, like your training runs, is saved in experiment artifacts.

> **Tip**
> Your *training experiment* that you ran to train many models is different from your *inferencing experiment* that you are running now. Make sure they have different names.

5. Run the single cell in section 2.0. This cell calls the inferencing dataset you created with the data preparation notebook; this is the data you will score with your trained model.

6.  In `section 3.0`, set your training **pipeline run ID** along with the training experiment name. You can find both of these in the `02_AutoML_Training_Pipeline.ipynb` notebook you ran earlier or in the **Experiments** section of AMLS. Your pipeline run ID is the ID for the experiment that trained all of your models:

```
training_pipeline_run_id ="your pipeline run id"
training_experiment_name = "your training experiment
name"
```

7.  Run the second cell in `section 3.0`. This cell configures the settings for your many models scoring pipeline. Most importantly, this is passing in your partition columns, your target column that you're trying to predict, and your time column, which determines the cadence of your predictions.

8.  Run the two cells in `section 4.0` to score new data. This is an ML pipeline run and your compute cluster will take some time to spin up. Once it spins up and the ML pipeline starts, however, scoring your data will be very fast.

9.  Run the single cell in `section 5.0` to view your results, as shown in the following screenshot:

| | Week Starting | Store | Brand | Quantity | Advert | Price | Revenue | Predicted |
|---|---|---|---|---|---|---|---|---|
| 0 | 1992-05-28 | 1001 | dominicks | 12736 | 1 | 2.37 | 30184.32 | 12655.926953 |
| 1 | 1992-06-04 | 1001 | dominicks | 17512 | 1 | 2.28 | 39927.36 | 17589.279167 |
| 2 | 1992-06-11 | 1001 | dominicks | 17769 | 1 | 2.18 | 38736.42 | 17616.802905 |
| 3 | 1992-06-18 | 1001 | dominicks | 17825 | 1 | 2.64 | 47058.00 | 18321.770558 |
| 4 | 1992-06-25 | 1001 | dominicks | 11105 | 1 | 2.02 | 22432.10 | 11428.825570 |
| 5 | 1992-07-02 | 1001 | dominicks | 15763 | 1 | 1.97 | 31053.11 | 15358.724956 |
| 6 | 1992-07-09 | 1001 | dominicks | 10904 | 1 | 2.33 | 25406.32 | 10827.578098 |
| 7 | 1992-07-16 | 1001 | dominicks | 16153 | 1 | 2.27 | 36667.31 | 15773.192383 |
| 8 | 1992-07-23 | 1001 | dominicks | 14260 | 1 | 2.03 | 28947.80 | 14397.971780 |
| 9 | 1992-07-30 | 1001 | dominicks | 9284 | 1 | 2.67 | 24788.28 | 8715.212884 |

Figure 7.3 – MMSA results

10. If you would like to publish your ML pipeline for later use, run the first cell in `section 6.0`. Avoid running the second cell, as this creates an automated schedule for your pipeline that can become quite costly over time.

You have now completed the MMSA OJ Sales notebooks from start to finish. You have prepped data and shaped it into the right format, splitting it into many files. Then, you trained 10 models in parallel and used those models to score the data.

It's time to do the same and score your sample dataset with a simplified notebook and see the output. Keep in mind that the output should not be especially good, as the sales numbers were randomly generated. This will, however, provide you with a template for generating results with your own data.

# Scoring your sample dataset with many models

In order to score data from your sample dataset, observe the following instructions:

1. Open the `solution-accelerator-many-models` folder.

2. Open the `Automated_ML` folder.

3. Open the `03_AutoML_Forecasting_Pipeline` folder.

4. Create a new Jupyter notebook and open it. Rename it `03_AutoML_Forecasting_Pipeline-My-Data.ipynb`.

5. Load in all of the libraries you have already used in this chapter with the following code:

```
from azureml.core import Workspace, Datastore, Dataset
from azureml.core import Experiment
import pandas as pd
import os
from azureml.core.compute import ComputeTarget
from azureml.contrib.automl.pipeline.steps import AutoMLPipelineBuilder
from azureml.pipeline.core import Pipeline
```

If you need a refresher on any of these, please refer to the *Training many models simultaneously* section.

6. Load in the libraries that are new to this section with the following code:

```
import shutil
import sys
from scripts.helper import get_forecasting_output
```

You have another helper function here, `get_forecasting_output`. This lets you easily retrieve the predictions generated by the MMSA without any hassle. Both `sys` and `shutil` are used by `get_forecasting_output`. While `shutil` lets you manipulate files and folders similar to `os`, `sys` lets you interact with the Python runtime environment.

7. Connect your Jupyter notebook to your AMLS workspace:

```
ws = Workspace.from_config()
```

If you are prompted to log in, do so by following the instructions.

8. Set your datastore to the default datastore that comes with your AMLS workspace:

```
dstore = ws.get_default_datastore()
```

This uses the same datastore variable name as the training notebook.

9. Set your experiment and give it a name with the help of the following code:

```
experiment = Experiment(ws, 'manymodels-forecasting-
pipeline-pandas-data')
```

10. Specify your training dataset with the following code:

```
filedst_10_models = Dataset.get_by_name(ws, name = 'MMSA_
Sample_inference')
filedst_10_models_input =\
filedst_10_models.as_named_input('MMSA_Sample_inference')
```

It doesn't matter what name you give to your named input. The important thing is the underlying dataset. The MMSA will find the correct dataset regardless.

11. Set your compute cluster, which will be used for remote training, with the following code:

```
compute = "compute-cluster"
```

12. Retrieve your experiment name and run ID from the ML pipeline you used to train the models. You can find the run ID in AML studio under **Experiments**:

```
training_experiment_name = "manymodels-training-pipeline-
pandas-data"
training_pipeline_run_id ="your-run-ID"
```

13. Set your partition column names:

```
partition_column_names = ['Store']
```

14. Pass in your MMSA configurations. Make sure that you set `time_column_name` to `Date`, `target_column_name` that you are trying to predict to `Sales`, `node_count` to the maximum number of nodes on your compute cluster, and `process_count_per_node` to the number of cores on a single VM with the help of the following code:

```
inference_steps =\
AutoMLPipelineBuilder.get_many_models_batch_inference_
steps(\
                        experiment=experiment,
                        inference_data=\
                        filedst_10_models_input,
                        compute_target=compute,
                        node_count=4,
                        process_count_per_node=4,
                        run_invocation_timeout=300,
                        train_experiment_name=\
                        training_experiment_name,
                        train_run_id=\
                        training_pipeline_run_id,
                        partition_column_names=\
                        partition_column_names,
                        time_column_name="Date",
                        target_column_name="Sales")
```

15. Submit your MMSA scoring run with the following code:

```
pipeline = Pipeline(workspace=ws, steps=train_steps)
run = experiment.submit(pipeline)
```

16. Get additional details about your MMSA scoring run with the following code:

```
run.wait_for_completion(show_output=True)
```

This should only take a few minutes to run.

17. Once your ML pipeline has finished, publish your ML pipeline with the following code:

```
published_pipeline = pipeline.publish(name = 'automl_
score_many_models_pandas',
                    description = \
                    'MMSA Solution using x data',
                    version = '1',
                    continue_on_step_failure = False)
```

Publishing your scoring pipeline will let you run it again very easily in the future. You will learn more about ML pipelines in *Chapter 9*, *Implementing a Batch Scoring Solution*.

18. View the first 10 rows of your results with the following code:

```
forecasting_results_name = "forecasting_results"
forecasting_output_name =\
"many_models_inference_output"
forecast_file = get_forecasting_output(run,\
forecasting_results_name, forecasting_output_name)
df = pd.read_csv(forecast_file, delimiter=" ",\
header=None)
df.columns = ["Date", "Store", "Sales", "Predicted" ]
df.head(10)
```

For this code to work, you need to manually enter the column names of your dataset. The last column will always be the predictions generated by your solution. Your results should resemble the following screenshot. Since the data was random, it shouldn't be good:

```
Prediction has  124  rows. Here the first 10.
```

| | Date | Store | Sales | Predicted |
|---|---|---|---|---|
| 0 | 2021-03-01 | San Francisco | 83 | 54.902630 |
| 1 | 2021-03-02 | San Francisco | 37 | 49.947213 |
| 2 | 2021-03-03 | San Francisco | 44 | 49.690911 |
| 3 | 2021-03-04 | San Francisco | 50 | 54.322844 |
| 4 | 2021-03-05 | San Francisco | 73 | 53.245385 |
| 5 | 2021-03-06 | San Francisco | 91 | 50.389134 |
| 6 | 2021-03-07 | San Francisco | 55 | 53.390174 |
| 7 | 2021-03-08 | San Francisco | 9 | 50.627610 |
| 8 | 2021-03-09 | San Francisco | 98 | 48.155031 |
| 9 | 2021-03-10 | San Francisco | 8 | 49.585355 |

Figure 7.4 – Many model results on the sample data

Success! You have reached the ultimate goal of creating a complete MMSA solution with sample data read in as a pandas dataframe. You are now in prime position to use the solution with your own data.

The first time you run the MMSA using only the OJ Sales data, it seems like it's really easy and there's nothing to it. Despite being easy, you will find that it produces superior results compared to the single model you trained in *Chapter 6, Building a Forecasting Solution*. By simply running a few notebooks in the correct order, you are able to produce a high performing model.

Experience has now taught you how you need to adjust the MMSA to work with your own data and that was pretty straightforward too. However, the first time you try to apply your own data to it, you may find it a bit tricky. Getting your data into just the right format can be frustrating. To help make your experience smooth, the final portion of this chapter covers tips and tricks to improve your solution.

# Improving your many models results

Now that you have adapted all three of the notebooks to run your own code, you should be feeling pretty confident in your ability to use the MMSA. Still, it's pretty easy to get stuck. Many models is a complicated framework and small errors in your data can lead to errors.

Additionally, sometimes it's really hard to know what your data will look like when you are dealing with thousands of files you wish to train. Here is some good advice to follow in order to ensure you do not come to an impasse when using your own data with the MMSA:

- Before using the accelerator, always try creating a single model first with your entire dataset. Check the performance of your model. Only use the MMSA if the single model's performance is subpar compared to your expectations or in a situation where obtaining the best accuracy is mission-critical for your project. Sometimes, the trade-off between complexity and performance isn't worth it.

- Spend a lot of time ensuring that your data is split correctly before using the accelerator. Each combination of partition columns needs to have its own file. Think carefully as to which columns you would like to use as your partitions. Alternatively, try out a few different combinations to see which gives the best performance.

- When splitting data for forecasting using a date column, absolutely make sure that it is in a datetime format as opposed to a string format. Oftentimes, data scientists will make the mistake of splitting on a string column. Sometimes when this happens, the first two notebooks will run as is and you will be able to train models. However, when you get to the third notebook to forecast data, you will get an error and have to start from the beginning.

- In the Data Preparation notebook, do not hardcode `split_date`. Instead, make it variable based on the current datetime, how much training data you expect to have, and how many hours, days, weeks, or months out you would like to forecast. This way, when you go to retrain the MMSA solution, you will get forecasts for the appropriate time periods. Keep in mind that this is only relevant for forecasting problems.

- For all problems, carefully study your data before passing it into the solution. While AutoML will handle null values and many other errors, it does less with other problems, such as large gaps in your forecasting problem's time column. Clean your data as much as possible before passing it into the MMSA.

- While the MMSA notebook was created using a forecasting example, it's quite easy to adapt the notebook for regression and classification problems. As these are inherently less complicated than forecasting, importing your own code for these problems is comparatively easier. You don't have to worry about dates.

- Become familiar with the log files. When you navigate them, make sure you first click on the pipeline step that failed. Then, click **Outputs + logs**. You want to look for a folder called `logs` and expand it. Then, look for a folder called `user`. Within the `user` folder, you need to search for the `error` folder. The `error` folder contains numerous folders that are a series of numbers separated by periods such as `10.0.0.5`.

  These folders hold the most important files for debugging purposes. Each file starts with `process` and ends with `.txt`. Open up these files and use them to find any errors in your code.

- Do not be afraid to use very large compute clusters when training models with the MMSA. Although larger VMs cost more per hour to use, they also train much quicker than their cheaper counterparts.

- Keep in mind that when you are training models using the MMSA, the compute cluster running it will be at maximum capacity for a comparatively long time depending on how many models you are training. As such, it makes sense to make sure that the compute cluster you use to train many models isn't responsible for running other jobs at the same time.

- The key problem that the MMSA solves is that, when you have multiple, high-dimensional categorical columns, many traditional ML algorithms underperform for mathematical reasons. As your business expands, your products expand, your locations expand, your workforce expands, and the MMSA becomes more and more appropriate for your business.

- Retrain your models frequently on a schedule. It's very difficult to monitor hundreds of thousands of ML models to determine which ones need to be retrained. Instead, retrain all of them on a weekly or monthly basis to ensure high performance.

Although you have received many tips and tricks that will help you build solutions using the MMSA, the best advice is simply to practice as much as possible. Explore the solution as much as possible and uncover as many caveats as you can.

More than anything, remember that the MMSA and AutoML perform best when you pass in clean data. This section concludes this chapter. You now have the expertise, knowledge, and practice to implement a truly game-changing solution in the world of automated ML.

# Summary

Advanced solutions like the MMSA are at the bleeding edge of ML and AI. It is a truly state-of-the-art technology and now it's another tool in your belt.

You've not only run all three notebooks on the OJ Sales data, but you have also converted the code to take in other datasets and understand how it works. Prepping data, training models, and forecasting the future using the MMSA are all things you have done and could do again. You may already have a use case to which you can apply it, or you may have to wait a few more years until your company is ready, but you are prepared.

*Chapter 8, Choosing Real-Time versus Batch Scoring*, continues your journey at the forefront of the ML world. Once you build a model in AutoML, the next step is to deploy it, and there are two options: batch versus real-time scoring. You will learn when to use batch scoring, when to use real-time scoring, and the main differences between the two. Mastering these concepts is key to successfully applying your AutoML models to real-world business scenarios.

# Section 3: AutoML in Production – Automating Real-Time and Batch Scoring Solutions

This third part trains you to productionalize your previously trained models. You will learn how to automate machine learning solutions in an end-to-end fashion.

This section comprises the following chapters:

# 8
# Choosing Real-Time versus Batch Scoring

As you have experienced in the previous chapters, training AutoML models is simple and straightforward. Whether you choose to train a model using the **Azure Machine Learning Studio (AMLS) GUI** or code an AutoML solution in Python using Jupyter, you can build highly accurate **machine learning (ML)** models in minutes. However, you still need to learn how to deploy them. In Azure, there are two main ways you can deploy a previously trained ML model to score new data: **real-time** and **batch**.

In this chapter, you will begin by learning what a **batch scoring solution** is, when to use it, and when it makes sense to retrain batch models. Continuing, you will learn what a **real-time scoring solution** is, when to use it, and when it makes sense to retrain real-time models. Finally, you will conclude by reading a variety of different scenarios and determining which type of scoring you should use. All scenarios are based on common problems faced by real companies.

By the time you finish this chapter, you will have gained an invaluable skill: being able to identify when you should build a batch scoring solution and when you should build a real-time solution.

Batch scoring scenarios require you to build ML pipelines, which you will learn about in *Chapter 9, Implementing a Batch Scoring Solution*. Real-time scoring scenarios, on the other hand, require you to build real-time scoring endpoints hosted on **Azure Kubernetes Service** (**AKS**), which are covered in *Chapter 11, Implementing a Real-Time Scoring Solution*. Many times, organizations mistakenly implement the wrong type of solution, but you will be available to avoid that pitfall.

In this chapter, we will cover the following topics:

- Architecting batch scoring solutions
- Architecting real-time scoring solutions
- Determining batch versus real-time scoring scenarios

# Technical requirements

*Chapter 7, Using the Many Models Solution Accelerator*, featured a lot of heavy Python coding. This chapter is a bit of a reprieve; you will not be coding, but you will be learning important skills through reading business scenarios and applying the proper solutions. As such, there are no technical requirements in this chapter.

# Architecting batch scoring solutions

**Batch inferencing** refers to scoring new data points in batches on a recurring time-based schedule. New data is collected over time and subsequently scored, generating new predictions. This is the most common way modern companies use ML models.

In this section, you will learn how to architect a complete, end-to-end batch scoring solution using Azure AutoML-trained models. You will also learn why, and in what situations, you should prioritize batch scoring over real-time scoring solutions.

# Understanding the five-step batch scoring process

Each batch scoring solution you make should follow a five-step process. This process begins by training and registering an ML model as you did in the previous chapters using AMLS. Regression, classification, and forecasting models all follow the same pattern. In order, the five steps are as follows:

1. **Train a model**. You can train a model either using the AMLS GUI as you did in *Chapter 3, Training Your First AutoML Model*, or using Python on a compute instance as you did in *Chapter 4, Building an AutoML Regression Solution*, *Chapter 5, Building an AutoML Classification Solution*, and *Chapter 6, Building an AutoML Forecasting Solution*.

2. **Register your model**. Once again, you can accomplish this either with the AMLS GUI or by using Python running on a compute instance. Registering a model saves it to your AMLS workspace and lets you reference it later.

3. **Determine a schedule**. Common schedules for batch inferencing are hourly, weekly, or monthly, although you may want to schedule it more or less frequently based on the needs of your business problem.

4. **Score data in batches**. Batch sizes run anywhere from a single data point to billions of data points at once. This step is where you run your batch inferencing code. In Azure, we use ML pipelines. You will learn how to code ML pipelines in *Chapter 9, Implementing a Batch Scoring Solution*.

5. **Deliver results**. Once you run your ML pipeline and make new predictions or forecasts, you need to send those results to either a report or a database. In Azure, sending results from AMLS to other databases is done with a tool called **Azure Data Factory** (**ADF**). You will learn how to use ADF in *Chapter 10, Creating End-to-End AutoML Solutions*.

*Figure 8.1* shows the whole end-to-end process. While you will implement a batch inference solution for your AutoML-trained models, you can use this same process to deploy any ML model. The key to ensuring the success of your solution lies in aligning your batch job schedule with the needs of your business:

Figure 8.1 – Batch scoring process

Now that you know the process, it's time to dive deeper into each of the steps. You're already familiar with training AutoML models and registering them to your AMLS workspace. Next, you will learn what to take into consideration when determining the schedule of your batch scoring solution.

## Scheduling your batch scoring solution

Ultimately, you have trained an AutoML model to meet some business goal. Perhaps you need to decide which products to keep in your lineup and which ones to drop. Maybe you need to forecast product demand over the next quarter. You may be in charge of a professional sports team and need to decide which players to draft for the upcoming season. In any case, you need to make sure that you schedule your batch inferencing job in a way that makes sense and meets your business needs.

The key to determining when you should schedule your job is based on three things:

- How often the business needs to make the decision
- Data availability
- How long your batch scoring job takes to run

First, you need to know how often the business makes the decision that your model is trying to assist. In the case of a professional sports team making a drafting decision, this means that you only need to run your job once a year. If you work for a business that decides its product mix on a quarterly basis, your product demand model should be scheduled to run four times a year. Likewise, if you built a model for a fast food restaurant that tells them what food they should prepare for the next hour, your batch inferencing solution should run every hour. How often you run your model is called **model cadence**.

Second, you need to make sure that new data is available for your model to score. This is called **data availability**. Even if your business problem requires new predictions to be made once an hour, if your data only refreshes once a day, you should build a model that scores data once a day. In other words, you would need to train a forecasting model that predicts 24 hours out and scores it once a day instead of a forecasting model that predicts 1 hour out that runs 24 times a day. Always figure out data availability at the onset of your project. It will save you a lot of time.

Lastly, you need to pay attention to how long your batch job runs. Even if you want to score data every 5 minutes and you have new data available every 5 minutes, if your batch scoring job takes 10 minutes to complete you'll be limited in how often you can score and deliver results. In this case, consider switching to a real-time solution.

Once you've determined your model cadence, data availability, and how long your batch job takes to run, the next step is to figure out when your job should run – down to the second.

In an ideal world, you would only run your model once all relevant data is available. For the professional sports example, you would want to have data on all players in the draft. For the hourly restaurant data, you would want up-to-the-minute foot-traffic, sales, weather, and traffic data to make your prediction.

In the real world, however, you should always expect that there will be data availability issues. Some player data will be randomly missing. Sometimes, weather or foot-traffic data will be late for no reason at all. Sales data may be corrupted by canceled orders or maxed-out credit cards. For this reason, you should simply schedule your job to run at the last possible second it can. Make sure you include a buffer to account for **compute cluster startup time**.

Compute cluster startup time can vary substantially, so it's important that you run a lot of tests on your solution to get an idea of the maximum time it will take to spin up. Set your buffer to the maximum time your cluster takes to start up, so long as it seems reasonable. Usually, this should be no more than 5 to 10 minutes. If it takes longer, open a support ticket. This way, you will ensure your job always runs on time.

> **Important tip**
>
> While you can set your minimum compute cluster nodes to 1 to achieve a faster, more consistent ramp-up time, this means that you are paying for usage 24 hours a day, 7 days a week, negating the cost savings advantage inherent to batch solutions. Setting compute cluster nodes to 0 will lead to substantial cost savings over time.

By scheduling your job to run right around the same time the business will be reviewing your predictions to assist their decision making, you give as much time as possible for systems upstream to collect, transform, and fix data. You also give the business the best predictions you can, based on the most up-to-date data. You also need to consider how to batch score data.

# Scoring data in batches and delivering results

Within AMLS, batch scoring takes place within an ML pipeline. ML pipelines require you to specify an environment, write a scoring script that accesses your model, and write results to a datastore, most likely to a filesystem sitting on a blob container in an Azure storage account in the form of a CSV file. You will learn how to do all of this in *Chapter 9, Implementing a Batch Scoring Solution*.

However, running an ML pipeline only generates and stores predictions. It is not the same as delivering results. Consulting the business directly is the best way to determine where your data should ultimately land. Sometimes, they will want you to store your predictions in a SQL database to which they have direct access. Other times, they will want to receive an Excel file in their email. Often, they will ask you to push the results to a web application accessible by their mobile device.

AMLS itself can write results directly to Azure Data Lake Storage accounts (Gen 1 and Gen 2), Azure SQL databases, Azure Blob storage, Azure file shares, Azure PostGreSQL, Azure Database for MySQL, and Databricks filesystems. ML pipelines can move data directly into these types of storage. That's all, though; you cannot directly move data out of Azure with an ML pipeline alone.

Usually, however, business people will request that you land the results of your AutoML models someplace else, such as an on-premises database or file share. ADF is the perfect tool for moving data both in to and out of Azure. You will learn how to use ADF in *Chapter 10, Creating End-to-End AutoML Solutions*, to solve this common task.

Understanding the process is the first step. The next is to understand when and why you should use batch scoring solutions over their real-time counterparts.

# Choosing batch over real time

Real-time solutions score new data points as they come in. Unlike with batching, there is no waiting for a compute cluster to spin up; real-time scoring clusters never spin down. As soon as new data comes in, new predictions are automatically generated. While this seems like an attractive alternative to batch scoring, there are two major reasons why you should prioritize batch inferencing over real-time inferencing: cost and complexity.

When using cloud computing, you are only paying for resources when you need them. With batch inferencing, when your job runs, a compute cluster spins up, and as soon as it finishes running the job, it spins down. With real-time inferencing, your cluster will be up and running 24 hours a day, 7 days a week. This means that real-time inferencing solutions are orders of magnitude more costly than their batch inferencing equivalents.

Complexity is also a key issue. With batch solutions, all you need to do is move new data into your Azure datastore, score it, and send it off to another database for final delivery. This is an easy, repeatable pattern applicable to a wide array of problems.

Real-time solutions, on the other hand, are never as straightforward. At the heart of any real-time solution is a **scoring endpoint**. These endpoints can be used anywhere in any piece of code. Sometimes, you'll want to integrate them with a web application; other times, you'll want to integrate them with an application that supports streaming data that never stops flowing in. Whereas batch scoring solutions follow a cookie cutter template, real-time solutions are usually more complex and unique.

To recap, batch scoring solutions have the following advantages over real-time solutions:

- They are cheaper to run.
- They are less complex.
- They are easy to replicate as they follow a boilerplate.

Now that you have a handle on what batch inferencing solutions are and why you should use them, it's time to look at real-time solutions. Real-time solutions aren't as prevalent as batch ones, but they do exclusively support plenty of use cases. They're also powerful, require thought, and are fun to create.

# Architecting real-time scoring solutions

**Real-time inferencing** refers to scoring new data points as they arrive instead of on a time-based schedule. New data flows in, new predictions come out. While not as common as batch inferencing, real-time inferencing is used by companies in a number of scenarios such as credit card fraud detection, anomaly detection on the factory floor, and recommending products when you're online shopping.

In this section, you will learn how to architect a complete, end-to-end real-time scoring solution using Azure AutoML-trained models. You will also learn why, and in what situations, you should prioritize real-time scoring over batch scoring solutions.

# Understanding the four-step real-time scoring process

Real-time scoring solutions follow a slightly different process than batch scoring solutions. There are only four steps. Like batch solutions, the process begins by training an ML model and registering it as you did in previous chapters. You can use any type of ML model, including regression, classification, and forecasting, all of which follow the same pattern. The four steps are as follows:

1. **Train a model**. When training a model for deployment in real time, pay extra attention to what data will be available to your model at the time of scoring. It's easy to mistakenly include data that, realistically, won't always be available to a real-time solution.

2. **Register your model**. You can register with either the AMLS GUI or with Python code running on a Jupyter notebook in a compute instance.

3. **Score data in real time**. This step is where you run your real-time inferencing code. In Azure, we use AKS to create a real-time scoring endpoint. You will learn how to create and use AKS and real-time scoring endpoints in *Chapter 11, Implementing a Real-Time Scoring Solution*.

4. **Deliver results**. Delivering results in real time is quite different from delivering results in batches, and is problem dependent. Usually, the results will be displayed on some user-facing app. In other cases, your results will be funneled to a database that triggers an alert if a condition is met. Think about how you may receive a text message if an algorithm detects fraudulent credit card usage on your account.

*Figure 8.2* shows the whole end-to-end process. While you will implement a real-time inference solution for your AutoML-trained models, you can use this same process to deploy any ML model in real time. The key to ensuring the success of your solution lies in aligning your real-time solution with the needs of your business:

Figure 8.2 – Real-time scoring process

Now that you know the process, it's time to dive deeper into each of the steps. First, you need to review the unique considerations of training a model for real-time deployment.

# Training a model for real-time deployment

When you train a model for deployment in real time using AutoML or a custom ML model, the single most important consideration is the availability of your data. Batch scoring solutions do not run that often; data builds up, and you pass it in all at once. With a real-time solution, data is constantly being generated and constantly being scored. Thus, you need to ask yourself if your solution will always have timely access to data.

A great example of this is real-time scoring for fast-food product demand on a minute-by-minute basis. One of the greatest predictors of demand is how many cars are currently lined up in the drive-thru line. If you have reliable video technology that can record the cars, count them, and deliver them to your real-time scoring endpoint on a minute-by-minute basis, by all means, you should use that data. If, however, the video feed takes 3-5 minutes to deliver that piece of data, you shouldn't use it for minute-by-minute scoring.

Therefore, at the onset of every project, you should spend a lot of time figuring out what data will be available to you and when. This is another type of data availability problem. If your data will be available to match the cadence at which it will be scored, use it. If not, discard it. Furthermore, if data is only sometimes available due to reliability issues, such as a weather API that often returns null values, discard it.

You should now have a firm understanding of the importance of data availability for real-time scoring. It's time to think about how you should score data and deliver results.

# Delivering results in real time

Creating a real-time solution with AMLS means creating an AKS-hosted real-time scoring endpoint. You will learn more on this topic in *Chapter 11, Implementing a Real-Time Scoring Solution*. A **scoring endpoint** is a web service into which you pass data to generate predictions. Once created, you can place these endpoints anywhere, in any piece of code.

Most often, the results of a real-time scoring solution are going to be embedded within an app. You should always consider three things when thinking about delivery:

- Is a human or an automated system receiving your predictions?
- How will a human receive your results?
- What will an automated system do with your predictions?

In the case where a human being receives your predictions, you need to determine how they expect to receive them. Usually, it is through some sort of application that they can access on their PC or mobile device. Predictions in a restaurant are likely to be displayed on an in-store app facing the workers. Predictions on a factory floor are likely to be sent to mobile devices.

In the case where your predictions are being sent to an automated system, you need to figure out if the system will send an alert to humans based on some events, or if the predictions will merely be used to control some process. If it is the latter, you only need to write code to move predictions to the appropriate database used by that process.

On the other hand, if the automated system needs to alert humans, you need to decide which events humans will be alerted to. Think of credit card fraud detection. You would only want to alert users of a fraudulent transaction; you wouldn't want to inundate them with alerts for every transaction.

With the importance of delivery in mind, you next need to develop a strong grasp of when to use real-time scoring solutions over their batch equivalents.

# Knowing when to use real-time scoring

Batch inferencing is the default type of scoring that data scientists use. This is because it's cheap, reliable, and easy to replicate. However, many situations mandate real-time inferencing. The key question to ask yourself is, "*Once the data becomes available, how much time do I have to give the business a prediction?*" This is really the only consideration. From the moment new data is available and ready to be scored, if users expect to have results in a period of time that cannot be achieved with batch scoring, you must use real-time scoring.

Consider the case where users send data to a web-based application and a prediction is returned on the screen. In this scenario, if you use batch processing, the prediction may take between 5 and 15 minutes to show up on the screen. This is because the compute cluster needs time to spin up, the environment takes a little bit of time to create, and your code requires time to run.

If you use real-time scoring, however, only your code needs to run, vastly reducing the total runtime. If your user expects near-instantaneous results, you need to build a real-time solution. If they are willing to wait, then you should build a cheaper batch solution instead.

> **Important tip**
> When choosing a CPU for a real-time solution, always go with the cheapest available that will score your data in a timely manner. While more powerful CPUs may save you time, they will also cost hundreds of extra dollars per month, every month your solution is in existence.

Other common scenarios that demand a real-time solution include **transactional fraud detection**, **anomaly detection** in a factory setting, and **recommendation engines**. This is because these situations require instant predictions as soon as the data becomes available. Once again, this is the key consideration. However, there are similar situations where batch processing would be more appropriate.

Consider the case of anomaly detection. If you have numerous machines running on a factory floor and need to know when one breaks so you can *immediately* replace it with a backup machine, that situation requires a real-time solution; the key word is *immediately*. The faster you replace the machine with a backup, the better your factory performs, the more money you save.

On the other hand, imagine that those machines also show signs of wear and tear and, a few days in advance, you can schedule an engineer to come and perform maintenance to keep them up and running. In this case, you would still use an anomaly detection ML solution to detect when a machine needs maintenance, but you should score the data in batches. This is because there is no pressing need to immediately fix the machine. Thus, you should score the data once a day, at the end of the day, and order an engineer as needed.

The more experience you gain in creating real-time scoring solutions, the more you will be able to tell when it is a requirement. Always ask yourself, *"How long can my customers wait for a prediction once my data becomes available?"* If they can wait, build a batch solution. If they cannot, build a real-time solution.

There are also some other considerations to take into account when deciding which type of solution to use.

## Choosing real-time over batch solutions

To recap, batch solutions should always be prioritized over real-time solutions if there is no pressing need to score data as soon it arrives. This is because real-time scoring solutions are inherently more expensive than batch scoring solutions, as your compute clusters never spin down. On the other hand, if there is a pressing need to score data as soon as it becomes available, you need to use a real-time solution to avoid the lag inherent with batch processes.

Complexity is also an issue. Batch scoring solutions always follow the same template: collect data, score data, send the results to some file or database. This is not the case with real-time solutions; they need to be thoughtfully integrated into an application. compares real-time and batch scoring solutions:

|  | Advantages | Disadvantages | When to use |
|---|---|---|---|
| Batch scoring | Cheap<br><br>Easy to replicate<br><br>Simple | Slow | When end users can wait for predictions with new data |
| Real-time scoring | Fast | Costly<br><br>Complex<br><br>Unique | When end users require predictions immediately |

Figure 8.3 – Comparing batch and real-time scoring

Being able to understand the differences between batch and real-time scoring solutions is one thing; being able to use that knowledge is another. In the next section, you will put your knowledge to the test.

# Determining batch versus real-time scoring scenarios

When confronted with real business use cases, it is often difficult to distinguish how you should deploy your ML model. Many data scientists make the mistake of implementing a batch solution when a real-time solution is required, while others implement real-time solutions even when a cheaper batch solution would be sufficient.

In the following sections, you will look at different problem scenarios and solutions. Read each of the six scenarios and determine whether you should implement a real-time or batch inferencing solution. First, you will look at every scenario. Then, you will read each answer along with an explanation.

## Scenarios for real-time or batch scoring

In this section, you are presented with six scenarios. Read each carefully and decide whether a batch or real-time scoring solution is most appropriate.

## Scenario 1 – Demand forecasting

A fast-food company is trying to determine how many bags of frozen French fries it needs to have on hand on any given day. The predictions generated by your ML regression algorithm will be used to determine how many bags of fries are delivered to each location. Once a week, fleets of trucks will deliver the French fries from centrally located warehouses to every store. Should your scoring solution be real-time or batch? If the solution is batch, how often should you score new data?

## Scenario 2 – Web-based supply chain optimization application

A chemical company is trying to optimize its supply chain and has operators located onsite at each of their warehouses. Once a day, they input data into a web-based application that will be used to determine delivery routes for the next day.

The predictions generated by your ML regression algorithm will predict total profitability for each of the possible routes and generate the best route. Operators are expected to manually enter data into the application once a day. Should this solution be batch or real-time? If the solution is real time, what benefits would it bring?

## Scenario 3 – Fraud detection

A credit card company is implementing a fraud detection algorithm. Recently, customers have been reporting many suspicious transactions and are leaving as a result. As soon as fraudulent activity is detected, the company would like to block the transaction and notify customers that their transaction was blocked.

The predictions generated by your ML classification algorithm will block any suspicious transactions and an application will send a text message to the customer's mobile phone. Should this solution be batch or real-time? If batch, how often should you score new data?

## Scenario 4 – Predictive maintenance

An automotive company is having difficulty with its machines breaking down. Every time a machine breaks down, it costs the company tens of thousands of dollars as the entire assembly line shuts down waiting for the machine to be fixed. About once a month, engineers perform maintenance on the machines, but there are only enough engineers to repair 20% of the machines.

Your ML classification algorithm will tell these engineers which machines to repair and order the repairs by priority. Should this solution be batch or real-time? If batch, how often should you score new data?

## Scenario 5 – Web-based product cost planning

An aerospace company is trying to predict the profitability of a new line of aircraft, and would like to predict the cost of raw materials and labor based on specifications. Pricing managers will enter relevant data manually into a web-based application and would like to see the projected price immediately from your ML regression algorithm. There is no set time that they are expected to do this, and they may run the application many times in a single session.

Should you design this solution to be batch or real-time? If batch, how often should you score new data?

## Scenario 6 – Recommendation engine

A retail store is building a website. As customers browse and add new items to their shopping cart, the store would like to recommend other items for those customers to purchase. Your ML regression algorithm will assign scores to items on the fly based on what customers browse, and the highest-scoring items will be automatically displayed to them. Should this solution be designed as a real-time or batch solution? If batch, how often should you score new data?

Think deeply about each scenario and then proceed to the next section.

# Answers for the type of solution appropriate for each scenario

In this section, you will review answers for each of the six scenarios. Read each explanation and then review the original scenario for clarity.

## Scenario 1 – Batch inferencing solution

Scenario 1 features a typical case for ML. The fast-food company wishes to forecast demand for French fries on a weekly basis. Data is collected from all of the stores and should be scored using a batch inferencing process once a week. Once the predictions are generated, French fries can be loaded onto trucks and delivered to all of their locations.

This is a *batch solution* because the data only needs to be scored once a week, and there's no pressing need to generate predictions as soon as new data becomes available.

## Scenario 2 – Batch inferencing solution

Scenario 2 could use either a real-time or batch inferencing solution. When operators manually pass data into the web-based application, it's simply a matter of how long they are willing to wait for results. Since this is a once-a-day operation and the results will not be used until the next day, it's best to trade time for money and go with a *batch inferencing process*. However, if you built a *real-time solution* in this scenario, there is a benefit. Operators would be able to see results right away instead of having to wait 10 to 15 minutes.

## Scenario 3 – Real-time inferencing solution

Scenario 3 is a classic real-time inferencing use case. Fraudulent transactions must be detected immediately, that is, as soon as data on the transaction becomes available. This speed enables both the transaction to be blocked and the customer to receive a notification as soon as possible.

There's no way that a batch inferencing solution could provide the necessary speed. Furthermore, each data point must be scored individually as it arrives. There's no time to lump data together in batches, or to spin up a compute cluster.

## Scenario 4 – Batch inferencing solution

Scenario 4 is tricky. Predictive maintenance can sometimes require real-time inferencing, particularly in cases where an anomalous detection indicates imminent failure and there are emergency staff on standby ready to fix the problem.

In this case, however, engineers are only available to service machines once a month. As a result, there is no pressing need for immediate results. A *once-a-month batch processing solution* is most appropriate for this scenario.

## Scenario 5 – Real-time inferencing solution

Scenario 5 is similar to `Scenario 2` with three major exceptions:

- The pricing managers do not run the scoring solution on a set schedule.
- The pricing managers may run the solution many times in a single setting.
- The pricing managers expect immediate results.

Immediate results should indicate to you a *real-time scoring solution*. If you designed this solution with a batch process, every single time the pricing managers ran their numbers, they would experience a long wait. One way you could alter the application to be more batch friendly is if it allowed the pricing managers to enter data for all of their scenarios at once, instead of one at a time.

## Scenario 6 – Real-time inferencing solution

Scenario 6 is another classic real-time inferencing scenario. Recommendation engines need to be extremely fast and change based on what users click, view, and add to their cart. They also need to change based on what customers purchase. Each time the screen changes, new data must be scored so that the appropriate items can be advertised to the user. Performance is also extremely important, as the algorithm must keep up with user actions. Every recommendation engine powered by ML should only be used in *real time*.

How did you do on the six scenarios? Were you able to achieve 100% accuracy? In either case, have a look at *Figure 8.4* to see how common scenarios map to real-time or batch scoring solutions:

| Scenario | Type of solution |
| --- | --- |
| Fraud detection | Real-time |
| Predictive maintenance | Dependent on when machines are serviced |
| Once a day, week, or month scoring | Batch |
| Recommendation engines | Real-time |
| Forecasting for the long term | Batch |
| Forecasting minute by minute | Real-time |
| Web-based applications | Dependent on user expectations |

Figure 8.4 – How common scenarios map to real-time or batch

If you were able to accurately decide which type of scoring solution fits each scenario on your first try, you have passed with flying colors. You now have a deep understanding of which situations warrant a real-time inferencing solution and which situations warrant a batch inferencing solution. If you made a mistake on one or more of the scenarios, reread all of them until you intuitively understand the differences.

Remember the most important factor in deciding which type of solution to use is how fast you need the prediction relative to when the data becomes available. If the end user can wait, use batch. If the application demands an immediate response, use real-time. Understanding the difference will not only make you a great data scientist, but it will also save you and your organization time, money, and work.

# Summary

You now have a firm understanding of batch and real-time inferencing, and when to use which type of scoring solution. This is important, as even seasoned data scientists occasionally make mistakes when designing end-to-end ML solutions.

Furthermore, most ML courses focus on training models instead of deploying them, but to be an effective data scientist, you must be proficient at both. In the upcoming chapters, you will learn how to code each of these inferencing methods in AMLS.

In *Chapter 9, Implementing a Batch Scoring Solution*, you will learn step by step how to use the ML models you've already built in batch scoring scenarios. You will create ML pipelines in AMLS and learn how to schedule them to run on a timer. This will allow you to easily productionalize your ML models and become a valuable asset to your company or organization.

# 9
# Implementing a Batch Scoring Solution

You have trained regression, classification, and forecasting models with AutoML in Azure, and now it's time you learn how to put them in production and use them. **Machine learning (ML)** models, after all, are ultimately used to make predictions on new data, either in real time or in batches. In order to score new data points in batches in Azure, you must first create an ML pipeline.

An ML pipeline lets you run repeatable Python code in the **Azure Machine Learning services (AMLS)** that you can run on a schedule. While you can run any Python code using an ML pipeline, here you will learn how to build pipelines for scoring new data.

You will begin this chapter by writing a simple ML pipeline to score data using the multiclass classification model you trained on the Iris dataset in *Chapter 5, Building an AutoML Classification Solution*. Using the same data, you will then learn how to score new data points in parallel, enabling you to quickly score models with millions to billions of data points simultaneously.

Once you have written these two pipelines, you will learn how to create an ML pipeline for retraining an AutoML model. Finally, you will learn how to retrigger ML pipelines both manually through the GUI and programmatically through the **Azure ML SDK**.

By the end of this chapter, you will be able to not only train AutoML models but also use them to score new data in a reproducible, automatable fashion. Furthermore, the code and techniques you learn here apply to all ML models, not just those that are AutoML-generated. Coding batch scoring solutions is a key skill for any ML engineer, and by working through the exercises in this chapter, you will be well on your way to mastering that skill.

In this chapter, we will cover the following topics:

- Creating an ML pipeline
- Creating a parallel scoring pipeline
- Creating an AutoML training pipeline
- Triggering and scheduling your ML pipelines

# Technical requirements

This chapter will feature a lot of coding using Jupyter notebooks within AMLS. Thus, you will need a working internet connection, an **AMLS workspace**, and a **compute instance**. ML pipelines also require a **compute cluster**. You will also need to have trained and registered the Iris multiclass classification model in *Chapter 5, Building an AutoML Classification Solution*.

The following are the prerequisites for the chapter:

- Access to the internet.
- A web browser, preferably Google Chrome or Microsoft Edge Chromium.
- A Microsoft Azure account.
- Have created an AMLS workspace.
- Have created the `compute-cluster` compute cluster in *Chapter 2, Getting Started with Azure Machine Learning Service*.
- Understand how to navigate to the Jupyter environment from an Azure compute instance as demonstrated in *Chapter 4, Building an AutoML Regression Solution*.
- Have trained and registered the `Iris-Multi-Classification-AutoML` ML model in *Chapter 5, Building an AutoML Classification Solution*.

The code for this chapter is available here: `https://github.com/PacktPublishing/Automated-Machine-Learning-with-Microsoft-Azure/tree/master/Chapter09`.

# Creating an ML pipeline

ML pipelines are Azure's solution for batch scoring ML models. You can use ML pipelines to score any model you train, including your own custom models as well as AutoML-generated models. They can only be created via code using the Azure ML Python SDK. In this section, you will code a simple pipeline to score diabetes data using the `Diabetes-AllData-Regression-AutoML` model you built in *Chapter 4, Building an AutoML Regression Solution.*

As in other chapters, you will begin by opening your compute instance and navigating to your Jupyter notebook environment. You will then create and name a new notebook. Once your notebook is created, you will build, configure, and run an ML pipeline step by step. After confirming your pipeline has run successfully, you will then publish your ML pipeline to a pipeline endpoint. **Pipeline endpoints** are simply URLs, web addresses that call ML pipeline runs.

The following steps deviate greatly from previous chapters. You will have to load in many more libraries and also write a custom Python file for scoring new data. You will also learn how to create **environments**, that is, artifacts that specify which Python packages, package versions, and software settings you are using.

In addition to creating an environment, you will need to containerize it. Finally, you will need to configure and run your ML pipeline, completing the process by publishing your pipeline to an endpoint. The entire process is shown in *Figure 9.1*:

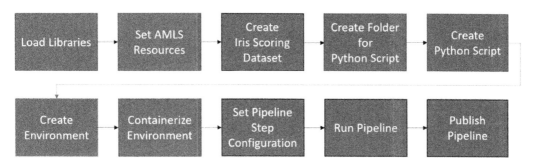

Figure 9.1 – Steps involved in creating your ML scoring pipeline

The `ML-Scoring-Pipeline.ipynb` file in the GitHub repository contains the code for all the steps.

# Coding the first three steps of your ML scoring pipeline

First, load in your libraries, set up your AMLS resources, and create a dataset to score with the following steps:

1.  Open **Azure Machine Learning studio** (**AML studio**) by navigating to `https://ml.azure.com/`.

2.  Click **Compute** and start up a compute instance. Any compute instance will work, as they all link to the same Jupyter notebook environment.

3.  Create a new Jupyter notebook and name it `machine-learning-pipeline`. If you need a refresher on how to do this, please review *Chapter 4, Building an AutoML Regression Solution*.

4.  Open your newly created notebook and begin by importing all of the standard Azure libraries you will need using the following code:

    ```
    from azureml.core import Workspace, Dataset, Datastore
    from azureml.core import Experiment, Environment, Model
    from azureml.core.compute import ComputeTarget
    ```

    *Chapter 4, Building an AutoML Regression Solution*, explains `Workspace`, `Dataset`, `Datastore`, `Experiment`, and `ComputeTarget`. `Environment` lets you create an object that contains information on which Python packages your ML pipeline will need to install to run successfully. `Model` lets you retrieve your previously trained ML models.

5.  Continuing on, import all of the Azure ML pipeline libraries with the following code:

    ```
    from azureml.core.runconfig import RunConfiguration,
    CondaDependencies, DEFAULT_CPU_IMAGE
    from azureml.pipeline.steps import PythonScriptStep
    from azureml.pipeline.core import Pipeline,
    PublishedPipeline
    from azureml.pipeline.core import StepSequence
    from azureml.widgets import RunDetails
    ```

RunConfiguration stores information that your ML pipeline will need to run, including the environment and base image. CondaDependencies lets you add Python packages to your environment. Default_CPU_Image is needed to specify which base image you will use in your run configuration. PythonScriptStep is a type of **ML pipeline step** for running non-specialized Python code.

There are additional specialized ML pipeline steps used for tasks such as training AutoML models that fall outside the scope of this chapter.

Pipeline is the core package to build ML pipelines. PublishedPipeline lets you publish ML pipelines to endpoints. StepSequence lets you set the order of your ML pipeline steps and RunDetails simply shows you the output of your ML pipeline as it runs.

> **Important note**
>
> If you are having trouble loading any Azure libraries, update the Azure ML SDK by running the Update AzureML SDK.ipynb notebook found here: https://github.com/PacktPublishing/Automated-Machine-Learning-with-Microsoft-Azure/blob/master/Update-AzureML-SDK.ipynb.

6.  Import pandas, numpy, and os. os will let you create and manipulate files and folders from your Jupyter notebook. random will let you generate random numbers, which is useful for simulating new Iris data:

```
import pandas as pd
import numpy as np
import os
import random as r
```

7.  Connect your Jupyter notebook to your AMLS workspace:

```
ws = Workspace.from_config()
```

If you are prompted to log in, follow the instructions.

8.  Set your compute cluster to the one you created in *Chapter 2, Getting Started with Azure Machine Learning Service*:

```
compute_name = 'compute-cluster'
compute_target = ComputeTarget(ws, compute_name)
```

9. Set your datastore:

```
datastore = Datastore.get_default(ws)
```

10. Next, you will create simulated Iris data to score. Begin by creating four variables that contain a list of numbers based on the minimum and maximum values of the original Iris dataset with the following code. These variables contain all the possible values contained within the Iris dataset:

```
sepal_length_range = np.arange(4.3, 7.9, 0.1)
sepal_width_range = np.arange(2, 4.4, 0.1)
petal_length_range = np.arange(1, 6.9, 0.1)
petal_width_range = np.arange(0.1, 2.5, 0.1)
```

11. Continuing with the creation of simulated Iris data, create an empty `pandas` DataFrame called IrisDF, with the appropriate column names. Also, create an empty list called `IrisList`:

```
columns =\ ['sepal_length','sepal_width','petal_
length','petal_width']
IrisDF = pd.DataFrame(columns=columns)
IrisList = []
```

12. Continuing with the creation of simulated Iris data, use the `choice` function from the `random` package within a `for` loop to create 100 new data points, rounding each value to `1` decimal place.

Combine each set of four data points with the column names in a Python dictionary within the `for` loop and append that dictionary to `IrisList` row by row:

```
for i in range(0,100):
    values = \
[round(r.choice(sepal_length_range),1),round(r.
choice(sepal_width_range),1),round(r.choice(petal_length_
range),1),round(r.choice(petal_width_range),1)]
    iris_dictionary = pd.DataFrame(dict(zip(columns,
values)),index=[0])
    IrisList.append(iris_dictionary)
```

This code will leave you with a list of randomly generated values from the original Iris dataset that can be turned into a `pandas` DataFrame.

13. Completing the creation of simulated Iris data, append `IrisList` to `IrisDF`:

```
IrisDF = IrisDF.append(IrisList,True)
```

14. Register your simulated Iris data with the following code:

```
Dataset.Tabular.register_pandas_dataframe(IrisDF,
datastore, 'Iris_Scoring')
```

This will save it to your datastore and create an Azure dataset named `Iris Scoring`.

# Creating a Python script to score data in your ML pipeline

In this section, you will create a folder and write a Python script that your ML pipeline will execute to score data using the following steps:

1. Make a folder to hold your scoring script using `os`:

   ```
   os.makedirs('Scoring_Scripts', exist_ok=True)
   ```

   For every ML pipeline step you make, you have to have an accompanying Python script.

2. Write a Python script to score new data. This script is long and has to be one block of code. Begin by writing out a new Python script file called `Iris_Scoring.py` using the `%%writefile` magic command. **Magic commands** are enhancements on top of normal Python that let you do common, useful tasks such as writing files.

   Everything you type in this cell will be written out as a single Python script. Begin by loading in your Azure libraries:

   ```
   %%writefile Scoring_Scripts/Iris_Scoring.py
   from azureml.core import Run, Workspace
   from azureml.core import Dataset, Datastore, Model
   ```

   You should recognize all of these packages with one exception. `Run` lets your program access the AMLS workspace you used to create the ML pipeline while running remotely on a compute cluster.

3. Continuing in the same cell as part of Iris_Scoring.py, import the other Python packages:

```
import joblib
import numpy as np
import pandas as pd
import os
```

The only new package here is joblib, which will let you load saved ML models.

4. Continuing in the same cell as part of Iris_Scoring.py, set a variable called run using the Run function. You can use this variable to set your AMLS workspace:

```
run = Run.get_context()
```

5. Continuing in the same cell as part of Iris_Scoring.py, we are going to create a function called main. This function will run the main part of your scoring code.

First, connect to your AMLS workspace using the run variable you created. Next, set your datastore to the default option and your dataset to Iris Scoring. Convert the Iris Scoring dataset into a pandas DataFrame called scoringDF:

```
def main():
    ws = run.experiment.workspace
    datastore = Datastore.get_default(ws)
    dataset = Dataset.get_by_name(ws,'Iris Scoring')
    scoringDF = dataset.to_pandas_dataframe()
```

6. Continuing in the same cell as part of Iris_Scoring.py, load your Iris-Multi-Classification-AutoML model with the Azure Model and joblib packages:

```
    model_path = Model.get_model_path('Iris-Multi-
Classification-AutoML')
    model = joblib.load(model_path)
```

7. Continuing in the same cell as part of `Iris_Scoring.py`, use your model to make predictions on `scoringDF`, save those predictions to a `pandas Series`, and add the predictions back to your `scoringDF` DataFrame in a new column called `Prediction`:

```
predictions = model.predict(scoringDF)
predSeries = pd.Series(predictions)
scoringDF['Prediction'] = predSeries
```

When you add the new column, the predictions will be in the correct order and match the corresponding row.

8. Continuing in the same cell as part of `Iris_Scoring.py`, make a folder called `Output_Folder` using `os`:

```
output_datastore_path = 'Output_Folder'
os.makedirs(output_datastore_path, exist_ok=True)
```

This will create a folder on your compute cluster to store your predictions temporarily so you can transfer them to your datastore.

9. Continuing in the same cell as part of `Iris_Scoring.py`, specify a file called `Iris_Predictions.csv`. Then, use `os` to specify a path on the compute cluster where you will write that file out. Finally, use `to_csv` to write out `scoringDF` to your compute cluster:

```
FileName = "Iris_Predictions.csv"
OutputPath = os.path.join(output_datastore_path,
FileName)
scoringDF.to_csv(OutputPath, index = False, sep=',')
```

This piece of code will write your output to your compute cluster. This is necessary to move it into your datastore.

10. Continuing in the same cell as part of `Iris_Scoring.py`, upload `Iris_Predictions.csv` to your datastore. This code will write it to a folder called `Output_Folder`, matching the directory structure on your compute cluster.

```
datastore.upload_files(files=[OutputPath], target_
path=output_datastore_path, overwrite=True)
```

11. Completing `Iris_Scoring.py`, use `os` to remove the file and folder from your compute cluster. Finish the cell with boilerplate code that will automatically run your `main` function when the Python script is called within the ML pipeline:

```
        os.remove(OutputPath)
        os.rmdir(output_datastore_path)
if __name__ == '__main__':
    main()
```

This completes your Python script. Write the next piece of code in a new cell.

## Creating and containerizing an environment

The difficult part is over and the rest is pure boilerplate, beginning with creating an environment. **Environments** are collections of Python packages that are required to run your code:

1. In a new cell, create an environment. Also, set a variable using `CondaDependencies`:

```
Env = Environment(name='AutoML Environment')
conda_dep = CondaDependencies()
```

All the packages and versions of packages that are required to run your Python script will be added to the `conda_dep` variable in the next step.

2. Attach Python packages to your `conda_dep` variable, beginning with the packages found in the `conda` package manager:

```
conda_dep.add_conda_package("numpy==1.18.5")
conda_dep.add_conda_package("joblib==0.14.1")
conda_dep.add_conda_package("pandas==0.25.3")
conda_dep.add_conda_package("packaging==20.7")
conda_dep.add_conda_package("xgboost==0.90")
```

There are two package managers, `conda` and `pip`. `conda` automatically resolves dependencies for you. So, if a package requires another package, you don't have to worry about it. `pip` requires you to resolve those dependencies yourself. As a result, if a package is available in both `conda` and `pip`, always install it via `conda`.

When installing packages, always specify the version. You can discover which version you are using by running the `!pip freeze` command in an empty cell. In addition to `numpy`, `joblib`, and `pandas`, AutoML-generated models also require `packaging` and `xgboost` to run.

3.  Attach Python packages to your `conda_dep` variable that are not available in `conda` using `pip` instead:

```
conda_dep.add_pip_package("azureml-defaults==1.19.0")
conda_dep.add_pip_package("azureml-automl-core==1.19.0")
conda_dep.add_pip_package("azureml-automl-runtime==1.19.0")
```

There are three packages; `azureml-defaults` enables you to use standard Azure ML SDK functions, while `azureml-automl-core` and `azureml-automl-runtime` are required to score any AutoML-generated models.

4.  Add the `conda_dep` variable to your environment and register the environment to your AMLS workspace by using the following code:

```
Env.python.conda_dependencies=conda_dep
RegisteredEnvironment = Env.register(workspace=ws)
```

Now that your environment is registered, you can call it anywhere in AMLS.

5.  Create a `RunConfiguration` object for containerizing your environment. Set your environment, enable Docker, and use `DEFAULT_CPU_IMAGE` as your base image:

```
run_config = RunConfiguration()
run_config.environment = Env
run_config.environment.docker.enabled = True
run_config.environment.docker.base_image =\
 DEFAULT_CPU_IMAGE
```

This will create a **Docker container**, a portable package of code that can be run anywhere as it contains all your code's scripts and dependencies. Your environment can now be utilized by your ML pipeline, which you will configure in the last series of steps.

# Configuring and running your ML scoring pipeline

With your environment built and containerized, your Python script written, and all your AMLS resources set, you're ready to configure and run your ML pipeline by following these steps:

1.  Configure your ML pipeline step with the following code. You need to give your step a name, `iris-scoring-step`, and specify your Python script name, Python script folder location, compute target, and run configuration. Always set `allow_reuse` to False:

    ```
    scoring_step = PythonScriptStep(name='iris-scoring-step',
    script_name='Iris_Scoring.py',
    source_directory='Scoring_Scripts',
    arguments=[],
    inputs=[],
    compute_target=compute_target,
    runconfig=run_config,
    allow_reuse=False)
    ```

    Setting `allow_reuse` to `True` is for debugging multi-step pipelines where you want to skip rerunning a successfully completed step.

2.  Set your **step sequence** and **pipeline object**:

    ```
    step_sequence = StepSequence(steps=[scoring_step])
    pipeline = Pipeline(workspace=ws, steps=step_sequence)
    ```

    The step sequence is the order in which your ML pipeline steps will run.

3.  Give your pipeline experiment run a name, `Iris-Scoring-Pipeline-Run`, and submit it with the following code:

    ```
    pipeline_experiment = Experiment(ws, 'Iris-Scoring-
    Pipeline-Run')
    pipeline_run = pipeline_experiment.submit(pipeline, show_
    output=True)
    ```

    Finally, this is what kicks your pipeline off!

4.  Use `RunDetails` to watch your pipeline get built and execute in real time:

    ```
    RunDetails(pipeline_run).show()
    pipeline_run.wait_for_completion(show_output=True)
    ```

As it runs, you will see a lot of logs. If your pipeline runs successfully, it will complete with the words **Finished**. You should see a graphic identical to the one in *Figure 9.2*:

iris-scoring-step - Finished

Figure 9.2 – Successful pipeline run graphic

5.  Publish your pipeline to an endpoint with the following code, specifying a name, description, and version number:

```
published_pipeline = pipeline_run.publish_pipeline(
    name='Iris-Scoring-Pipeline',\
    description='Pipeline that Scores Iris Data',
version= '1.0')
published_pipeline
```

All published pipelines require version numbers set by the creator. Running this code will give you a published pipeline ID as well as a link to the endpoint, as seen in *Figure 9.3*:

Figure 9.3 – Successfully published pipeline

Now that you have executed and published your scoring pipeline, you can examine and download your scoring file. It was saved to a folder called Output_Folder in a file called Iris_Predictions.csv. Access the file directly by navigating to your storage account. You can do this either from the Azure portal (https://portal.azure.com) or via **AML studio**.

# Accessing your scored predictions via AML studio

To access Iris_Predictions.csv and download it to your desktop, you first have to locate your storage account. You can find your storage account through AML studio.

The following steps will have you locate your datastore through the AML studio, access your storage account, navigate to the correct file, and download it to your local machine. This way, you can use the AI-generated predictions for any purpose you wish:

1.  Navigate to AML studio at `https://ml.azure.com`.

2.  Click **Datastores** on the left-hand panel.

3.  Click the blue link to **workspaceblobstore** (default) in the center of the page.

4.  Click the blue link to your storage account under **Account name**. Each person will have a unique storage account name, prefixed with `automlexamplew` followed by a string of numbers. This will take you to your storage account resource in Azure.

5.  Once in your storage account, click the blue link to **Containers** in the center-left of your screen. Clicking anywhere in the box will work.

6.  You will now see a list of folders. Click the folder that begins with `azureml-blobstore-` followed by a unique identifier ID.

7.  Click **Output_Folder**. You should also see folders named `azureml`, `managed-dataset`, and `UI`. These folders hold logs for your experiments, among other objects. *Figure 9.4* shows the folder structure you need to follow to reach your file:

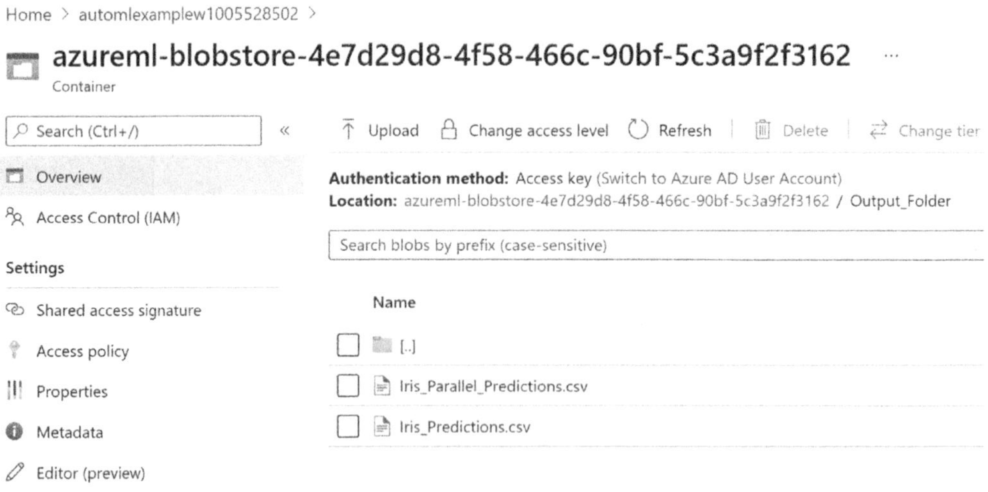

Figure 9.4 – Path to your output files

8.  Click **Iris_Predictions.csv**.

9.  Click the **Download** button near the top of your screen to download `Iris_ Predictions.csv` to your local machine. It is a comma-separated file with headers.

10. Open up your file with Microsoft Excel or similar software to look at your data.

That was a lot of work, but now you have a working pipeline endpoint that can score new data points in batch. This is a huge accomplishment, as many organizations have trouble setting up such workflows. You can also easily reuse this code in multiple projects, as the vast majority is boilerplate. While you have to alter the Python script and add packages as appropriate, this template can also be used to score both AutoML and custom ML models.

Next, you will learn how to score 10,000,000 data points in no time at all using a parallel scoring pipeline.

# Creating a parallel scoring pipeline

Standard ML pipelines work just fine for the majority of ML use cases, but when you need to score a large amount of data at once, you need a more powerful solution. That's where `ParallelRunStep` comes in. `ParallelRunStep` is Azure's answer to scoring big data in batch. When you use `ParallelRunStep`, you leverage all of the cores on your compute cluster simultaneously.

Say you have a compute cluster consisting of eight `Standard_DS3_v2` virtual machines. Each `Standard_DS3_v2` node has four cores, so you can perform 32 parallel scoring processes at once. This parallelization essentially lets you score data many times faster than if you used a single machine. Furthermore, it can easily scale vertically (increasing the size of each virtual machine in the cluster) and horizontally (increasing the node count).

This section will allow you to become a *big data* scientist who can score large batches of data. Here, you will again be using simulated Iris data, but instead of 100 rows, you will be scoring 10 million rows at once.

Furthermore, this is an advanced solution that utilizes two pipeline steps, a step that scores data in parallel and a step that transfers data to an output folder. By working through this example, you'll understand how to create advanced multi-step pipeline runs to solve difficult problems.

> **Important note**
>
> Parallel runs score data in batches, dividing your dataset into many small parts. If you have any data preprocessing that relies on calculations made with previous rows, this preprocessing should be done in a separate `PythonScriptStep` before being passed on to `ParallelRunStep`.

Much of this code is similar to the *Creating an ML pipeline* section. However, there are two pipeline steps to create instead of one. Furthermore, you will be introduced to new concepts such as **pipeline data** and using the `input` and `output` pipeline configuration options. At the end of this section, you will also publish your pipeline to an endpoint. *Figure 9.5* shows the entire process:

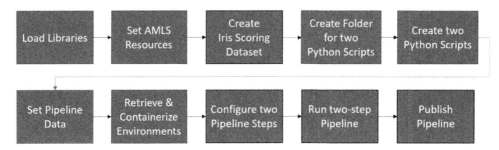

Figure 9.5 – Steps involved in creating a parallel scoring pipeline

If you need a refresher on any of the steps, please refer to the *Creating an ML pipeline* section. You can find the code for all the steps in the `ML-Parallel-Pipeline.ipynb` file in the GitHub repository.

## Coding the first three steps of your ML parallel scoring pipeline

To create your parallel scoring pipeline, begin with the following steps:

1.  Navigate to your Jupyter environment on your compute instance and create a new Jupyter notebook. Name it `ml-parallel-pipeline`.

2.  Open your newly created notebook and import your standard Azure libraries:

```
from azureml.core import Workspace, Dataset, Datastore
from azureml.core import Experiment, Environment, Model
```

3. From `azureml.core.compute`, import `ComputeTargetNext` and import all of the Azure ML pipeline libraries with the following code:

```
from azureml.core.runconfig import RunConfiguration,
CondaDependencies, DEFAULT_CPU_IMAGE
from azureml.pipeline.steps import PythonScriptStep,
ParallelRunStep, ParallelRunConfig
from azureml.pipeline.core import Pipeline,
PublishedPipeline, PipelineData
from azureml.pipeline.core import StepSequence
from azureml.widgets import RunDetails
```

There are three additional packages compared to the previous section. `ParallelRunStep` is an ML pipeline step that lets you run Python code in parallel. `ParallelRunConfig` lets you configure `ParallelRunStep`. `PipelineData` lets you pass intermediate data from one step to another.

> **Important note**
>
> If you are having trouble loading any Azure libraries, update the Azure ML SDK by running the `Update AzureML SDK.ipynb` notebook found here: `https://github.com/PacktPublishing/Automated-Machine-Learning-with-Microsoft-Azure/blob/master/Update-AzureML-SDK.ipynb`.

4. Import pandas, numpy, os, and random:

```
import pandas as pd
import numpy as np
import os
import random as r
```

5. As always, connect your Jupyter notebook to your AMLS workspace:

```
ws = Workspace.from_config()
```

If you are prompted to log in, follow the instructions.

6. Set your compute cluster with the following code:

```
compute_name = 'compute-cluster'
compute_target = ComputeTarget(ws, compute_name)
```

7. Set your datastore:

```
datastore = Datastore.get_default(ws)
```

8. Use the following code to create simulated Iris data:

```
sepal_length_range = np.arange(4.3, 7.9, 0.1)
sepal_width_range = np.arange(2, 4.4, 0.1)
petal_length_range = np.arange(1, 6.9, 0.1)
petal_width_range = np.arange(0.1, 2.5, 0.1)
```

9. Continuing with the creation of simulated Iris data, create an empty `pandas` DataFrame and list:

```
columns =\
['sepal_length','sepal_width','petal_length','petal_
width']
IrisDF = pd.DataFrame(columns=columns)
IrisList = []
```

10. Continuing with the creation of simulated Iris data, use the `choice` function from the `random` package within a `for` loop to create 10,000,000 new data points, rounding each value to `1` decimal place:

```
for i in range(0,10000000):
    values =\
[round(r.choice(sepal_length_range),1),round(r.
choice(sepal_width_range),1),\
round(r.choice(petal_length_range),1),round(r.
choice(petal_width_range),1)]
    iris_dictionary = pd.DataFrame(dict(zip(columns,
values)),index=[0])
    IrisList.append(iris_dictionary)
```

This will take a while, so give it some time to run.

11. Completing the creation of simulated Iris data, append `IrisList` to `IrisDF`:

```
IrisDF = IrisDF.append(IrisList,True)
```

12. Register your simulated Iris data with the following code:

```
Dataset.Tabular.register_pandas_dataframe(IrisDF,
datastore, 'Iris_Scoring')
```

This will save it to your datastore and create an Azure dataset named `Iris Parallel Scoring`. You're now ready to write your Python script.

# Creating Python scripts to score data in your ML parallel pipeline

Next, create a folder and write two Python scripts that your ML pipeline will execute to score data. You will need one step to make predictions and another step to transfer your output to a final destination on your datastore:

1.  Make a folder to hold your scoring script using `os`:

    ```
    os.makedirs('Scoring_Scripts', exist_ok=True)
    ```

    This folder should already exist from the previous section, but this code will not error out since `exist_ok` is set to `True`. This folder will hold both the scripts you will write for your parallel pipeline run.

2.  Write a Python script to score new data in parallel:

    ```
    %%writefile Scoring_Scripts/Iris_Scoring.py
    from azureml.core import Run, Workspace
    from azureml.core import Dataset, Datastore, Model
    ```

    This script is significantly different from the previous script, but also has to be in one cell. Begin by writing a new Python script file called `Iris_Parallel_Scoring.py` using the `%%writefile` magic command. Begin by loading in your Azure libraries. You should recognize all of them from the previous section.

3.  Continuing in the same cell as part of `Iris_Parallel_Scoring.py`, import other Python packages, including the new `argparse` package:

    ```
    import os
    import joblib
    import argparse
    import numpy as np
    import pandas as pd
    ```

    This package lets you pass arguments into your script. **Arguments** are flexible pieces of code that you can pass into your pipeline at runtime. For example, you can use arguments to pass in different datastores or datasets.

4. Continuing in the same cell as part of `Iris_Parallel_Scoring.py`, set a variable called `run` using the Run function:

```
run = Run.get_context()
```

5. Continuing in the same cell as part of `Iris_Parallel_Scoring.py`, create a function called `init`. This function will pass in your arguments and load your ML model, setting it to a global variable.

   **Global variables** can be accessed across functions. Set a variable called `parser` to store your arguments and add the `model_name` argument to that variable. `ParallelRunStep` also passes hidden arguments behind the scenes, so you also need to set `unknown_args`. Once that is done, use `joblib` to load your model using the `model_name` argument, as shown in the following code:

```
def init():
    parser = argparse.ArgumentParser()
    parser.add_argument('--model_name',\
    dest="model_name", required=True)
    args, unknown_args = parser.parse_known_args()
    global model
    model_path = Model.get_model_path(args.model_name)
    model = joblib.load(model_path)
```

6. Continuing in the same cell as part of `Iris_Parallel_Scoring.py`, create a function called `main`. This function will score your data and return the result, which will be automatically stored in a file called `parallel_run_step.txt`. `model` with the Azure `Model` and `joblib` packages.

   First, you will use the `predict` function on your `model` variable to make predictions. Notice that the data is automatically passed into this function as a `pandas` DataFrame called `input_data`.

   You then convert these predictions into a series and add it back to `input_data` as a column called `Prediction`. Completing `Iris_Parallel_Scoring.py`, you return the finished `input_data` DataFrame to be automatically written to the text file:

```
def run(input_data):
    predictions = model.predict(input_data)
    predSeries = pd.Series(predictions)
    input_data['Prediction'] = predSeries
```

```
print('Data written to parallel_run_step.txt')
    return input_data
```

7.  Write a Python script to transfer your results to the output location of your choice. `ParallelRunStep` outputs a file called `parallel_run_step.txt`. This will be stored as pipeline data.

Pipeline data is data that is saved in your datastore as an intermediate step to be passed on to another ML pipeline step. Furthermore, `parallel_run_step.txt` has no headers and you need to add them.

Begin by writing out a new Python script file called `Iris_Parallel_Output_Creation.py` using the `%%writefile` magic command. Start by loading in your Azure libraries as usual:

```
%%writefile Scoring_Scripts/Iris_Parallel_Output_
Creation.py
from azureml.core import Run, Workspace
from azureml.core import Dataset, Datastore
```

8.  Continuing in the same cell as part of `Iris_Parallel_Output_Creation.py`, load in all of the standard Python packages you need:

```
import pandas as pd
import numpy as np
import os
import argparse
```

You will once again need `argparse` to pass in arguments, namely the folder that holds `parallel_run_step.txt`.

9.  Continuing in the same cell as part of `Iris_Parallel_Output_Creation.py`, set a variable called `run` using the `Run` function:

```
run = Run.get_context()
```

10.  Continuing in the same cell as part of `Iris_Parallel_Output_Creation.py`, pass in your arguments to access the folder that holds `parallel_run_step.txt`:

```
parser = argparse.ArgumentParser()
parser.add_argument("--input_data_folder",type=str)
args = parser.parse_args()
```

Call the `input_data_folder` argument and pass it in as an argument when you configure this pipeline step.

11. Continuing in the same cell as part of `Iris_Parallel_Output_Creation.py`, write a function called `main`. This function will transfer your predictions from an intermediate pipeline data location to its final destination.

    Begin by using `os` and `input_data_folder` to find the path holding `parallel_run_step.txt`. Then, read it in as a space-delimited text file with no headers in a `pandas` DataFrame called `result` using the following code:

    ```
    def main():
        FileName = "parallel_run_step.txt"
        input_data_path =\
      os.path.join(args.input_data_folder, FileName)
        result =\
      pd.read_csv(input_data_path, delimiter=" ", header=None)
    ```

12. Continuing in the same cell as part of `Iris_Parallel_Output_Creation.py`, as part of your `main` function, add columns to your `result` DataFrame:

    ```
        columns =\
      ['sepal_length','sepal_width','petal_length','petal_
      width', 'Prediction']
        result.columns = columns
    ```

    It's important to remember that `parallel_run_step.txt` never has headers, so you need to enter the columns manually in the correct order as shown in the preceding code.

13. Continuing in the same cell as part of `Iris_Parallel_Output_Creation.py`, as part of your `main` function, connect to your AMLS workspace using the `run` variable and set a variable for your datastore:

    ```
        ws = run.experiment.workspace
        datastore = Datastore.get_default(ws)
    ```

    This is the datastore that will hold your final output file.

14. Continuing in the same cell as part of `Iris_Parallel_Output_Creation.`
    `py`, as part of your `main` function, use `os` to create a folder called `Output_`
    `Folder` on your compute cluster, and write a CSV file called `Iris_Parallel_`
    `Predictions.csv`:

```
output_datastore_path = 'Output_Folder'
os.makedirs(output_datastore_path, exist_ok=True)
FileName = "Iris_Parallel_Predictions.csv"
OutputPath = os.path.join(output_datastore_path,
FileName)
result.to_csv(OutputPath, index = False, sep=',')
```

Even though the original `parallel_run_step.txt` file was space-delimited,
you can set the delimiter on your final output file to whatever you wish.

15. Completing `Iris_Parallel_Output_Creation.py`, upload `Iris_`
    `Parallel_Predictions.csv` to your datastore in a folder called `Output_`
    `Folder`.

    Then, use `os` to remove both `Iris_Parallel_Predictions.csv` and
    `Output_Folder` from your compute cluster. Finally, trigger your `main` function
    as you did in the *Creating an ML pipeline* section:

```
datastore.upload_files(files=[OutputPath], target_
path = output_datastore_path, overwrite=True)
os.remove(OutputPath)
os.rmdir(output_datastore_path)
if __name__ == '__main__':
    main()
```

With both steps written, the rest of the code is pure boilerplate to containerize your
environment and to configure and run your pipeline.

# Configuring and running your ML parallel scoring pipeline

Since you've already built your environment in the *Creating an ML pipeline* section, all that's really left is configuring your ML pipeline steps. Use the following steps:

1.  In a new cell, retrieve the environment that you created in the *Creating an ML pipeline* section with the following code:

    ```
    Env = Environment.get(ws, 'AutoML Environment')
    ```

2.  Next, define a variable that defines your pipeline data and assigns it to a datastore:

    ```
    parallel_run_output =\
    PipelineData(name='parallel_predictions',
    datastore=datastore)
    ```

    This is the location that will hold `parallel_run_step.txt` between your first and second steps. You must also give this pipeline data object a name.

3.  Enable Docker on your environment and specify `DEFAULT_CPU_IMAGE` as your base image for your `ParallelRunStep`:

    ```
    parallel_environment = Env
    parallel_environment.docker.enabled = True
    parallel_environment.docker.base_image = DEFAULT_CPU_
    IMAGE
    ```

    You do not need to specify a `RunConfiguration` object for `ParallelRunStep`.

4.  Create a `RunConfiguration` object for your output creation step:

    ```
    run_config = RunConfiguration()
    run_config.environment = Env
    run_config.environment.docker.enabled = True
    run_config.environment.docker.base_image = DEFAULT_CPU_
    IMAGE
    ```

5.  Set your parallel run configurations with the following code:

    ```
    parallel_run_config = ParallelRunConfig(
        source_directory='Scoring_Scripts/',
        entry_script="Iris_Parallel_Scoring.py",
        mini_batch_size="1MB",
    ```

```
    error_threshold=5,
    output_action="append_row",
    environment=parallel_environment,
    compute_target=compute_target,
    run_invocation_timeout=60,
    node_count=4,
    logging_level="DEBUG")
```

You need to input the name of your Python script as well as the source directory that holds it. You need to specify how much data will be scored in parallel with `mini_batch_size`. For all **tabular data**, that is, data with rows and columns, the recommended setting is 1 MB.

`error_threshold` is how many times the step can fail in parallel before the entire pipeline fails. Next, setting `output_action` to `append_row` will automatically generate `parallel_run_step.txt` for you. Other options for `output_action` are labor-intensive.

Set your compute target to the appropriate compute cluster and specify your environment. Leave `run_invocation_timeout` at 60 seconds so your run will fail if it idles for too long and set `node_count` equal to the number of nodes in your compute cluster to ensure maximum parallelization. Lastly, set `logging_level` to DEBUG for informative logs.

6. Set the two variables that you will need to create your parallel scoring step, your dataset, and your model name:

```
dataset = Dataset.get_by_name(ws,'Iris Parallel Scoring')
input_data =\
dataset.as_named_input('Iris_Parallel_Scoring')
model_name = 'Iris-Multi-Classification-AutoML'
```

Datasets need to be passed in with the `as_named_input` code and appear as the `input_data` variable in your Python script.

7. Create your parallel scoring step using the following code:

```
parallel_scoring_step = ParallelRunStep(
    name="iris-parallel-scoring-step",
    parallel_run_config=parallel_run_config,
    inputs=[input_data],
    output=parallel_run_output,
```

```
arguments=['--model_name', model_name],
allow_reuse=False)
```

You need to give the step a name, `iris-parallel-scoring-step`. No spaces are allowed. Pass in your configurations using `parallel_run_config` and pass in your dataset using `inputs`. Set `output` to your pipeline data object and pass in your model name as an argument. As always, set `allow_reuse` equal to `False`.

8.  Create your output creation step using the following code:

```
output_step =\
  PythonScriptStep(name='iris-output-step',
script_name='Iris_Parallel_Output_Creation.py',
source_directory='Scoring_Scripts',
arguments=\
["--input_data_folder", parallel_run_output,],
inputs=[parallel_run_output],
compute_target=compute_target,
runconfig=run_config,
allow_reuse=False)
```

Give this step the name `iris-output-step` and pass in your script name and source directory. For `arguments` and `input`, you need to pass in `parallel_run_output`. This lets your output creation step use `parallel_run_step.txt` generated by your parallel scoring step. Then, set your compute target, specify your run configuration, and set `allow_reuse` to `False`.

9.  Set your step sequence and create a pipeline object:

```
step_sequence =\
  StepSequence(steps=[parallel_scoring_step, output_step])
  pipeline = Pipeline(workspace=ws, steps=step_sequence)
```

This time, you have two steps to set, `parallel_run_step` and `output_step`.

10. Give your pipeline experiment run a name, `Iris-Parallel-Scoring-Pipeline-Run`, and submit it to your compute cluster:

```
pipeline_experiment = \
Experiment(ws, 'Iris-Parallel-Scoring-Pipeline-Run')
pipeline_run = \
pipeline_experiment.submit(pipeline, show_output=True)
```

11. Use `RunDetails` to watch your pipeline execute in real time:

```
RunDetails(pipeline_run).show()
pipeline_run.wait_for_completion(show_output=True)
```

Notice how fast this scores your data. If your pipeline runs successfully, it will complete with the word **Finished**. You should see a graphic identical to the one in *Figure 9.6*:

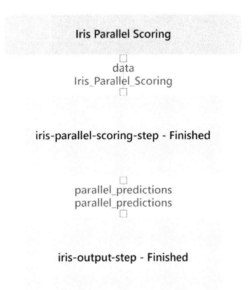

Figure 9.6 – Successful parallel pipeline run graphic

12. Publish your pipeline to an endpoint as you did in the previous section, naming it `Iris-Parallel-Scoring-Pipeline` or whatever you wish:

```
published_pipeline = pipeline_run.publish_pipeline(
    name='Iris-Parallel-Scoring-Pipeline',\
    description='\
Pipeline that Scores Iris Data in Parallel', version=
'1.0')
published_pipeline
```

Running this code will give you your published pipeline ID as well as a link to the endpoint, as seen in *Figure 9.7*:

```
published_pipeline = pipeline_run.publish_pipeline(
    name='Iris-Parallel-Scoring-Pipeline',\
    description='Pipeline that Scores Iris Data in Parallel', version= '1.0')

published_pipeline
```

| Name | Id | Status | Endpoint |
|---|---|---|---|
| Iris-Parallel-Scoring-Pipeline | c58a16ea-5abc-4d42-b25c-21fa9967895f | Active | REST Endpoint |

Figure 9.7 – Successfully published parallel pipeline

You can now examine and download your scoring file as you did in the previous section. Look inside `Output_Folder` in your datastore for a file called `Iris_Parallel_Predictions.csv`. It's quite a bit larger than your last file, at around 30 MB.

With both a standard scoring pipeline and a parallel run pipeline built, you are now at the cutting edge of AMLS. Both of these pipelines can be used to score not only AutoML-generated ML models, but custom models as well.

Even experienced data scientists have a hard time building these batch scoring solutions. So, you have acquired a desirable, marketable skill that will enable you to work alongside seasoned experts.

In the next section, you will learn how to build a pipeline for training AutoML models instead of scoring.

# Creating an AutoML training pipeline

Sometimes, it's necessary to retrain a model that you trained in AutoML. ML models can degrade over time if the relationship between your data and your target variable changes. This is true for all ML models, not just ones generated by AutoML.

Imagine, for example, that you build an ML model to predict demand for frozen pizza at a supermarket, and then one day, a famous pizza chain sets up shop next door. It's very likely that consumer buying behavior will change, and you will need to retrain the model. This is true for all ML models.

Luckily, AMLS has specialized ML pipeline steps built specifically for retraining models. In this section, we are going to use one of those steps, the AutoML step. The **AutoML step** lets you retrain models easily whenever you want, either with a push of a button or on a schedule.

Here, you will build a two-step ML pipeline where you will first train a model with an AutoML step and register it with a typical Python script step. This will enable you to build complete end-to-end solutions with automated scoring and training, completing your skillset. Furthermore, this will familiarize you with the AutoML step and all of its caveats.

> **Important note**
> Not all ML models require retraining, particularly those that predict physical phenomena, as the relationship between your data and the target variable is unlikely to change over time. However, most ML models will improve with additional data points, so it does make sense to retrain models as you collect and label more data.

By now, you should know what to expect in terms of creating ML pipelines. Most of the steps will be familiar to you, but you will have to work with specialized forms of pipeline data that pass data from your training step to your model registration step.

The Python scripts involved in this pipeline are much simpler than those involved in scoring pipelines, and thus require less customization when you try it with your own data. At the end of this section, like others, you will also publish your AutoML training pipeline to an endpoint. *Figure 9.8* outlines the process:

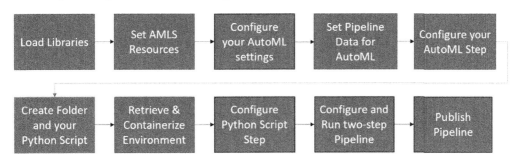

Figure 9.8 – Steps involved in setting up an AutoML retraining pipeline

This process is a little bit different than the other pipelines, as you need to configure your AutoML settings early on. You can find the code for all the steps in the ML-Retraining-Pipeline.ipynb file in the GitHub repository.

# Coding the first two steps of your AutoML training pipeline

To create your AutoML training pipeline, begin with the following steps:

1. Navigate to your Jupyter environment on your compute instance and create a new Jupyter notebook. Name it `automl-training-pipeline`.

2. Open your newly created notebook and import the usual set of Azure libraries along with `AutoMLConfig`:

```
from azureml.core import Workspace, Dataset, Datastore
from azureml.core import Experiment, Environment, Model
from azureml.core.compute import ComputeTarget
from azureml.train.automl import AutoMLConfig
```

`AutoMLConfig` lets you configure AutoML training runs.

3. Continuing on, import the necessary Azure ML pipeline libraries with the following code:

```
from azureml.core.runconfig import RunConfiguration,
CondaDependencies, DEFAULT_CPU_IMAGE
from azureml.pipeline.steps import PythonScriptStep,
AutoMLStep
from azureml.pipeline.core import Pipeline,
PublishedPipeline, PipelineData, TrainingOutput
from azureml.pipeline.core import StepSequence
from azureml.widgets import RunDetails
```

There are two new packages. `AutoMLStep` is an ML pipeline step that lets you run AutoML training runs. `TrainingOutput` lets you access the output from your AutoML step to pass on to your model registration step.

4. Import `os`:

```
import os
```

This is the only non-Azure Python package you will need to make this pipeline, and it will be used to create a new folder.

5. Connect your Jupyter notebook to your AMLS workspace:

```
ws = Workspace.from_config()
```

Log in if prompted by following the instructions.

6.  Set your compute cluster:

```
compute_name = 'compute-cluster'
compute_target = ComputeTarget(ws, compute_name)
```

7.  Set your datastore:

```
datastore = Datastore.get_default(ws)
```

8.  Retrieve your Iris Training dataset with the following code. You will pass this dataset into your AutoML configuration settings:

```
dataset = Dataset.get_by_name(ws, 'Iris Training')
```

9.  Retrieve the environment named AutoML Environment that you created in the *Creating an ML pipeline* section of this chapter:

```
Env = Environment.get(ws,'AutoML Environment')
```

This will be used only for your model registration step; your AutoML training step will use a standard, autogenerated environment.

## Configuring your AutoML model training settings and step

Next, you'll configure everything related to your AutoML training step with the following code:

1.  Set variables to pass into your AutoML configuration settings:

```
target_column = 'species'
task = 'classification'
primary_metric = 'accuracy'
featurization = 'auto'
num_classes = 3
iterations = 4
```

Explanations for these settings can be found in *Chapter 5, Building an AutoML Classification Solution*. One new setting is iterations. This will be used to determine how many AutoML models should be trained concurrently; this value should equal the number of nodes on your compute cluster to ensure maximum parallelization.

2.  Configure your AutoML training run:

```
config = AutoMLConfig(task=task,
                    primary_metric=primary_metric,
                    num_classes=num_classes,
                    featurization=featurization,
                    compute_target=compute_target,
                    training_data=dataset,
                    label_column_name=target_column,
                    experiment_timeout_minutes=15,
                    enable_early_stopping=True,
                    max_concurrent_iterations =
iterations,
                    n_cross_validations=5,
                    model_explainability=True,
                    enable_stack_ensemble=True,
                    enable_voting_ensemble=True)
```

An explanation for these settings can be found in *Chapter 4, Building an AutoML Regression Solution*. If you would like higher accuracy, adjust `experiment_timeout_minutes` to give AutoML more time to train. Note that you are passing in your dataset here.

3.  Set the output for AutoML metrics:

```
metrics_data =PipelineData(name='metrics_data',\
  datastore=datastore,pipeline_output_name='metrics
output',\
        training_output=TrainingOutput(type='Metrics'))
```

This code is standard boilerplate used in every AutoML step. It saves metrics from your AutoML run as intermediate pipeline data that you can use to pass on to other steps in your ML pipeline.

4.  Set the output for your best model:

```
model_data = PipelineData(\
name='model_data', datastore=datastore, pipeline_output_
name='best_model_output',\
        training_output=TrainingOutput(type='Model'))
```

This code is standard boilerplate used in every AutoML step. It saves information about the best model from your AutoML run as intermediate pipeline data to pass on to your model registration step.

5. Configure your AutoML step:

```
automl_training_step = AutoMLStep(
    name='Multiclass_AutoML_Step',
    automl_config=config,
    outputs=[metrics_data, model_data],
    allow_reuse=False)
```

All you need to do is give it a name, pass in your AutoML configuration settings, and specify `metrics_data` and `model_data` as output. As always, set `allow_reuse` to `False`.

# Creating a Python script to register your model

With your AutoML training step configured, you now need to write another script to extract and register your model using the following steps:

1. Make a folder to hold your training script using `os`:

```
os.makedirs('Training_Scripts', exist_ok=True)
```

2. Write a Python script to register your model. This script is very short compared to the others you wrote. Begin by writing out a new Python script file called `Iris_Model_Registration.py` using the `%%writefile` magic command and loading in your Azure libraries and `argparse`:

```
%%writefile Training_Scripts/Iris_Model_Registration.py
from azureml.core import Run, Workspace, Model
from azureml.core import Dataset, Datastore
import argparse
```

3. Continuing in the same cell as part of `Iris_Model_Registration_Scoring.py`, set a variable called `run` using the `Run` function:

```
run = Run.get_context()
```

4. Continuing in the same cell as part of `Iris_Model_Registration_Scoring.py`, pass in your arguments to access the best model as trained by AutoML as well as the dataset you used to train the model. For this, you will need three arguments, `model_name`, `model_path`, and `dataset_name`:

```
parser = argparse.ArgumentParser()
parser.add_argument("--model_name", dest="model_name")
parser.add_argument("--model_path", dest="model_path")
parser.add_argument("--dataset_name", dest="dataset_name")
args = parser.parse_args()
```

5. Continuing in the same cell as part of `Iris_Model_Registration_Scoring.py`, write a function called `main`. This function will register your best model. Begin by connecting to your AMLS workspace using the `run` variable:

```
def main():
    ws = run.experiment.workspace
```

6. Continuing in the same cell as part of `Iris_Model_Registration_Scoring.py`, as part of your `main` function, retrieve your dataset through the `dataset_name` argument:

```
    ds = Dataset.get_by_name(ws, args.dataset_name)
    dataset = [(Dataset.Scenario.TRAINING, ds)]
```

Use the `Dataset.Scenario.Training` line of code to specify the scenario in which it was used. This information will be saved when you register your model.

7. Continuing in the same cell as part of `Iris_Model_Registration_Scoring.py`, as part of your `main` function, register your model using the `model_path` and `model_name` arguments:

```
    model = Model.register(workspace=ws,
                          model_path=args.model_path,
                          model_name=args.model_name,
                          datasets=dataset)
if __name__ == '__main__':
    main()
```

While `model_name` is something you specify, `model_path` will be automatically generated from `model_data`. The dataset you used to train your model will also be saved using this code. Finally, complete `Iris_Model_Registration_Scoring.py` with the boilerplate code that triggers `main`.

# Configuring and running your AutoML training pipeline

All that's left is to containerize your environment, configure your model registration step, and run and publish your pipeline by following these steps:

1.  Create a `RunConfiguration` object for the model registration step:

    ```
    run_config = RunConfiguration()
    run_config.environment = Env
    run_config.environment.docker.enabled = True
    run_config.environment.docker.base_image = DEFAULT_CPU_
    IMAGE
    ```

    Note that this uses `AutoML Environment`, but you can get away with using a simpler environment without `pandas` or NumPy if you so desire.

2.  Set variables for your model name and dataset name:

    ```
    model_name = 'Iris-Multi-Classification-AutoML'
    dataset_name = 'Iris Training'
    ```

    Your model name will be used to register the best model that AutoML produces and is your choice. Your dataset name, on the other hand, should match the dataset you used to train your model.

3.  Configure your model registration step:

    ```
    model_registration_step = \
    PythonScriptStep(script_name="Iris_Model_Registration.
    py",\
                     source_directory = 'Training_Scripts',\
                     name = "Model-Registration-Step",\
                     allow_reuse = False,\
                     arguments = ["model_name",model_name,\
       "--model_path", model_data, "--dataset_name",\
         dataset_name],\
    ```

```
               inputs = [model_data],\
               compute_target = compute_target,\
               runconfig = run_config,\
               allow_reuse = False)
```

Here, you must pass in three arguments, model_name, model_data, and dataset_name, and pass in model_data as input. This is because model_data is pipeline data generated by your AutoML training step, while model_name and dataset_name are simple string variables. As always, set allow_reuse to False.

4.  Set your step sequence and create a pipeline object:

    ```
    step_sequence =\
     StepSequence(steps=[parallel_scoring_step, output_step])
     pipeline = Pipeline(workspace=ws, steps=step_sequence)
    ```

    This time, you have two steps to set, automl_training step and model_registration_step.

5.  Give your pipeline experiment run a name, Iris-AutoML-Training-Pipeline-Run, and submit it to your compute cluster:

    ```
    pipeline_experiment =\
     Experiment(ws, 'Iris-Parallel-Scoring-Pipeline-Run')
     pipeline_run =\
     pipeline_experiment.submit(pipeline, show_output=True)
    ```

    This will take much longer than your other pipelines, perhaps around a half hour.

6.  Use RunDetails to watch your pipeline execute in real time:

    ```
    RunDetails(pipeline_run).show()
     pipeline_run.wait_for_completion(show_output=True)
    ```

    If your pipeline runs successfully, it will complete with the word **Finished**. You should see a graphic identical to the one in *Figure 9.9*:

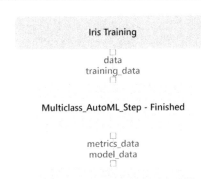

Figure 9.9 – Successful AutoML training pipeline

7.  Publish your pipeline to an endpoint as you did in the previous section, naming it Iris-AutoML-Training-Pipeline or whatever you wish:

```
published_pipeline = pipeline_run.publish_pipeline(
    name='Iris-AutoML-Training-Pipeline',\
    description=\
'Pipeline that Trains Iris Data with AutoML', version=
'1.0')
published_pipeline
```

Running this code will give you your published pipeline ID as well as a link to your endpoint, as seen in *Figure 9.10*:

| Name | Id | Status | Endpoint |
|---|---|---|---|
| Iris-AutoML-Training-Pipeline | bdafc5af-4964-40ac-bb01-50dd49b6dcb5 | Active | REST Endpoint |

Figure 9.10 – Successfully published AutoML training pipeline

> **Important note**
> Sometimes when you're running an ML pipeline, your computer will crash.
> However, your pipeline run will continue to run and you will still be able
> to publish it upon completion. To retrieve a completed pipeline so you can
> publish it, use the following code:

```
from azureml.pipeline.core import PipelineRun
experiment = Experiment(ws, 'your-experiment_name')
pipeline_run = PipelineRun(experiment, 'your-pipeline-run-id')
```

You have now built three ML pipelines, a standard scoring pipeline, a parallel run pipeline, and an AutoML training pipeline. This was not a trivial effort, but all that hard work has paid off. You have mastered one of the most complex parts of AMLS.

While making these pipelines is quite an undertaking, once you have them, they are very easy to manually rerun or automatically schedule, as you will see in the next section.

# Triggering and scheduling your ML pipelines

One of the biggest problems data scientists face is creating easy, rerunnable, production-ready code and scheduling it in an automatic, reliable manner. You've already accomplished the first part by creating your three ML pipelines. Now, it's time to learn how to do the second part.

In this section, you will first learn how to manually trigger the pipelines you've created through the GUI. Then, you will learn how to trigger the pipelines via code, both manually and on an automated schedule. This will enable you to put your ML pipelines into production, generating results on an hourly, daily, weekly, or monthly basis.

## Triggering your published pipeline from the GUI

Triggering your published pipeline from the AML studio GUI is easy. However, you cannot set up an automated schedule for your ML pipelines at this time. As such, it is most useful for triggering training pipelines when you notice that your results seem off. Use the following steps to manually trigger your ML pipeline through the AML studio:

1. Navigate to `https://ml.azure.com` to access AML studio.

2. Click **Pipelines** under **Assets** on the left-hand side.

3. Click **Pipeline endpoints** near the top of the page.

4. Click the blue link to **Iris-AutoML-Training-Pipeline**.

5. Click **Submit**. This will open up a dialog box.

6. Select an experiment name from the drop-down box under **Existing Experiment**. Use `Iris-AutoML-Training-Pipeline-Run`.

7. Click **Submit**.

8. Click **Pipelines** under **Assets** again and, on the top line, you should see a new run, as shown in *Figure 9.11*:

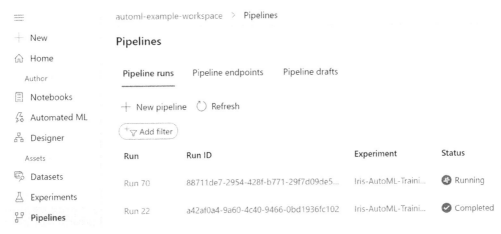

Figure 9.11 – Pipeline run submitted through the GUI

Compared to making an ML pipeline, resubmitting it is very easy. Next, we will look at ways to trigger our pipeline through code and create an automatic schedule.

# Triggering and scheduling a published pipeline through code

Triggering a published ML pipeline through code first requires you to obtain your pipeline ID. These were generated at the end of the previous sections whenever you published a pipeline. You can also find your pipeline ID by clicking on individual pipelines found under **Pipeline endpoints** through the AML studio. You will also need your pipeline IDs to set up schedules through code.

All the code for this section can be found in the `ML-Pipeline-Scheduling.ipynb` file in the GitHub repository. Begin by opening a Jupyter notebook and following these steps:

1. Create a new Jupyter notebook as you have before. Name it `pipeline-scheduling`.

2. Open your notebook and import the required Azure libraries, three of which are new. `PublishedPipeline` lets you access any ML pipelines you have published. `Schedule` and `ScheduleRecurrence` let you schedule ML pipelines:

```
from azureml.core import Workspace, Datastore
from azureml.pipeline.core import Pipeline,
```

```
PublishedPipeline
from azureml.core.experiment import Experiment
from azureml.pipeline.core.schedule import
ScheduleRecurrence, Schedule
```

3. To manually trigger an ML pipeline, use the following code by replacing your-published-pipeline-id with the ID of your published AutoML training pipeline. That's it:

```
experiment =\
Experiment(ws,'AutoML-Retraining-Code-Trigger')
published_pipeline =\
PublishedPipeline.get(workspace=ws, id='your-published-pipeline-id')
pipeline_run = experiment.submit(published_pipeline)
```

4. To create a schedule for running your ML pipeline, first determine an interval with the following code. The interval options are Minute, Hour, Day, Week, or Month. You can also specify start_time and time_zone as optional arguments. Another optional argument is status, which you can set to Disabled to turn off your schedule:

```
recurrence =\
ScheduleRecurrence(frequency="Day", interval=1)
```

5. Create your schedule by giving it a name and passing in your recurrence settings, experiment name, published pipeline ID, and a description:

```
schedule = \
Schedule.create(ws, name="IrisTrainingSchedule",
                description="AutoML Training",
                pipeline_id='your-pipeline-id',
                experiment_name='Iris-Retraining',
                recurrence=recurrence)
```

You have now created a schedule that will automatically trigger your AutoML training pipeline once a day. This schedule will automatically spin up your compute cluster, train a model, and spin down. Many companies spend years trying to figure out how best to schedule ML training and scoring runs in a timely, reliable manner, and you've accomplished this task in a mere chapter!

# Summary

You have now implemented a fully automated ML batch scoring solution using an AutoML trained model. You've created pipelines that can score models, pipelines that can process big data in parallel, and pipelines that can retrain AutoML models. You can trigger them whenever you want and you can even set up an automated scoring schedule. This is no small feat, as many organizations have spent years trying to learn best practices for these tasks.

In *Chapter 10, Creating End-to-End AutoML Solutions*, you will cement your knowledge as you learn how to ingest data into Azure, score it with ML pipelines, and write your results to whatever location you want.

# 10
# Creating End-to-End AutoML Solutions

Now that you have created **machine learning** (**ML**) pipelines, you can learn how to use them in other Azure products outside of the **Azure Machine Learning Service** (**AMLS**). Perhaps the most useful is Azure Data Factory.

**Azure Data Factory** (**ADF**) is Azure's premier code-free data orchestration tool. You can use ADF to pull data from on-premise sources into the Azure cloud, to run ML pipelines, and push data out of Azure by creating an **Azure Data Factory pipeline** (**ADF pipeline**). ADF pipelines are an integral part of creating end-to-end ML solutions and are the end goal of any non-real-time AutoML project.

You will begin this chapter by learning how to connect AMLS to ADF. Once you have accomplished this task, you will learn how to schedule an ML pipeline using the parallel pipeline you created in *Chapter 9, Implementing a Batch Scoring Solution*.

Next, you will learn how to pull data from your local machine and load it into the Azure cloud using ADF. Finally, you will pull everything you have together to create an end-to-end AutoML solution, creating an ADF pipeline for scoring incoming data, and another ADF pipeline for retraining AutoML models.

By the end of this chapter, you will be able to integrate AMLS with ADF to create ADF pipelines and be able to fashion complete end-to-end AutoML solutions, from ingesting and scoring data, to retraining ML models. This is an invaluable, in-demand skillset that will set you apart from your peers.

If you're already a trained data scientist, you will acquire software engineering skills that are rare in your field. If you're a trained engineer, you will learn how to incorporate ML into a familiar field you already understand.

In this chapter, we will cover the following topics:

- Connecting AMLS to ADF
- Scheduling a machine learning pipeline in ADF
- Transferring data using ADF
- Automating an end-to-end scoring solution
- Automating an end-to-end training solution

# Technical requirements

In this chapter, you will create an ADF resource and use the ML pipeline objects you created in *Chapter 9, Implementing a Batch Scoring Solution.* As such, you will need a working internet connection, an Azure account, and access to your AMLS workspace.

With your Azure account, you will also need permissions to create a service principal in Azure Active Directory. If you're using a personal Azure account, you should have this access. If you're using a work account, speak with your Azure administrator for this level of permission.

The following are the prerequisites for the chapter:

- Have access to the internet
- Have a web browser, preferably Google Chrome or Microsoft Edge Chromium
- Have a Microsoft Azure account
- Have created an AMLS workspace
- Have created the `compute-cluster` compute cluster in *Chapter 2, Getting Started with Azure Machine Learning Service*
- Understand how to navigate to the Jupyter environment from an Azure compute instance as demonstrated in *Chapter 4, Building an AutoML Regression Solution*

- Have trained and registered the `Iris-Multi-Classification-AutoML` ML model in *Chapter 5, Building an AutoML Classification Solution*

- Have created all three of the ML pipelines in *Chapter 9, Implementing a Batch Scoring Solution*. The three ML pipelines are *Iris-Scoring-Pipeline, Iris-Parallel-Scoring-Pipeline*, and *Iris-AutoML-Training-Pipeline*.

- Have necessary permissions to create service principals in Azure Active Directory. If you're using a personal account, you will have these permissions.

The code for this chapter is available here: `https://github.com/ PacktPublishing/Automated-Machine-Learning-with-Microsoft- Azure/tree/master/Chapter10`.

# Connecting AMLS to ADF

ADF is a code-free data orchestration and transformation tool. With it, you can create ADF pipelines that can copy data into Azure, transform data, run ML pipelines, and push data back onto certain on-premise databases and file shares. It's incredibly easy to make and schedule ADF pipelines using ADF's code-free pipeline editing tool. As you create an ADF pipeline with the drag and drop interface, you're actually writing JSON code, which ADF uses to execute jobs.

> Tip
> **Azure Synapse Analytics**, Microsoft Azure's premier data warehousing and integrated analytics service, also has a feature nearly identical to ADF pipelines: **Azure Synapse pipelines**. Anything that you do in this chapter with ADF pipelines you can also achieve with Azure Synapse pipelines using a very similar interface.

In this section, you will create an ADF resource and connect it to AMLS. You will do this using a **linked service**, an object similar to a connection string that ADF requires to connect to other Azure and non-Azure services and data stores. Linked services require authentication, and AMLS requires service principal authentication.

A **service principal** is a security identity that Azure uses to grant permissions across Azure resources. Once you grant your service principal access to both ADF and AMLS, it's easy to connect them together and start running ML pipelines.

# Creating an ADF

An ADF can be created by using the GUI or using Azure PowerShell through the Azure **Command Line Interface (CLI)** that you used in *Chapter 2, Getting Started with Azure Machine Learning Service*. **PowerShell** is a series of cmdlets for managing Azure resources through the CLI. Here, you will first learn how to create an ADF resource using the Azure portal GUI. Then, you will learn how to create an ADF resource through PowerShell.

To create an ADF resource using the GUI, do the following:

1. Navigate to the Azure portal at `https://portal.azure.com`.

2. Click on **Create a resource** in the top-left corner.

3. In the search box, type in `Data Factory` and click **Data Factory** from the drop-down box.

4. Click on **Create**, the blue box in the top-left corner under **Data Factory**.

5. Now fill out the **Data Factory creation** form. Begin by selecting the same **Resource group** that holds your AMLS workspace. If you used the suggested **Resource group** in *Chapter 2, Getting Started with Azure Machine Learning Service*, this will be **automl-example-resource-group**.

6. Select the same Azure **Region** that holds your AMLS workspace. If you used the suggested Azure **Region** in *Chapter 2, Getting Started with Azure Machine Learning Service*, this will be **North Central US**.

7. Give your ADF a name in the **Name** field. As it has to be globally unique across Microsoft Azure, try `automl-adf` followed by a number string. The following screenshot shows what your completed settings should look like. Leave **Version** as **V2**:

## Create Data Factory    ...

⚠ Changes on this step may reset later selections you have made. Review all options prior to deployment.

**Basics**    Git configuration    Networking    Advanced    Tags    Review + create

### Project details

Select the subscription to manage deployed resources and costs. Use resource groups like folders to organize and manage all your resources.

Subscription * ⓘ

| Dennis Sawyers Internal MS Learning Account | ⌄ |

Resource group * ⓘ

| auto-ml-example-resource-group | ⌄ |

Create new

### Instance details

Region * ⓘ

| North Central US | ⌄ |

Name * ⓘ

| automl-adf713 | ✓ |

Version * ⓘ

| V2 | ⌄ |

Figure 10.1 – Data factory settings

8.  Click the **Git configuration** tab and check the **Configure Git later** box.

9.  Click **Review + create** and hit **Create**. Your data factory is now created.

Another way to create an ADF resource is through PowerShell. Follow these steps:

1.  Navigate to the Azure portal at `https://portal.azure.com`.

2.  Click the computer screen icon at the top right of your screen as shown in the following screenshot. When you hover over the icon, the words **Cloud Shell** will appear:

Figure 10.2 – Navigating to PowerShell

3.  Select **PowerShell** from the drop-down box.

4.  Type in the following code:

```
$DataFactory =\
Set-AzDataFactoryV2 -ResourceGroupName 'auto-ml-example-
resource-group' -location 'northcentralus' -Name 'automl-
adf713'
```

ResourceGroupName sets your resource group. Set-AzDataFactoryV2 sets your version, while location sets your Azure region. Name gives your ADF a name. Your data factory has now been created.

Now that you have created an ADF, the next step is to create a service principal and give it access to both your ADF and AMLS workspace. This will grant ADF access to use ML pipelines.

## Creating a service principal and granting access

Service principals are security identities that Azure uses to grant Azure resources access to other Azure resources. You can use service principal authentication across many areas of Azure, including AMLS. In order to connect AMLS to ADF, however, a service principal is required. To create one using the Azure portal, you must first navigate to **Azure Active Directory**, Azure's premier identity and authentication service, by following these steps:

1.  Navigate to the Azure portal at https://portal.azure.com.

2.  Search for Azure Active Directory in the top search bar and click **Azure Active Directory** under the **Services** heading.

3.  Click **App registrations** on the left-hand side of the screen.

4.  Click **New registration** at the top left of the screen.

5.  Give the service principal a name, adf-service-principal, and click **Register**. Leave all other settings as is.

6.  You will now be taken to a page with all of the information about your service principal. Copy **Application (client) ID** and paste it in Notepad or a similar text editor. You will need this ID later.

7.  Click **Certificates & secrets** on the left-hand side of the screen. This will let you create a password for your service principal.

8.  Click **New client secret**. *Secret* is another word for a password in Azure.

9. Give the secret a name, ADF-Secret, and set it so that it never expires as shown in *Figure 10.3*. Click **Add**:

Home > Microsoft > adf-service-principal

## 🔑 adf-service-principal | Certificates & secrets   📌   🖨

🔍 Search (Ctrl+/)          ≪          ♡  Got feedback?

🏠 Overview

🪄 Quickstart                              ### Add a client secret

🏎 Integration assistant                   Description

                                          ADF-Secret|

**Manage**
                                          Expires
🖼 Branding                                ◯  In 1 year

🔁 Authentication                          ◯  In 2 years

🔑 Certificates & secrets                  ⦿  Never

‖ Token configuration                      [ Add ]   [ Cancel ]

Figure 10.3 – Naming your service principal secret

10. Copy the **Value** field of your secret. This is your password and you will only be able to see it for a short time before it disappears. Once it vanishes, you will never be able to see it again. Paste it into Notepad or a similar text editor, as you will need it later when creating your ADF linked service.

11. With your service principal created, you must now grant it access to both AMLS and ADF. Navigate to the front page of the Azure portal at https://portal.azure.com.

12. Open your AMLS resource by clicking the **Machine Learning** icon near the top of your screen under **Azure Services**. You should see it if you have recently used AMLS, as shown in *Figure 10.4*:

Azure services

Create a resource | Azure Active Directory | Subscriptions | Data factories | Machine Learning | Monitor | Resource groups | Event Hubs | Azure Databricks | More services

Figure 10.4 – Azure services panel

13. Click the name of your AMLS workspace to access the resource.

14. Click **Access Control (IAM)** on the left-hand panel.

15. Click **Add role assignments**.

16. Select **Contributor** for **Role**, assign access to **User, group, or service principal**, search for `adf-service-principal` and click it as shown in *Figure 10.5*. Then, click **Save**:

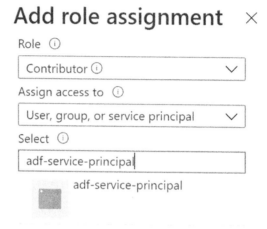

Figure 10.5 – Granting permission to your service principal

17. You have now granted your service principal access to AMLS. Now, you must do the same thing for ADF. Begin by navigating to the front page of the Azure portal by clicking **Home** in the top-left corner of your screen.

18. Click the **Data factories** icon at the top of your screen under **Azure Services**. If you have used ADF lately, you will see this icon.

19. Click the name of the data factory you made to open up the resource.

20. Repeat *steps 14-16* for ADF. These steps are identical to AMLS. You have now granted your service principal access to both ADF and AMLS.

## Creating an ADF resource through the Azure CLI

You can also create a service principal and grant it access to ADF and AMLS through the Azure CLI with the following steps:

1. Open up the Azure CLI by clicking the computer screen icon at the top right of your screen and select **Bash** from the drop-down menu.

2. Type in the following code to create your service principal, assigning it a name:

```
az ad sp create-for-rbac --name adf-service-principal
```

3. Copy both the `appid` and `password` fields. You will never see the value for your password again, so make sure to copy it. This maps to **Application (client) ID** and the secret.

4. Use the following code to grant your service principal access to all resources in the resource group containing both AMLS and ADF. Change to match your resource group if necessary. Use `assignee` to pass in your service principal application ID. Use `role` to pass in the correct level of access, in this case, **Contributor**. Use `resource-group` to assign access to the correct **Resource group**:

```
az role assignment create --assignee "your-service-
principal-id" --role "Contributor" --resource-group
"auto-ml-example-resource-group"
```

With your service principal created and granted access to the appropriate resources, your next step is to open ADF and create the linked service. Make sure you have Notepad open as you will need both the service principal ID as well as the secret you created. Having these readily available will make the next set of steps easy.

# Creating a linked service to connect ADF with AMLS

Moving forward, now you'll get a chance to open up ADF and get used to its interface. ADF is designed largely as a code-free platform, but everything you create is also written as JSON files under the hood. To link ADF with AMLS, follow these steps:

1. Navigate to the Azure portal at `https://portal.azure.com`.

2. Click the **Data factories** icon at the top of your screen under **Azure Services**. If you have used ADF lately, you will see this icon. If not, use the search bar at the top of your screen.

3. Click the name of the data factory you made that starts with the name `auto1-adf`.

4. Click **Author & Monitor** in the middle of the screen. You should now see the ADF user interface, shown in *Figure 10.6*:

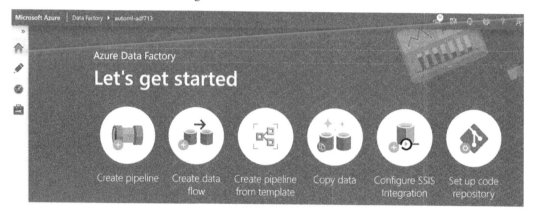

Figure 10.6 – ADF UI

5. Click the toolbox icon on the left-hand side. When you hover over the icon for a few seconds, the word **Manage** will appear to indicate the section you're navigating to.

6. Click **Linked Services** under **Connections** in the top-left corner.

7. Click **Create linked service**.

8. Click **Compute** and select **Azure Machine Learning** as shown in *Figure 10.7*:

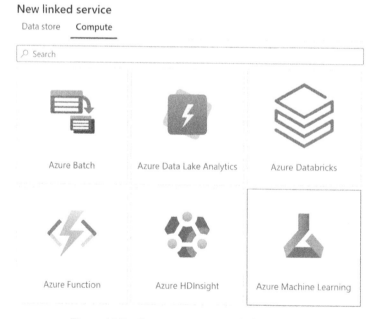

Figure 10.7 – Create an Azure ML linked service

9.  Click **Continue**.

10. Now it's time to fill out the linked service creation form. Begin by giving your linked service a name such as `AMLS Linked Service`.

11. Select **AutoResolveIntegrationRuntime** from the dropdown under **Connect via integration runtime**. An **integration runtime** is simply the compute that ADF uses under the hood to move data and run your jobs. The **Azure integration runtime (Azure IR)** is a serverless, elastic compute fully managed by ADF.

12. Select your Azure subscription from the drop-down box under **Azure subscription**.

13. Select your AMLS workspace from the drop-down box under **Azure Machine Learning workspace name**.

14. Paste your service principal application (client) ID into the **Service principal ID** textbox. You copied this ID into a text editor earlier.

15. Paste your service principal secret into the **Service principal key** textbox.

16. Click **Test connection**.

17. If the result of the test is **Connection successful**, click **Create**.

18. Your linked service has been created. Hover over your new linked service and click the { } icon to view the underlying JSON code.

You have successfully connected your ADF to AMLS. In this short section, you have learned a lot. Not only have you learned how to create an ADF, but you have also learned how to create service principals, grant access, and create linked services. With this infrastructure created, you can now learn how to easily run and schedule ML pipelines inside of an ADF pipeline.

# Scheduling a machine learning pipeline in ADF

Perhaps ADF's best feature is its ease of use. By clicking and dragging objects across a screen, you can easily orchestrate a flow of seamless data ingestion, transformation, and ML through an ADF pipeline. Moreover, with a few more clicks, you can schedule that ADF pipeline to run whenever you want. Gaining this skill will enable you to create code-free data orchestration runs quickly and easily.

First, you will schedule and run the simplest ML pipeline you created in *Chapter 9, Implementing a Batch Scoring Solution*, the `Iris-Scoring-Pipeline`. To do so, follow these steps:

1. Navigate to your ADF resource and click **Author & Monitor**.

2. Click the pen icon on the left-hand side. When you hover over this icon, the word **Author** will appear to indicate which section you're navigating to.

3. Click the blue cross icon next to the search box under **Factory Resources** in the top-left corner. When you hover over this icon, the words **Add new resource** will appear.

4. Click **Pipeline** from the resulting dropdown as shown in *Figure 10.8*:

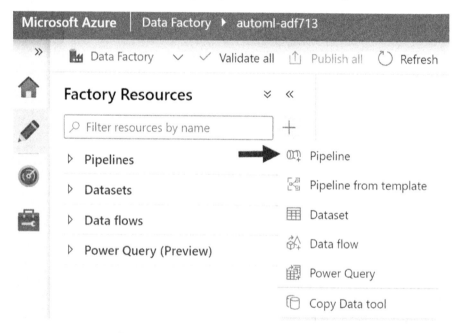

Figure 10.8 – Creating your first ADF pipeline

5. Click **Machine Learning** under **Activities** in the center-left of the screen.

6. Click and drag the blue flask icon onto the canvas as shown in *Figure 10.9*. This is the **Machine Learning Executive Pipeline** activity:

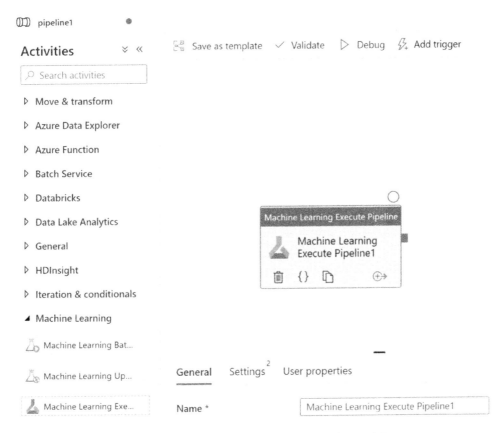

Figure 10.9 – Machine Learning Execute Pipeline activity

7. Click **General** underneath the canvas and give your activity a new name, `Execute Iris Scoring Pipeline`.

8. Click **Settings** underneath the canvas.

9. Select **AMLS Linked Service** from the first drop-down box to connect your linked service.

10. Select **Iris-Scoring-Pipeline** from the **Machine Learning pipeline name** drop-down box.

11. Select a pipeline ID from the **Machine Learning pipeline ID** drop-down box. There should only be one pipeline ID unless you published multiple ML pipelines with the same name.

12. Click the abacus icon in the top right-hand corner to open the **Properties** box. Rename your ADF pipeline from `pipeline1` to `Iris Scoring Pipeline`. Spaces are allowed.

13. Click **Publish All** near the top left of your screen. Then, click **Publish** in the bottom right-hand corner to create your ADF pipeline.

> **Important tip**
> In order to save your work in ADF, you need to publish your changes. Make sure you publish multiple times as you're developing new ADF pipelines.

14. To schedule your newly created ADF pipeline, click **Add trigger** near the top of your screen.

15. Click **New/Edit** from the resulting dropdown.

16. Click the **Choose Trigger** dropdown and select + **New**.

    Like the AML Python SDK, there are multiple types of triggers within ADF. Execute **schedule-based triggers** on a timetable. Execute **event-based triggers** when a file is created or deleted in an Azure blob container.

    **Tumbling window triggers** are similar to schedule-based triggers, but they are more advanced and have options such as retrying failed runs and backfilling past time periods. For this exercise, create a simple schedule-based trigger.

17. Give your trigger a name such as `Once Monthly`.

18. Select **Schedule** under **Type**.

19. Pick a start date and the appropriate time zone from the respective drop-down boxes.

20. Under **Recurrence**, type in `1` and select **Month** from the drop-down box.

21. Click **OK** twice.

22. Click **Publish All** near the top left of your screen, followed by **Publish** in the bottom right-hand corner. You are now finished. Your completed ADF pipeline should look something like *Figure 10.10*. To see the JSON code, click the { } icon at the top right-hand side of your screen:

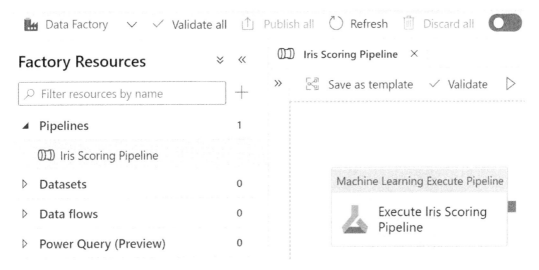

Figure 10.10 – Your first completed ADF pipeline

While you have created and scheduled your first ADF pipeline, it does not mean much. After all, while this ADF pipeline will trigger your ML pipeline on a monthly basis, you still need to automate the ingestion of new data. Thankfully, data ingestion is where ADF excels. You will see just how easy transferring data is using ADF in the next section. No matter where the data lies, ADF can pull it in.

# Transferring data using ADF

Moving data from on-premise to the cloud and from the cloud to on-premise is a key skill for any data engineer or data scientist. ADF accomplishes this task with the **Copy data** activity. This is ADF's most basic and most powerful function.

In this section, first, you will download a **self-hosted integration runtime** (**SHIR**) to your local machine, allowing your computer to serve as a compute resource to load data into Azure. Then, you will create a linked service for your **Azure storage account** and your local PC.

Next, you will download a file from the GitHub repository and save it to your PC. Finally, you will create a **Copy data** activity in ADF that will take data from your PC and put it into the same Azure blob container that's connected to your AML datastore.

Going through these exercises will give you the data engineering skills that will allow you to create an end-to-end solution in the next section.

# Installing a self-hosted integration runtime

Before you can copy data into Azure, you first need to install a SHIR on your local machine. Begin with the following steps:

1.  Navigate to your ADF resource and click **Author & Monitor**.

2.  Click the toolbox icon on the left-hand side. When you hover over this icon, the word **Manage** will appear to indicate which section you're navigating to.

3.  Click **Integration runtimes** under **Connections**.

4.  Click **+New** at the top center of your screen.

5.  Select **Azure, Self-Hosted** and click **Continue** as shown in *Figure 10.11*:

### Integration runtime setup

Integration Runtime is the native compute used to execute or dispatch activities. Choose what integration runtime to create based on required capabilities. Learn more ⬚

### Azure, Self-Hosted

Perform data flows, data movement and dispatch activities to external compute.

### Azure-SSIS

Lift-and-shift existing SSIS packages to execute in Azure.

Figure 10.11 – Selecting the right integration runtime to install a SHIR

6.  Select **Self-Hosted** and click **Continue**.

7.  Give your new SHIR a name, `IntegrationRuntime`, and click **Create**.

8.  On the next screen, you will see two options to install the SHIR. Choose **Option 1: Express setup** by clicking **Click here to launch the express setup for this computer**.

> **Important note**
>
> If you are using your work machine, ask your IT security organization for permission before installing the SHIR. It does open up a connection between your machine and the public-facing Azure cloud.

9.  This will download the SHIR installation file to your compute. Open the file and click **Yes**. Installation should take between 5 and 10 minutes.

10. Once the installation is finished, click **Close**. Your SHIR should now appear as shown in *Figure 10.12*:

## Integration runtimes

The integration runtime (IR) is the compute infrastructure to provide the following data integration capabilities

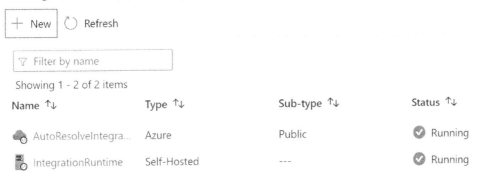

Figure 10.12 – Self-hosted integration runtime

With an SHIR installed on your local machine, you're now able to move data from your PC directly into Azure using ADF. Just as you created a linked service for AMLS, next you will create a linked service for Azure Blob storage.

# Creating an Azure Blob storage linked service

To create a linked service connecting ADF to **Azure Blob storage**, follow these steps:

1. Click **Linked services** under **Connections** in the top-left corner of your screen.

2. Click **+New** at the top center of your screen.

3. Select **Azure Blob Storage** and click **Continue** to see the linked service creation form.

4. Give your linked service a name such as `AMLSDatastoreLink`.

5. Select **AutoResolveIntegrationRuntime**.

6. Select your Azure subscription from the drop-down box under **Azure subscription**.

7. Select your storage account from the drop-down box under **Storage account name**. This should be the storage account linked to your AMLS workspace; if you followed the naming convention, it should begin with `automlexamplew` followed by a string of numbers.

8. Click **Test connection**.

9. If your test was successful, click **Create**.

10. Download `Iris_Scoring_Data_for_ADF.csv` from the GitHub repository:

    `https://github.com/PacktPublishing/Automated-Machine-Learning-with-Microsoft-Azure/blob/master/Chapter10/Iris_Scoring_Data_for_ADF.csv`

11. Create a folder on your PC called `Iris`. Move `Iris_Scoring_Data_for_ADF.csv` there.

# Creating a linked service to your PC

Next, it's time to create a linked service to your PC. This linked service will make use of your SHIR. Use the following steps:

1. Click **Linked Services** and **+New** as you did to create the other linked services.

2. Click **File**, select **File System**, and click **Continue** to see the linked service creation form.

3. Give your linked service a name such as `LocalPCLink`.

4. Select your SHIR from the drop-down box under **Connect via integration runtime**.

5. Under **Host**, type in the full file path, starting with your disk drive, to the Iris folder.

6. Fill in the username and password that you use to log into your PC. To find your username, search for **System Information** in your PC's search bar and click it; your user name can be found under **System Summary**.

7. Click **Test connection**.

8. If your test was successful, click **Create**.

# Creating an ADF pipeline to copy data

With an SHIR, Azure Blob storage linked service, and a linked service connecting to your local PC, you are now ready to build an ADF pipeline using the **Copy data** activity with the following steps:

1. Click the pen icon on the left-hand side of your ADF.

2. Click the blue cross icon next to the search box under **Factory Resources** in the top-left corner. When you hover over this icon, the words **Add new resource** will appear.

3. Click **Copy Data tool** from the resulting dropdown as shown in *Figure 10.13*:

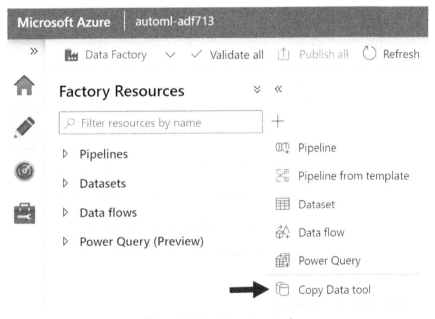

Figure 10.13 – Copy Data tool

4.  Under **Task name**, enter `Copy Iris Data to Azure` and click **Next**.

5.  You now have to select your source datastore. Select the linked service to your PC, **LocalPCLink**, and click **Next**.

6.  Choose the data you wish to transfer into Azure by clicking **Browse**, selecting `Iris_Scoring_Data_for_ADF.csv`, and clicking **Choose**.

7.  Click **Next**.

8.  Under **File format settings**, check the box for **First row as header** and click **Next**.

9.  You now have to select your destination datastore. Select the linked service to your Azure storage account, **AMLSDatastoreLink**.

10. Under **File name**, type `Input_Folder/Iris_Scoring_Data.csv` and click **Next**. This will write your data to a file called `Iris_Scoring_Data.csv` in a folder called `Input_Folder`. The folder will be created if it does not exist.

11. Under **File format settings**, check the box for **Add header to file** and click **Next**.

12. Click **Next** under **Settings** without changing any of the defaults.

13. Click **Next** under **Summary**. Your ADF pipeline will now be created and run.

14. Click **Finish**. You will now be transported to the main ADF pipeline authoring tool.

15. Click `Copy Iris Data to Azure` under **Pipelines**. You will notice that your **Copy data** activity will be poorly named.

16. Click your activity and rename it `Copy Iris Data from PC` as shown in *Figure 10.14*:

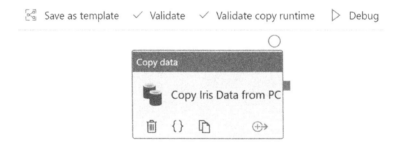

Figure 10.14 – Finished ADF pipeline with the Copy data activity

17. Save your change to the pipeline by clicking **Publish All** and then **Publish**.

You have now successfully transferred data from your PC into Azure using ADF. This is a foundational skill for data engineering and allows you to transfer all sorts of data into the cloud. Like the ADF pipeline you created in the previous section for executing ML pipelines, you can schedule this to run on any time schedule you wish.

We are now going to bring together all of the skills you have learned in this chapter to write a truly productionalizable ADF pipeline. This pipeline will ingest data from your computer, score it, and then write results back to your local machine. Even though it's not a trivial task by any means, you will be able to churn out pipeline after pipeline by the end of this chapter.

# Automating an end-to-end scoring solution

Ultimately, the end goal of any AutoML project is to create an automated scoring solution. Data gets pulled in from a source, scored automatically using the model you trained, and the results get stored in a location of your choice. By combining everything you've learned in the previous three sections, you can accomplish this task easily.

You will begin this section by opening up AMLS, creating a new dataset, and slightly altering your existing `Iris-Scoring-Pipeline`. Then, after republishing your pipeline with a new name, you will combine it with the **Copy data** activity you created to load data into Azure.

Next, you will create another Copy Data activity to transfer your results from Azure to your PC and schedule the job to run once a week on Mondays. This is a very common pattern in ML, and it's one you can accomplish without any code at all using ADF.

## Editing an ML pipeline to score new data

First, you need to create a new ML pipeline by editing `Iris-Scoring-Pipeline` you created in *Chapter 9*, *Implementing a Batch Scoring Solution*, with the following steps:

1. Access your AML studio at `https://ml.azure.com`.

2. Use the GUI to create a new dataset as you did in *Chapter 3*, *Training Your First AutoML Model*. Begin by clicking **Datasets** under **Assets** on the left-hand panel.

3. After clicking **Create dataset**, select **From datastore** and name your new dataset `Iris Local Scoring Data`.

4. Select **workplaceblobstore** as your datastore and navigate to `Iris_Data.csv` in `Input_Folder`. This is the data you copied over from your PC.

5. Finish creating the dataset, making sure to set the option under the **Column headers** dropdown to **Use headers from the first file** in order to pull in column names.

6. With your dataset created, navigate to your **Compute instance** and open up your `machine-learning-pipeline` Python notebook in Jupyter.

7. Click **File** at the top left and select **Make a Copy** from the drop-down box.

8. Rename your copied notebook to `machine-learning-pipeline-local-scoring`.

9. Delete the cells that make `Iris` data and register it as a dataset.

10. Rename your Python script from `Iris_Scoring.py` to `Iris_Scoring_Local.py` in the first line of your script that writes the file as follows:

```
%%writefile Scoring_Scripts/Iris_Scoring_Local.py
```

11. In `Iris_Scoring_Local.py`, retrieve your `Iris Local Scoring Data` dataset instead of the `Iris Scoring` dataset as shown in the following line of code:

```
dataset =\
Dataset.get_by_name(ws,'Iris Local Scoring Data')
```

12. When configuring your ML pipeline step, replace `Iris_Scoring.py` with `Iris_Scoring_Local.py` as shown in the following code:

```
scoring_step =\
PythonScriptStep(name='iris-scoring-step',\
                 script_name= 'Iris_Scoring_Local.py',\
                 source_directory='Scoring_Scripts',\
                 arguments=[],\
                 inputs=[],\
                 compute_target=compute_target,\
                 runconfig=run_config,\
                 allow_reuse=False)
```

13. In `Iris_Scoring_Local.py`, retrieve your `Iris Local Scoring Data` dataset instead of the `Iris Scoring` dataset in the following line of code:

```
dataset =\
Dataset.get_by_name(ws,'Iris Local Scoring Data')
```

14. Rename your published pipeline from `Iris-Scoring-Pipeline` to `Iris-Local-Scoring-Pipeline` in the following lines of code:

```
published_pipeline =\
pipeline_run.publish_pipeline( name='Iris-Local-Scoring-
Pipeline',\
        description='Pipeline that Scores Iris Data',
version= '1.0')
```

15. Run all cells in your notebook to create your new ML pipeline, `Iris-Local-Scoring-Pipeline`. This will take a few minutes. You have now created an ML pipeline that scores data loaded into Azure from your PC.

# Creating an ADF pipeline to run your ML pipeline

With a new ML pipeline created, you are now ready to create a new ADF pipeline that automates the end-to-end scoring process using these steps:

1. Open up ADF and click the pen icon on the left-hand side to open the ADF pipeline authoring tool.

2. Click **Pipelines** under **Factory Resources** to see your existing ADF pipelines. Click the three dots next to `Copy Iris Data to Azure` and select **Clone** from the drop-down box.

3. Rename your new pipeline to `End-to-End Iris Scoring`.

4. Click **Machine Learning** under **Activities** and drag a **Machine Learning Execute Pipeline** activity onto the canvas. Connect it to your `Copy Iris Data from PC` activity by clicking the green square, holding your mouse button so an arrow appears, and connecting the arrow to your **Machine Learning Execute Pipeline** activity as shown in *Figure 10.15*:

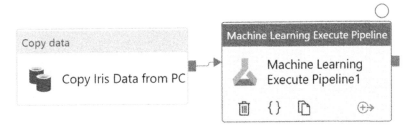

Figure 10.15 – Connecting activities in an ADF pipeline

5. Configure your **Machine Learning Execute Pipeline** activity as you did earlier in this chapter. Rename your activity to `Score Iris Data` by selecting the activity and opening the **General** tab.

   Then, after opening the **Settings** tab, set your linked service to **AMLS Linked Service**. Subsequently set your **Machine Learning pipeline name** field to `Iris-Scoring-Local-Pipeline` and select the only **Machine Learning pipeline ID** that appears in the drop-down box.

6. Click **Publish All** and **Publish** to save your work.

7. Click **Move & transform** under **Activities** and drag a new Copy Data activity onto your canvas. Connect it to the end of your ADF pipeline.

8. After selecting the new activity, click **General** and rename it to `Copy Results to PC`.

9. Click **Source** and click **+New** to begin the creation of a new input data file.

10. Select **Azure Blob Storage** as your source destination and **DelimitedText** as your file format. Click **Continue**.

11. Fill out the ADF dataset creation form. Name this object `ScoringResults`. Select **AMLSDatastoreLink** as your linked service. Navigate to `Iris_Predictions.csv` in `Output_Folder` on your AML datastore. When finished, the form should match *Figure 10.16*. Click **OK**:

## Set properties

**Name**

> ScoringResults

**Linked service** *

> AMLSDatastoreLink

**Connect via integration runtime** *  ⓘ

> AutoResolveIntegrationRuntime

**File path**

> azureml-blobstore-4e7d2  /  Output_Folder  /  Iris_Predictions.csv

**First row as header** ☐

**Import schema**

⦿ From connection/store   ◯ From sample file   ◯ None

▷ Advanced

Figure 10.16 – ADF dataset creation form

12. Click **Sink** and click **+New** to begin the creation of a new output data file.

13. Select **Azure Blob Storage** as your source destination and **DelimitedText** as your file format. Click **Continue**.

14. Click **File,** select **File system**, and click **Continue**.

15. Select **DelimitedText** as your file format. Click **Continue**.

16. Fill out the ADF dataset creation form. Name this object `ScoringLocalOutput`. Select **LocalPCLink** as your linked service. Check the box for **First row as header**. Click **OK**. This will save your file in the same folder on your PC as your input data.

17. Click **Sink** and click **Open**. This will open a new tab where you can edit the destination data.

18. Edit **File path**, specifying `Iris_Scoring_Results.csv` as the filename.

19. Click **Publish All** and **Publish** to save your work.

# Adding a trigger to your ADF pipeline

The last step in creating an ADF pipeline is adding a trigger to automate pipeline runs:

1. Next, add a trigger as you did earlier in the chapter. Click **Add trigger** and select **New/Edit**.

2. Click **Choose trigger** and select **+New**.

3. Name your trigger `Monday Trigger` and set it to run once a week on Mondays at 11:00 A.M. Make sure you set your time zone to your local time zone. Click **OK** twice.

4. Click **Publish All** and **Publish** to save your work. Test your new ADF pipeline by clicking **Trigger (1)** and **Trigger Now**. Your pipeline should run successfully as shown in *Figure 10.17*:

Figure 10.17 – Successful end-to-end scoring pipeline

You have now created a fully automated AutoML scoring solution that will pull in data from your local PC every Monday at 11:00 A.M. and produce a scoring file. In a real situation, this solution would pull data from a database that gets updated on a routine basis.

This technique is applicable to any ML project; you can use custom trained models, vision models, AutoML models, or any other type of ML model. This pattern is reusable for any batch scoring scenario, and it is the most common deployment scenario across all industries. Practice it.

With an automated scoring solution in your toolkit, your final task is to craft an automated training solution. ML models, for many reasons, often need to be retrained and should be retrained when new data becomes available. By using the same techniques and patterns you used in this section, this will be an easy task.

# Automating an end-to-end training solution

Like any other ML model, once an AutoML model is deployed and runs for a few months, it can benefit from being retrained. There are many reasons for this, in order of importance:

- ML models break if the pattern between your input data and target column changes. This often happens due to extraneous factors such as changes in consumer behavior. When the pattern breaks, you need to retrain your model to retain performance.

- ML models perform better the more relevant data you feed them. Therefore, as your data grows, you should periodically retrain models.

- Retraining models on a consistent basis means that they're less likely to break if patterns change slowly over time. Consequently, it's best practice to retrain as data is acquired.

In this section, you are going to put your skills to the test. You will be given a set of instructions similar to when you created an end-to-end scoring solution. However, this time, there will be significantly less guidance. If you find yourself lost, carefully reread the instructions throughout this chapter.

## Creating a pipeline to copy data into Azure

First, you need to create an ADF pipeline to copy data from your PC into Azure:

1. Download `Iris_Training_Data_for_ADF.csv` from the GitHub repository and put it in your `Iris` folder on your PC:

   ```
   https://github.com/PacktPublishing/Automated-Machine-
   Learning-with-Microsoft-Azure/blob/master/Chapter10/Iris_
   Training_Data_for_ADF.csv
   ```

2.  Create a new ADF pipeline called `End-to-End Iris Training`.

3.  Within the pipeline, create a **Copy data** activity called `Copy Iris Training Data from PC` where you copy `Iris_Training_Data_for_ADF.csv` into `Input_Folder` on your Azure storage account.

    Refer to the `Copy Iris Data from PC` activity you created in the *Automating an end-to-end scoring solution* section.

4.  Run this pipeline once to move data into Azure.

## Editing an ML pipeline to train with new data

Next, copy and edit the `automl-training-pipeline` you created in *Chapter 9, Implementing a Batch Scoring Solution*:

1.  Open AMLS and create a new dataset called `Iris Local Training Data`.

2.  Open your Jupyter notebook called `automl-training-pipeline`. Make a copy and rename it `automl-local-training-pipeline`.

3.  Replace the `Iris Training` dataset with the `Iris Local Training Data` dataset within the ML pipeline. Run and publish the ML pipeline with the name `Iris-AutoML-Training-Local-Pipeline`.

## Adding a Machine Learning Execute Pipeline activity to your ADF pipeline

Finally, you'll add an activity to your ADF pipeline to execute the ML pipeline you just created as follows:

1.  In ADF, add a **Machine Learning Execute Pipeline** activity to your **End-to-End Iris Training** pipeline. Name this activity `Retrain Iris Model`.

2.  Add a trigger called `Tuesday Trigger` to your **End-to-End Iris Training** pipeline. Schedule this trigger to run every Tuesday at 6:00 A.M. local time.

3.  Publish your changes to save your work. Your finished pipeline should be a two-step process resembling *Figure 10.18*:

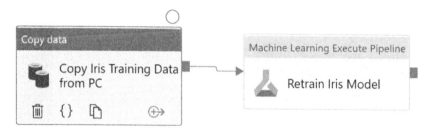

Figure 10.18 – Completed retraining pipeline

That's it! You've created a solution that will automatically retrain models on a weekly basis with new data. In the real world, this would be pulling from a database that is routinely updated instead of from your local PC.

Remember that your ML pipeline for training automatically registers models, and your ML pipeline for scoring automatically reuses the latest version of your ML model. As such, there's no need to manually update either of the pipelines from this point on.

# Summary

Automating ML solutions in an end-to-end fashion is no easy task and if you've made it this far, feel proud. Most modern data science organizations can easily train models. Very few can implement reliable, automated, end-to-end solutions as you have done in this chapter.

You should now feel confident in your ability to design end-to-end AutoML solutions. You can train models with AutoML and create ML pipelines to score data and retrain models. You can easily ingest data into Azure and transfer it out of Azure with ADF. Furthermore, you can tie everything together and create ADF pipelines that seamlessly ingest data, score data, train data, and push results to wherever you'd like. You can now create end-to-end ML solutions.

*Chapter 11*, *Implementing a Real-Time Scoring Solution*, will cement your ML knowledge by teaching you how to score data in real time using Azure Kubernetes Service within AMLS. Adding real-time scoring to your batch-scoring skillset will make you a more complete applied ML expert, able to tackle a wide variety of problems.

# 11
# Implementing a Real-Time Scoring Solution

While most **machine learning (ML)** projects involve **batch scoring**, the most complex ML projects use **real-time solutions**. Think about models that determine whether a credit card transaction is fraudulent, models that decide which ads to show online shoppers, and models that decide whether a customer at a car dealership is creditworthy or not. These situations all demand a real-time scoring solution and it's incredibly important that your model be both fast and accurate.

Luckily, creating a fast, reliable real-time scoring solution in AutoML is easy whether you decide to code it with Python or use the **Azure Machine Learning** (**AML**) Studio **graphical user interface** (**GUI**).

You will begin this chapter by creating a real-time scoring endpoint through the AML studio GUI. **Real-time scoring endpoints** are web services through which you can pass data and quickly receive results. Continuing, you will then create real-time scoring endpoints through Python code using the AzureML SDK in a Jupyter notebook. Lastly, you will learn how to improve the performance of your real-time scoring endpoints to better serve your end users.

By the end of this chapter, you will have a more complete data science skillset. Being able to train models, score models in batch, retrain models on a schedule, and score models in real time are all fundamental ML engineering skills that you will have in your repertoire. This skillset is in high demand. Moreover, you will be able to craft real-time scoring endpoints that you can embed in complex scenarios.

In this chapter, we will cover the following topics:

- Creating real-time endpoints through the UI
- Creating real-time endpoints through the SDK
- Improving performance on your AKS cluster

# Technical requirements

In this chapter, you will be creating an **Azure Kubernetes Service** (**AKS**) instance through AML studio and creating real-time scoring endpoints using the `Diabetes-AllData-Regression-AutoML` that you created in *Chapter 4, Building an AutoML Regression Solution*.

As such, you will need a working internet connection, an **Azure Machine Learning Service** (**AMLS**) workspace, and a compute instance. You will also need permission to create an AKS cluster. If you are using a personal account, this will not be an issue.

The following are the prerequisites for the chapter:

- Have access to the internet
- Have a web browser, preferably Google Chrome or Microsoft Edge Chromium
- Have a Microsoft Azure account
- Have created an AMLS workspace
- Have created the `compute-cluster` compute cluster in *Chapter 2, Getting Started with Azure Machine Learning Service*
- Understand how to navigate to the Jupyter environment from an Azure compute instance as demonstrated in *Chapter 4, Building an AutoML Regression Solution*
- Have trained and registered the `Diabetes-AllData-Regression-AutoML` ML model in *Chapter 4, Building an AutoML Regression Solution*

The code for this chapter is available here: `https://github.com/PacktPublishing/Automated-Machine-Learning-with-Microsoft-Azure/tree/master/Chapter11`.

# Creating real-time endpoints through the UI

The crux of any real-time scoring solution is a real-time scoring endpoint, a web URL through which you can pass data and immediately retrieve ML predictions. Endpoints are hosted on containerized services that are up and running 24 hours a day, 7 days a week, waiting for incoming requests.

**Requests** send data to the endpoint for scoring and can be written in any computer language including Python. As soon as a request comes through, your endpoint will automatically execute the underlying code and return results.

You can use these endpoints anywhere; any coding language from C# to Python to Java can make use of real-time scoring endpoints. Thus, once you obtain the URL that hosts the endpoint, you are free to implement it in any other piece of code. Commonly, real-time scoring endpoints are incorporated in streaming jobs, web applications, and mobile apps.

When using real-time scoring endpoints based on AutoML models, there are a few key points to keep in mind that make them quite different from the batch scoring pipelines you created in *Chapter 9, Implementing a Batch Scoring Solution*. They are as follows:

- First, when passing data into an endpoint that's scoring data using an AutoML-trained model, you must pass input data in a JSON format, the most common format for sending data through an endpoint. Pandas dataframes or any format other than JSON will fail.

- Second, you do not have to write a Python script for scoring AutoML-trained models. Azure AutoML automatically generates one for you. Because of this, the data you pass into the endpoint must be in the proper shape needed to score. You cannot do data preprocessing within your endpoint itself unless you want to alter the underlying scripts generated by AutoML.

There are two main services that AMLS uses to host endpoints, **Azure Container Instances** (**ACI**) and AKS. Both are containerized and use Docker. Both can be created either using the GUI within AML studio or using the Python SDK through a Jupyter notebook. ACI is lightweight, cheap, and used largely for testing. AKS is powerful, expensive, and used for production.

> **Important note**
> A key difference between ACI and AKS is authentication. ACI supports **key-based authentication** only whereas AKS supports both key-based and **token-based authentication**.

In this section, you will use the AML studio GUI to create an endpoint using the `Diabetes-AllData-Regression-AutoML` ML model you built in *Chapter 4, Building an AutoML Regression Solution*, hosted on ACI. Then, you will create an **AKS cluster** through the UI; an AKS cluster is a group of **virtual machines** (**VMs**) that run 24/7 to host your endpoints. You will wrap up this section by creating an endpoint hosted on your AKS cluster.

Overall, the goal of this section is to introduce you to endpoints and show how you can easily create them with AutoML trained models in just a few clicks.

## Creating an ACI-hosted endpoint through the UI

First, create an Azure container instance using the AI using the following steps:

1.  Open up your AML studio by navigating to `https://ml.azure.com/`.

2.  Click on **Models** on the left-hand panel under **Assets**.

3.  You will see a list of all of the ML models you have trained on this AMLS workspace. Click the blue link to `Diabetes-AllData-Regression-AutoML`.

4.  Click the blue link under **Run ID** to take you to the experiment used to train your model. It should begin with `AutoML_` followed by a GUID, a unique string of characters.

5.  Click **Deploy** near the top of your screen.

6.  Give your endpoint the name `diabetes-aci-gui`. Endpoint names may only consist of lowercase letters, numbers, and dashes.

7.  Select **Azure Container Instance** for **Compute type**.

8. After confirming that your settings match the following screenshot, click **Deploy**:

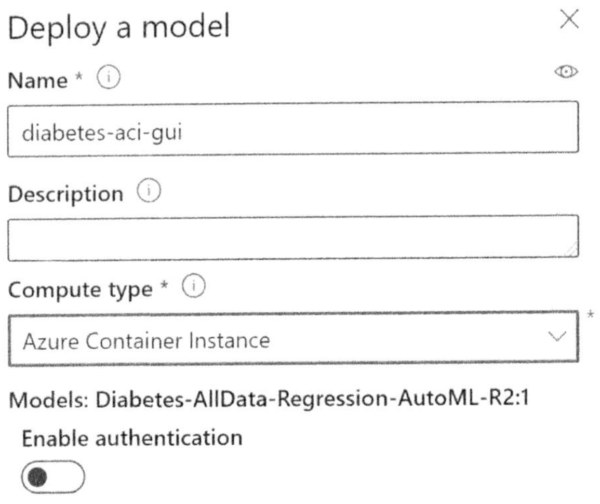

Deploy a model                                    ✕

Name * ⓘ                                          ◎

diabetes-aci-gui

Description ⓘ

Compute type * ⓘ

Azure Container Instance                    ⌄   *

Models: Diabetes-AllData-Regression-AutoML-R2:1

Enable authentication

⬤⃝

Figure 11.1 – ACI settings

9. Your model will take a few minutes to deploy. After waiting a sufficient amount of time, click **Endpoints** on the left-hand panel under **Assets**.

> **Important note**
>
> The first time you create an endpoint in either ACI or AKS, AMLS will create a container registry to host them. Do not, under any circumstances, delete this registry as you will be unable to deploy endpoints from that point on.

10. Click the blue link to `diabetes-aci-gui`.

11. Click **Consume** near the top of your screen.

12. Copy the `REST` endpoint URL into a text editor such as Notepad. Notice that there is also code to use the model in C#, Python, and R. You have now created a functioning scoring endpoint hosted on ACI.

With an ACI built, you now have a working endpoint that you can use to score new data. ACI is great for testing purposes, but to create a production-ready solution, you need AKS.

# Creating an AKS cluster through the UI

Before you can host an endpoint on AKS, you first need to build an AKS cluster. Follow these steps to create one using the GUI:

1. Click **Compute** on the left-hand panel under **Manage**.

2. Click **Inference clusters** near the top of your screen.

3. Click **Create**.

4. Select **North Central US** for **Location** or whatever Azure location your AMLS workspace is located in.

5. Use the search box on the right-hand side to search for `Standard_DS3_v2`.

6. Select `Standard_DS3_v2` for your VM and click **Next**.

7. Give your AKS cluster a name. Call it `aks-amls-cluster`. It can only be 16 characters long.

8. Select **Dev/test** for **Cluster purpose**.

9. Set **Number of nodes** to 3.

> **Important note**
>
> When creating an AKS cluster, ensure that the number of cores on your VM type multiplied by the number of nodes is equal to or greater than 12. `Standard_DS3_v2` VMs have 4 cores each, thus we set the number of nodes to 4. This is a minimum requirement.

10. Once you compare your settings to the following screenshot and ensure they match, click **Create**:

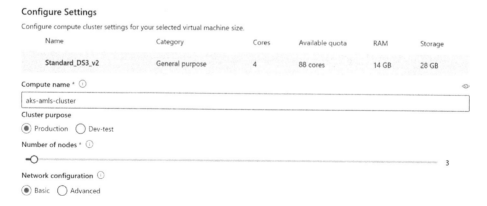

Figure 11.2 – AKS cluster settings

You have now successfully created an AKS cluster. You can use this cluster to host a large number of ML models. While ACI is suitable only for running models up to 1 GB in size, you can use AKS clusters to host much larger models. Next, you will create an endpoint on this cluster.

## Creating an AKS-hosted endpoint through the UI

In order to create a real-time scoring endpoint hosted on AKS, you need to follow nearly the exact same steps that you used to create one hosted on ACI. Begin with the following:

1.  Open up your AML studio by navigating to `https://ml.azure.com/`.

2.  Click on **Models** on the left-hand panel under **Assets**.

3.  You will see a list of all of the ML models you have trained on this AMLS workspace. Click the blue link to open `Diabetes-AllData-Regression-AutoML`.

4.  Click the blue link under **Run ID** to take you to the experiment used to train your model. The run ID of your experiment will begin with `AutoML_` followed by a GUID, a unique string of characters.

5.  Click **Deploy** near the top of your screen.

6.  Give your endpoint the name `diabetes-aks-gui`. Endpoint names may only consist of lowercase letters, numbers, and dashes.

7.  Select **Azure Kubernetes Service** for **Compute type**.

8.  Switch **Enable Authentication** on.

9.  Select **Key-based authentication** for **Type**.

10. After confirming that your settings match with the following screenshot, click **Deploy**:

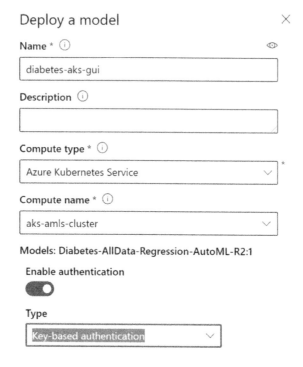

Figure 11.3 – AKS settings

11. Your model will take a few minutes to deploy, the same as your ACI-hosted model. Once it's ready, click **Endpoints** on the left-hand panel under **Assets**.

12. Click the blue link to open `diabetes-aks-gui`.

13. Click **Consume** near the top of your screen.

14. Copy the REST endpoint URL into a text editor such as Notepad. Also, copy one of the keys. You can use either the primary key or the secondary key. Either will work for authentication.

Via this section, you have now created two real-time scoring endpoints, one hosted in ACI and the other in AKS. You have also created an AKS cluster to host your endpoints and assigned key-based authentication to secure your AKS-hosted endpoint. Through AML studio, by clicking **Consume**, you can also easily find code to deploy your endpoint in C#, Python, and R.

In the next section, you will do the same thing with code. Additionally, you will also test your endpoints to see how they work.

# Creating real-time endpoints through the SDK

One-click deployment through AML studio is really easy, but most organizations will require you to develop your solutions via code. Luckily, creating real-time scoring endpoints for AutoML models via the AzureML Python SDK is almost as easy as creating them through the UI. Furthermore, you'll gain a deeper understanding of how your endpoints work and how to format your JSON testing to pass data into the endpoint as a request.

In this section, you'll begin by entering your Jupyter environment and creating a new notebook. First, you will deploy your `Diabetes-AllData-Regression-AutoML` model via ACI, test it, and, once you've confirmed that your test is a success, create a new AKS cluster via code and deploy it there. You will conclude this section by testing your AKS deployment and confirm that everything works as expected.

The goal of this section is to further your understanding of real-time scoring endpoints, teach you how to create everything in code, and enable you to craft and test complex real-time solutions.

## Creating and testing a real-time endpoint with ACI through Python

Anytime you intend to deploy a ML model in real time, you should begin by deploying your model to ACI and testing it. This way, you can get an idea of how your data needs to be formatted, how long your endpoint will take to respond with a score, and whether your model works. Begin by creating an endpoint.

### Creating a real-time scoring endpoint hosted on ACI

Much like previous chapters, you first need to open a Jupyter notebook on your compute instance. Then, build a real-time scoring endpoint with the following steps:

1. Open up your AML studio by navigating to `https://ml.azure.com/`.

2. Click **Compute**, start up a compute instance, and open a Jupyter environment.

3. Create a new Jupyter notebook and name it `real-time-endpoints`. If you need a refresher, please review *Chapter 4*, *Building an AutoML Regression Solution*.

4. Import your standard Azure libraries with the following code:

```
from azureml.core import Workspace, Dataset, Datastore
from azureml.core import Experiment, Environment, Model
from azureml.core.compute import ComputeTarget,
AksCompute
```

All of these packages should be familiar to you by now except `AksCompute`. If you need a refresher, consult *Chapter 4*, *Building an AutoML Regression Solution*, for `Workspace`, `Dataset`, `Datastore`, `Experiment`, and `ComputeTarget`, and *Chapter 9*, *Implementing a Batch Scoring Solution*, for `Environment` and `Model`. `AksCompute` allows you to create an AKS cluster via code.

5. Import your Azure libraries specific to creating an endpoint with ACI with the following code:

```
from azureml.core.model import InferenceConfig
from azureml.core.webservice import AciWebservice
from azureml.core.webservice import AksWebservice

from azureml.train.automl.run import AutoMLRun
```

`InferenceConfig` lets you specify the Python script and environment you will use to create your endpoint deployment. This package is used with both AKS and ACI-based deployments.

`AciWebservice` is what you use to actually create endpoints deployed on ACI and `AksWebservice` is what you use to create endpoints deployed on AKS. `AutoMLRun` will let you access previous AutoML training runs. You will need to recover the Python script created when you trained your model.

> **Important tip**
> If you are having trouble loading Azure libraries, update the AzureML SDK by running the `Update AzureML SDK.ipynb` notebook, found here: `https://github.com/PacktPublishing/Automated-Machine-Learning-with-Microsoft-Azure/blob/master/Update-AzureML-SDK.ipynb`.

6. Import the non-Azure libraries with the following code:

```
import pandas as pd
import numpy as np
import random as r
import requests
import json
import os
```

You are already familiar with `pandas`, `numpy`, `os`, and `random`. If you need a refresher, please consult *Chapter 4, Building an AutoML Regression Solution*, or *Chapter 9, Implementing a Batch Scoring Solution*, for `os` and `random`.

Onto the new packages, `requests` lets you make web requests to your deployed endpoints. This package will let you test your deployment and score data using your endpoint, while `json` lets you transform your data into the JSON format used by web requests.

7. Connect your Jupyter notebook to your AMLS workspace with the following code:

```
ws = Workspace.from_config()
```

If you are prompted to log in, follow the instructions.

8. Set your datastore to the default with the first line of code. If you want to use a different datastore, use the second and third lines of code instead, replacing `workspaceblobstore`:

```
datastore = Datastore.get_default(ws)
my_datastore_name = 'workspaceblobstore'
my_datastore = Datastore.get(ws, my_datastore_name)
```

9. Set your compute cluster to the one you created in *Chapter 2, Getting Started with Azure Machine Learning Service*, with the following code:

```
compute_name = 'compute-cluster'
compute_target = ComputeTarget(ws, compute_name)
```

10. Set your environment to `AzureML-AutoML` with the following code:

```
environment = Environment.get(ws, 'AzureML-AutoML')
```

`AzureML-AutoML` is a standard environment that comes with the AzureML SDK. You can use this environment for any real-time AutoML deployment.

> **Tip**
> There are many different standard environments that come with the AzureML SDK. You can access a list of them by using the `Environment.list` function.

11. Set your `Diabetes-AllData-Regression-AutoML` model with the following code:

```
model = Model(ws, 'Diabetes-AllData-Regression-AutoML')
```

This is the model you will deploy to an endpoint to score diabetes data in real time.

12. Navigate to your AML studio and click **Models** on the left-hand panel. You need to retrieve the experiment and run the ID associated with your model.

13. Click the blue link to open `Diabetes-AllData-Regression-AutoML`.

14. Copy **Experiment name** and **Run ID** to a text editor such as Notepad. The name of your experiment should be `Diabetes-Sample-Regression` if you followed the instructions word for word in *Chapter 4, Building an AutoML Regression Solution*.

15. Set your experiment and run ID with the following code:

```
experiment = Experiment(ws, 'Diabetes-Sample-Regression')
runID = 'AutoML_your_run_ID'
```

16. Retrieve your AutoML run with the following code:

```
run = AutoMLRun(experiment, runID)
```

The reason you are retrieving your old run is so you can pull the Python script out of it that was used to deploy the models. This is the same script that was used to deploy your models using the GUI.

> **Important tip**
> You can always retrieve old model runs using this code. This is important if you forgot to register models. You can similarly retrieve old ML pipeline runs.

17. Extract the best model fitted by AutoML with the following code:

```
best_run, fitted_model = run.get_output()
```

This code retrieves two objects, the best run as well as the model. You will only use the best run, but `get_output()` requires you to pass two objects or the function will return an error.

18. Make a folder to hold all of your real-time scripts with the following code:

```
os.makedirs('Real_Time_Scripts', exist_ok=True)
```

19. Retrieve the Python script you will use for scoring data in real time with the following code:

```
script_path =\
'Real_Time_Scripts/Diabetes_Inference.py'
best_run.download_file('outputs/scoring_file_v_1_0_0.py',
script_path)
```

When AutoML trains a model, it outputs a scoring file for real-time inferencing. This file is always called `scoring_file_v_1_0_0.py` and is located in the `outputs` folder. This code grabs that file and saves it as `Diabetes_Inference.py`.

20. Set a variable to name your ACI deployment:

```
aci_service_name = 'diabetes-scoring-aci'
```

21. Configure your endpoint to use your Python script and `Azure-AutoML` environment with the following code:

```
inference_config =\
InferenceConfig(entry_script=script_path,\
environment = environment)
```

22. Configure your ACI deployment with the following code:

```
aci_config =\
AciWebservice.deploy_configuration(\
cpu_cores = 1, memory_gb = 1,\
tags = {'Project': 'Diabetes'},\
description = 'Diabetes Real-Time ACI Deployment')
```

Notice you need to set the number of cores to use for the deployment as well as the amount of memory to reserve. You can also set tags and add a description.

23. Create your ACI endpoint with the following code:

```
aci_service =\
Model.deploy(ws, aci_service_name,\
[model], inference_config, aci_config,overwrite=True)\
aci_service.wait_for_deployment(True)
```

This code requires you to pass your AMLS workspace, the name of your ACI deployment, your ML model, your endpoint (inference) configuration, your ACI configuration, and to set an `overwrite` flag to `True` or `False`. Your endpoint should take between 5 and 10 minutes to deploy.

## Testing your real-time scoring endpoint

Now that you have created a real-time scoring endpoint on ACI, it's time to test it. First, you'll need to create some data to test it with, then you need to convert it to JSON and pass it into the endpoint with the following steps:

1.  To create some random `Diabetes` data, first, create a range of possible values for each variable using the minimum and maximum values from the `Diabetes` sample dataset you created in *Chapter 2, Getting Started with Azure Machine Learning Service*, with the following code:

    ```
    AGE_range = np.arange(19,79,1)
    SEX_range = np.arange(1,2,1)
    BMI_range = np.arange(18.0,42.2,0.1)
    BP_range = np.arange(62, 133, 1)
    S1_range = np.arange(97, 301, 1)
    S2_range = np.arange(41.6, 242.4, 0.1)
    S3_range = np.arange(22, 99, 1)
    S4_range = np.arange(2, 9.09, 0.01)
    S5_range = np.arange(3.258, 6.107, 0.001)
    S6_range = np.arange(58, 124, 1)
    ```

2.  Create an empty list to help generate the sample data. This is similar to the method you used to create sample `Iris` data in *Chapter 9, Implementing a Batch Scoring Solution*. Also, create an empty pandas dataframe and assign columns to it with the following code:

    ```
    DiabetesList = []
    columns =\
    ['AGE', 'SEX', 'BMI', 'BP', 'S1', 'S2', 'S3', 'S4', 'S5',
    'S6']
    DiabetesDF = pd.DataFrame(columns=columns)
    ```

3.  Use the following code to create sample diabetes data using a `for` loop:

```
for i in range(0,5):
    values = [r.choice(AGE_range),\
r.choice(SEX_range),r.choice(BMI_range),\
r.choice(BP_range), r.choice(S1_range),\
r.choice(S2_range), r.choice(S3_range),\
r.choice(S4_range), r.choice(S5_range),\
r.choice(S6_range)]
    DiabetesDict = pd.DataFrame(dict(zip(columns,
values)), index=[0])
    DiabetesList.append(DiabetesDict)
DiabetesDF = DiabetesDF.append(DiabetesList,True)
```

This code is identical to the code you used to create `Iris` data. Please refer to *Chapter 9, Implementing a Batch Scoring Solution*, for a detailed explanation.

4.  Register your sample data with the name `Diabetes Scoring` with the following code:

```
Dataset.Tabular.register_pandas_dataframe(\
DiabetesDF, datastore, 'Diabetes Scoring')
```

This will write the underlying data to your default datastore and register it as a dataset called `Diabetes Scoring`.

5.  Convert `DiabetesDF` into a JSON object beginning with `{"data":` and ending with `}`. Every AutoML real-time deployment requires data in this format:

```
test = '{"data":' +\
DiabetesDF.to_json(orient='records') + '}'
```

---

**Important tip**

When creating a JSON file, always set `orient` to `records`. Any other JSON format risks errors.

---

6.  View your data to understand what your incoming data should look like:

```
Test
```

Your data should resemble *Figure 11.4*, although the values will be different based on your data. The key point is that the JSON values need to be in a key-value pair to guarantee a correct prediction:

'{"data":[{"AGE":68,"SEX":1,"BMI":41.3,"BP":119,"S1":145,"S2":65.7,"S3":27,"S4":8.51,"S5":4.823,"S6":94},{"AGE":59,"SEX":1,"BMI":32.1,"BP":104,"S1":104,"S2":187.6,"S3":97,"S4":6.87,"S5":3.438,"S6":120},{"AGE":64,"SEX":1,"BMI":30.4,"BP":67,"S1":220,"S2":169.0,"S3":86,"S4":4.79,"S5":5.704,"S6":86},{"AGE":57,"SEX":1,"BMI":32.3,"BP":113,"S1":290,"S2":116.5,"S3":58,"S4":5.35,"S5":3.872,"S6":101},{"AGE":36,"SEX":1,"BMI":26.5,"BP":131,"S1":131,"S2":122.5,"S3":57,"S4":6.9,"S5":5.634,"S6":111}]}'

Figure 11.4 – JSON format

7. Navigate to your AML studio front page and click **Endpoints**.

8. Click the blue link to `diabetes-scoring-aci` and click **Consume**. Copy the URL that links to your endpoint and paste it in a text editor such as Notepad.

9. Going back to your code, set the URL and headers as variables:

```
aci_url = 'your-aci-endpoint-url'
headers = {'Content-Type': 'application/json'}
```

While you need to enter your URL, the headers will be the same for every deployment.

10. Test your ACI deployment with the following code:

```
response =\
requests.post(aci_url, test, headers=headers)
print(resp.text)
```

You have now coded a real-time scoring endpoint hosted on ACI and have successfully tested it. Additionally, you understand how your data needs to be shaped and formatted in JSON in order to be scored. Once you have confirmed that your real-time endpoint is working in ACI, the next step is to create an AKS cluster and deploy the production version there as you will do next.

# Creating an AKS cluster through Python

Creating an AKS cluster through code is just as easy and straightforward as creating it through the GUI. Many organizations require all infrastructure to be created as code, and you can use the following steps as a template:

1. Continuing in your Jupyter notebook, set variables for your VM size, the number of nodes required, your AKS cluster location, and your AKS cluster name:

```
aks_cluster_name = 'aks-code-cluster'
vm_type = 'Standard_DS3_v2'
```

```
node_count = 3
AKS_location = 'northcentralus'
```

2. Set your AKS cluster configurations with the following code:

```
prov_config =\
AksCompute.provisioning_configuration(vm_size =\
vm_type, agent_count = node_count, location =\
AKS_location)
```

When setting your configurations, keep in mind that your node count multiplied by the number of cores on each VM must be greater than or equal to 12. Also, think about where the incoming data will be coming from when setting your Azure location.

3. Create your AKS cluster with the following code:

```
aks_target =\
ComputeTarget.create(workspace = ws, name =\
aks_cluster_name, provisioning_configuration =\
prov_config)
aks_target.wait_for_completion(show_output = True)
```

You have to pass in your AMLS workspace, AKS cluster name, and AKS cluster provisioning configurations. It should take about 5-10 minutes to spin up your cluster.

You have just created an AKS cluster via code. Once it is up and running, you can deploy your scoring endpoint to your AKS cluster and test it using many of the same variables you have already created. For this reason, it's recommended that you create both the ACI and AKS endpoint in the same Jupyter notebook. It will save you a lot of work copying over code.

# Creating and testing a real-time endpoint with AKS through Python

Your last task in this section is to deploy your real-time scoring endpoint to your AKS cluster, grab the URL and access key, and test your deployment. There are only a few steps, as you have already created most of the code when deploying to ACI.

At the end of this chapter, remember to delete your AKS endpoints and cluster as they can be quite expensive and rack up a bill. Within the same Jupyter notebook, continue with the following steps:

1.  Set your target AKS cluster with the following code:

```
aks_cluster = AksCompute(ws, 'aks-code-cluster')
```

2.  Set a variable for the name of your AKS deployment:

```
aks_service_name = 'diabetes-scoring-aks'
```

3.  Configure your AKS deployment with the following code:

```
aks_config =\
AksWebservice.deploy_configuration(cpu_cores = 1,\
                    memory_gb = 1, tags = {'Project':\
                    'Diabetes'}, description =\
                    'Diabetes Real-Time ACI Deployment')
```

    Notice that these configurations are identical to those used for your ACI deployment.

4.  Create your AKS endpoint with the following code:

```
aks_service =\
Model.deploy(ws, aks_service_name, [model],\
inference_config, aks_config, aks_cluster,\
overwrite=True)
aks_service.wait_for_deployment(show_output = True)
```

    Notice that this code is nearly identical to the code you used to create the ACI deployment; the one difference is that you also must pass in the AKS cluster. This is because AKS is hosted on a cluster of VMs that you manage, whereas ACI is a serverless container service.

5.  Navigate to your AML studio front page and click **Endpoints**.

6.  Click the blue link to open `diabetes-scoring-aks` and click **Consume**. Copy the URL that links to your endpoint and paste it in a text editor such as Notepad. Do the same thing for your access key, using either the primary or secondary key. Either will work.

7. Going back to your code, set your URL, key, and headers as variables:

```
aks_url = 'your-aks-endpoint-url'
key = 'your-aks-key'
headers = {'Content-Type': 'application/json'}
headers['Authorization'] = f'Bearer {key}'
```

Here, you need to add in one additional header for authorization. **Bearer functions** work by granting access to anyone who provides the correct key.

> **Important tip**
>
> In a production setting, make sure you store all of your keys in **Azure Key Vault** and do not expose your passwords and keys in open code. This is a best practice that will protect you.

8. Test your AKS deployment with the following code:

```
resp = requests.post(aks_url, test, headers=headers)
print(resp.text)
```

You should see the same results as your ACI test as they use the same input data. Make sure the output matches and you can call your test a success.

You have now learned everything you need to learn in order to successfully create a real-time scoring endpoint in Azure. These endpoints can be used anywhere in any other piece of code. Make sure that any data that gets pushed into the endpoint is in the correct JSON format and your projects will be successful.

The last part of this chapter deals with optimizing the performance of your AKS clusters. There is some fine-tuning involved that can greatly enhance the response time of your scoring solution.

# Improving performance on your AKS cluster

Sometimes you will deploy an endpoint on AKS and it doesn't perform how you'd like. Maybe it times out, maybe it's too slow, maybe an endpoint that was previously working fine suddenly gets a lot more traffic that it cannot handle. These situations happen, and you must be prepared to face them.

Thankfully, AKS deployments have a lot of additional configurations that you can take advantage of to solve these problems. This section covers some of the more common situations as follows:

- Depending on how complex your model is, how many data points you are trying to score, and the size of your VMs, AKS models can sometimes take a while to score or even timeout. In this situation, there are many things you can do.

  First, you can try increasing the size of your VM, selecting one with more RAM. Next, you can add an additional setting to your deployment configuration, `scoring_timeout_ms`. This setting defaults to `60000` milliseconds, or 1 minute. You can adjust it to a maximum of `300000` milliseconds, or 5 minutes. Sometimes, adjusting `memory_gb` or upping the number of `cpu_cores` can help too.

- Check the size of your model using AML studio. You can do this by clicking **Models**, selecting your model, and clicking **Artifacts**. There, you will find a pickle file containing your model. If it's quite large, try increasing the `memory_gb` setting on your deployment configurations.

- In the case where your endpoint is suddenly encountering surges in traffic that it cannot handle, try turning on autoscaling and increasing its ability to scale. **AKS autoscaling** creates replicas of your application, scaling out horizontally. Autoscale is on by default, but you can explicitly set `autoscale_enabled` to `True` in your deployment configurations.

  You can also manually adjust the minimum and maximum number of replicas autoscaling will create using `autoscale_min_replicas` and `autoscale_max_replicas`. These default to `1` and `10`, respectively. Try upping both of these to increase performance in the case of heavy traffic.

Armed with this information, you can easily create powerful AKS deployments that meet your business and performance requirements. When traffic is heavy, up the autoscaling. When your application times out, adjust the timeout setting. When your AKS endpoint runs slowly, try using a larger VM or adjusting the memory settings. Above all, always test your deployment in ACI before deploying it in AKS, and make sure that input data is coming in the correct JSON format in key-value pairs.

# Summary

You have now created and tested real-time scoring solutions using an AutoML trained model. Deploying first on ACI and then on AKS, you understand the full end-to-end process of creating a real-time scoring endpoint.

Furthermore, you understand how data must be shaped and formatted in order to generate predictions using these endpoints, which can be incorporated into any piece of code using a wide variety of computer languages to create powerful, innovative solutions.

In the next chapter, *Chapter 12, Realizing Business Value with AutoML*, the final chapter of the book, you will learn how to present AutoML solutions in a way that will gain the trust of your non-technical business partners. Their trust and acceptance, after all, is the foundation to unlocking the power and value of ML and artificial intelligence in your organization.

# 12
# Realizing Business Value with AutoML

You have acquired a wide variety of technical skills throughout this book. You're now able to train regression, classification, and forecasting models with AutoML. You can code AutoML solutions in Python using Jupyter notebooks, you know how to navigate **Azure Machine Learning Studio**, and you can even integrate machine learning pipelines in **Azure Data Factory** (**ADF**). Yet, technical skills alone will not guarantee the success of your projects. In order to realize business value, you have to gain the trust and acceptance of your end users.

In this chapter, you will begin by learning how to present end-to-end architectures in a way that makes it easy for end users to understand. Then, you will learn which visualizations and metrics to use to show off your model's performance, after which you will learn how to visualize and interpret AutoML's built-in explainability function.

You will also explore options to run AutoML outside of **Azure Machine Learning Service** (**AMLS**) and end the chapter with a section on gaining end user trust by aligning your message with the type of solution you are providing.

By the end of this chapter, you will be primed for success. You will have gained some of the soft skills necessary to communicate your solution to end users, increasing the likelihood that your end-to-end solution is adopted and used by your organization. Failing to gain end user trust is a major reason why data science projects fail, and by following the guidelines in this chapter, you will be much more successful at creating excitement for your solution.

In this chapter, we will cover the following topics:

- Architecting AutoML solutions
- Visualizing AutoML modeling results
- Explaining AutoML results to your business
- Using AutoML in other Microsoft products
- Realizing business value

# Technical requirements

In this chapter, you will use models that you created in previous chapters to retrieve graphs, charts, and metrics. As such, you will need a working internet connection, an Azure account, and an AMLS workspace. You will also need to complete the exercises in *Chapter 4, Building an AutoML Regression Solution*, and *Chapter 5, Building an AutoML Classification Solution*.

The following are the prerequisites for the chapter:

- Access to the internet.
- A web browser, preferably Google Chrome or Microsoft Edge Chromium.
- A Microsoft Azure account.
- An AMLS workspace.

- You need to have trained and registered the `Diabetes-AllData-Regression-AutoML` machine learning model in *Chapter 4, Building an AutoML Regression Solution.*

- You need to have trained and registered the `Iris-Multi-Classification` machine learning model in *Chapter 5, Building an AutoML Classification Solution.*

There is no new code for this chapter.

# Architecting AutoML solutions

**Architecting AutoML** solutions refers to drawing end-to-end diagrams. These act as blueprints for how you should build out your solution, and also can be used to explain to your end users how everything works. While many IT solutions are complex and can take many forms, AutoML-based solutions follow standard patterns that require you to make a few important decisions.

In this section, you'll first learn what decisions to make before architecting a decision. Then, you will learn how to architect an end-to-end batch scoring solution and an end-to-end real-time scoring solution that's easy to explain to end users. Although the architecture may be simplified, the more standard it is, the easier it is to implement, explain, and understand.

## Making key architectural decisions for AutoML solutions

When drawing an architectural diagram, there are several key considerations you need to make, the most important being whether you need to make a batch or real-time solution. Batch solutions have very different requirements than real-time solutions and mostly follow a template involving AMLS and ADF. Real-time solutions, on the other hand, are more customizable.

First, we'll examine key questions to ask for batch solutions as they're easier to understand. You only need to worry about where your data comes from, how often your solution should score new data, when should you retrain models, and how your end users will receive results. That's it.

There is also the question of how you should orchestrate your various **machine learning** (**ML**) pipelines as you schedule them in either AMLS or ADF. ADF is generally the best choice since you can use it to move data in and out of Azure easily. The following table provides a summary of key questions and answers for architecting a batch solution:

| Key questions to ask | Common answers to key questions |
|---|---|
| Where is my input data coming from? | On-premise database, cloud database |
| How often should my solution score? | On certain days at certain times |
| How do end users access results? | Report generated by an on-premise database |
| When should I retrain my model? | Once a month as new data becomes available |
| How should I orchestrate my solution? | Azure Data Factory |

Figure 12.1 – Key considerations for batch solutions

Real-time solutions, on the other hand, are much more complicated. You still have to ask where your input data is coming from and how often you should retrain your AutoML model. Additionally, you should figure out where your endpoint will score data. This can be exceptionally complicated, as you use your endpoint nearly anywhere. Most commonly, this will be some sort of web application or serverless piece of code.

Lastly, you need to figure out how many requests will your endpoint have to serve at once, how fast of a response your end users require, and what size your **Azure Kubernetes Service** (**AKS**) cluster should be to accommodate demand for your solution. The following table provides a summary of key questions and answers for architecting a real-time solution:

| Key questions to ask | Common answers to key questions |
|---|---|
| Where is my input data coming from? | On-premise database, cloud database |
| How often should I retrain my model? | Whenever model performance degrades |
| Where is my endpoint located? | A user-facing web app, an Azure function |
| How many requests are coming in at once? | A maximum of 100 requests per minute |
| How fast do end users expect a response? | Within 10 seconds of submitting a request |
| How large should my AKS cluster be? | Large VM size for faster performance |

Figure 12.2 – Key considerations for real-time solutions

Once you've asked and answered these questions, you're ready to start building out an architectural diagram. First, you'll learn a common pattern for batch solutions.

# Architecting a batch solution

AutoML batch solutions are fairly easy to build once you have answered where your input data is coming from and where you will land your results. They always follow roughly the same pattern. First, you will ingest data from both on-premises and cloud sources through ADF and land the data in an **Azure Data Lake Storage Gen 2 (ADLS Gen 2)** storage account. This makes your data accessible to AMLS.

Once it's in the data lake, you use AutoML in AMLS to train and register an ML model. Your next step is to take that model and use it to create both a scoring pipeline and a training pipeline. You then orchestrate both ML pipelines through ADF, deciding on one schedule for your scoring pipeline and another schedule for your training pipeline.

Training pipelines automatically register a new version of your model in AMLS, but you need to decide where to land the final output of your scoring pipeline. Natively, scoring pipelines are designed to land data in ADLS Gen 2. Once it's there, you should set up an ADF copy activity to move data from the data lake to its final destination. The full end-to-end architecture is presented in the following diagram:

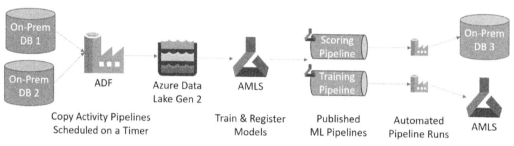

Figure 12.3– Common batch architecture

Make similar diagrams for every batch AutoML solution you make, and reuse them as often as needed. Following a template architecture will make you and your team more productive over time.

Next, you'll learn a common architecture for real-time solutions. Take careful note of the similarities and differences. While the beginning is identical to batch architecture, the end is quite different.

## Architecting a real-time solution

Real-time solution architectures require more careful consideration. How will your end users interact with your endpoint, if at all? Are you designing a web app where users score data whenever they want? Do you have a streaming system sending thousands of signals into your endpoint at once? Once you have these questions answered, you can fully flesh out the architecture.

As for batch solutions, the first step involves ingesting data with ADF into ADLS Gen 2 and training and registering AutoML models using AMLS. That part is identical. Once your model is trained, you need to create a real-time scoring endpoint and an ML training pipeline. You'll schedule the retraining in ADF as usual to update your model on some sort of cadence.

You also need to decide where your endpoint will live. In this architecture, it sits on a user-facing web application. Users can pass data into the web app at any time during the day, at which point the results will be displayed on the screen and also immediately sent to ADLS Gen 2. The following diagram displays the full end-to-end architecture:

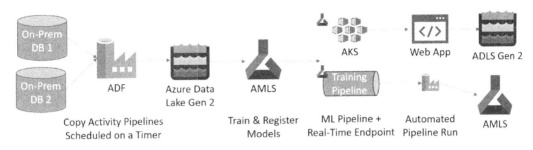

Figure 12.4 – Common real-time architecture

Presenting architectures to your end users is a key part of gaining acceptance for your solution. End users need to understand, in a general way, how everything connects and works. After presenting your architecture, you should then focus on presenting the results of your AutoML model. Teaching users how all the pieces fit together is just an introduction. Displaying your model's results in a way that end users can understand will go a long way in getting them to champion your solution.

# Visualizing AutoML modeling results

Presenting the results of your AutoML model to your business is integral to the adoption of your solution. After all, your end users are unlikely to adopt your solution unless they can be sure that it meets certain standards of performance. There are many ways of presenting the results of ML models; the most effective way of presenting your results is through visualizations.

Thankfully, AutoML runs provide automatic visualizations for results of regression, classification, and forecasting. Regression and forecasting share identical visualizations, while classification is quite different. In each case, you only want to share a single visualization with your end user; multiple views of the same results are likely to only cause confusion.

In this section, you'll first uncover what to show your end user for classification before moving onto regression and forecasting.

# Visualizing the results of classification

Confusion matrices, as shown in *Chapter 5, Building an AutoML Classification Solution,* are the key to presenting results from AutoML classification training runs. Ultimately, what end users usually care about is how accurate your model is, and whether there is a tendency toward false positives or false negatives. In order to get this information, follow these steps:

1. Navigate to AML studio at `https://ml.azure.com`.

2. Click **Experiments** under **Assets** on the left-hand panel.

3. Click the blue link to `Iris-Multi-Classification`. This is the experiment you used to train a classification model in *Chapter 5, Building an AutoML Classification Solution*.

4. Click the blue link to your latest run. This link is found under **Run ID** and begins with `AutoML_` followed by a unique identifier string. If there are multiple runs, use your latest.

5. Click **Models** near the top of your screen.

6. Click the blue link to the name of your highest-performing model under **Algorithm name**. It is likely either **StackEnsemble** or **VotingEnsemble**. You will know it's your highest-performing model because it will be the only one with the **View explanation** link.

7. Click **Metrics** near the top of your screen.

8. Check the boxes for **accuracy** and **confusion_matrix**.

9. On the confusion matrix, click the drop-down box and select **Normalized**. You should see a chart similar to the one in the following figure:

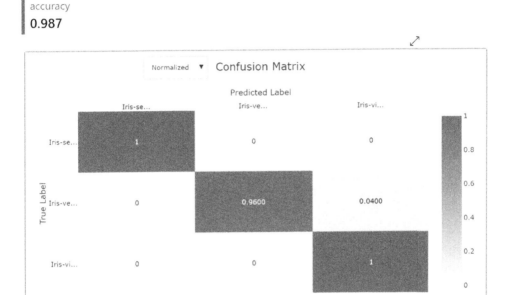

Figure 12.5 – Classification results for your business users

This chart contains all of the information your end users are looking for. First, the model is 98.7% accurate. Next, it always identifies *Iris-setosa* and *Iris-virginica* correctly. Lastly, there's a 4% chance that your model will incorrectly identify an *Iris-versicolor* as an *Iris-virginica*.

Keep it at that level of detail when explaining your results to your business users. Explain that this was based on training data, and you expect that the results may be a little worse when applied to data that the model has never seen before.

> **Important tip**
> The larger the sample size and the more representative your sample data is of the real world, the more applicable your training results will be to scoring new data points. This is one reason why it's always important to collect as much good data as you can and to make sure that your data is free from sampling bias.

Most commonly, this chart will satisfy most of your end users' questions about your model's performance. Since the AutoML-generated graph can be difficult to read, one thing you can do to improve it is recreate this graph in another tool such as PowerPoint. Regression and forecasting also have one chart that is quite powerful for presenting results.

# Visualizing the results of forecasting and regression

The predicted versus true graph, first introduced in *Chapter 4, Building an AutoML Regression Solution*, is key to presenting the results of both problem types. This graph shows the performance of your model over a range of scores. It's a little bit more difficult to explain than the confusion matrix, however, and requires you to carefully explain it to your end users. To access it, follow these steps:

1.   Navigate to AML studio at `https://ml.azure.com`.

2.   Click **Experiments** under **Assets** on the left-hand panel.

3.   Click the blue link to open `Diabetes-Sample Regression`. This is the experiment you used to train a regression model in *Chapter 4, Building an AutoML Regression Solution*.

4.   Click the blue link to open your latest run. This link is found under **Run ID** and begins with `AutoML_` followed by a unique identifier string. If there are multiple runs, use your latest run.

5.   Click **Models** near the top of your screen.

6.   Click the blue link to open the name of your highest-performing model under **Algorithm name**. It is likely either **StackEnsemble** or **VotingEnsemble**. You will know it's your highest-performing model because it will be the only one with the **View explanation** link.

7.   Click **Metrics** near the top of your screen.

8.   Check the boxes for **mean_absolute_percentage error** and **predicted_true**. You should see a chart similar to the one in the following figure:

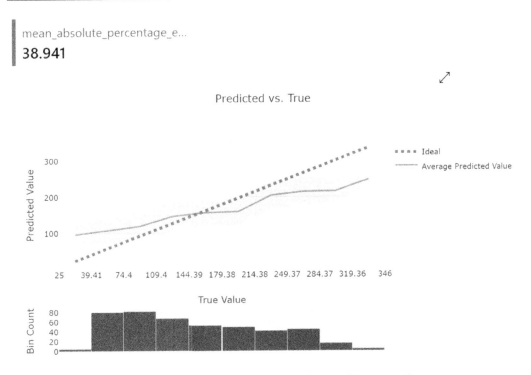

mean_absolute_percentage_e...
**38.941**

Figure 12.6 – Regression/forecasting results for your business end users

**Mean absolute percentage error** (**MAPE**) is usually the best regression metric to use with business errors. In this case, it shows that your AutoML model is usually 39.4% off, not especially impressive compared to your near-perfect Iris model. Business people tend to find MAPE to be the easiest metric to understand, as it doesn't require a background in statistics or a deep understanding of standard deviation or variance.

The predicted versus true graph shows how well your model performs at predicting scores across a range of values. Ideally, you want your blue line (**Average Predicted Value**) to match your green line (**Ideal**). At the very least, you want most of your green line (**Ideal**) to fall within the shaded boundaries around the blue line (**Average Predicted Value**).

You want to explain that for scores of 74.4 to around 250, your model does a pretty good job of predicting the true score. Outside of that range, your model performs worse, tending to overpredict true scores beneath 74.4 and underpredict scores above 250. Use the following histogram to point out how the training data was distributed. Perhaps collecting more sample data points at the higher end and lower end of the spectrum will improve your model.

Occasionally, someone with a background in statistics may be among your end users. If this is the case, you also want to show them the residuals graph that you can obtain by checking the **Residuals** box. They will want to know if your model shows evidence of bias, and by showing a bell-shaped residuals histogram as shown in the following figure, you can put their minds at ease:

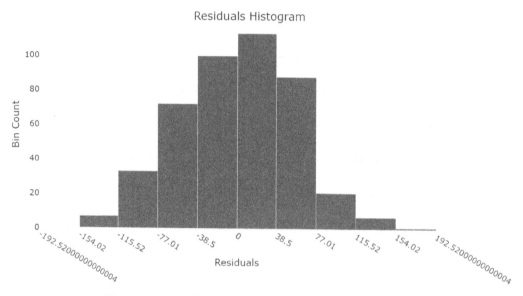

Figure 12.7 – Residuals histogram for regression and forecasting

Forecasting is identical to regression in terms of presenting results; they use identical graphs. By showing the right visualization to your end users, you can assuage them of any concerns they have about performance. However, they usually ask a follow-up question. *How does your model actually work?* To answer that question, you need to use AutoML's built-in explainability features.

# Explaining AutoML results to your business

To realize business value, your AutoML models must be implemented and used by the business. A common obstacle to implementation is a lack of trust stemming from a lack of understanding of how ML works. At the same time, explaining the ins and outs of how individual ML algorithms work is a poor way to gain trust. Throwing math symbols and complicated statistics at end users will not work unless they already have a deep background in mathematics.

Instead, use AutoML's inbuilt explainability. As long as you enable explainability when training models, you can say exactly which features AutoML is using to generate predictions. In general, it's a good practice to do the following four things:

- Always enable explainability when training any AutoML model.
- When presenting results to the business, first show performance, then show explainability.
- Rank the features in order of most to least important.
- Drop any unimportant features from future training runs.

Simpler models are easier to understand and lead to faster acceptance among end users. For this reason, you should always emphasize which features the model is using to train.

In order to access explainability, use the following steps:

1. Navigate to AML studio at `https://ml.azure.com`.
2. Click **Experiments** under **Assets** on the left-hand panel.
3. Click the blue link to open `Diabetes-Sample Regression`. This is the experiment you used to train a regression model in *Chapter 4, Building an AutoML Regression Solution.*
4. Click the blue link to open your latest run. This link is found under **Run ID** and begins with `AutoML_` followed by a unique identifier string. If there are multiple runs, use your latest.
5. Click **Models** near the top of your screen.
6. Click **View explanation**.
7. Click the first ID number under **Explanation ID**. These are explanations for your raw features that AutoML used to train your model.
8. Click **Aggregate feature importance** to see which raw features were most important in training your AutoML model.

9.  Use the scroller to see the top 10 features used to train your model as in the following figure:

**Top 1-10 features**

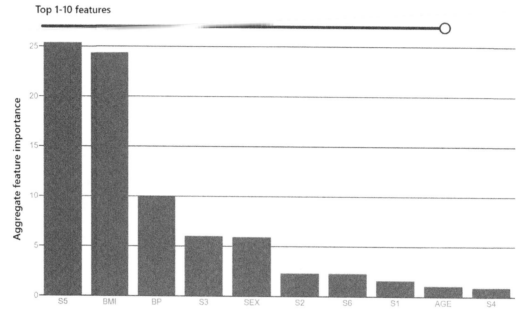

Figure 12.8 – Explainability visualization

This visualization shows that the two most important features used to train the `Diabetes-AllData-Regression-AutoML` model were S5 and BMI. Blood pressure (BP), S3, and SEX were also important, but not nearly as much as S5 and BMI. To train the model, S5 and BMI were both nearly 5 times as important as SEX. The remaining five features, S2, S6, S1, AGE, and S4, were only minor contributors to your ML model; the model didn't find them important.

> **Important tip**
>
> It's very likely that your business partners will try to infer causation from this graph. It's important to keep in mind that, without controlled scientific experimentation, explainability within any ML models can only show correlation, not causation.

Present this chart to your end users to gain their trust; it's easy to understand and shows them exactly which features are being used by AutoML to make predictions. Not only can you show them which features are being used, but you can also show them the relative importance of each of the columns of your dataset. Use this chart to tell a story that's engaging and makes sense; you can even begin by showing this chart to your business audience and asking them for their interpretations. Let them tell the story and make the solution on their own.

It's best to show explainability slides after you have explained architecture and performance. Architecture explains how the solution works in an end-to-end format without diving too deep into technical details. Performance gives your users confidence in how accurate they can expect the model to be at any given time. Logically, your users will then inquire as to how your AutoML model is making predictions. This is where you show the explainability chart instead of making the mistake of diving deep into statistics and algorithms.

Having covered architecture, performance visualizations, and explainability, you now have all of the tools you need to gain the trust and acceptance of your end users. The next section is going to expand upon the various places you can use AutoML to expand the breadth of solutions that you can develop. Even when using AutoML outside of AMLS, keep in mind to always use explainability.

# Using AutoML in other Microsoft products

In this book, you've learned how to use AutoML on Azure, but you can also use AutoML in a wider suite of Microsoft products. While you can easily create and productionalize just about any AutoML solution following the architectural patterns in the *Architecting AutoML solutions* section of this chapter, there are certain scenarios in which you may want to use AutoML on other Microsoft platforms. You can find AutoML in the following places:

- PowerBI
- Azure Synapse Analytics
- ML.NET
- HDInsight
- SQL Server
- Azure Databricks

Even though AutoML is available for these services, there are many differences of which you should be aware. Some services are code-free while others are code-only. Some services preclude you from training forecasting algorithms and others are based on entirely different ML frameworks. In this section, you will be guided through the general capabilities service by service.

# Using AutoML within PowerBI

**PowerBI** is Microsoft's business analytics solution that lets users visualize data to gain rapid insights. It's one of the most popular and powerful dashboarding tools on the market, and both the *Power BI Premium* and *Power BI Embedded* licenses of the software allow you to use AutoML directly with the tool. This is a no-code version of AutoML that works similarly to the AutoML GUI you can find in AML studio, as seen in *Figure 12.7*:

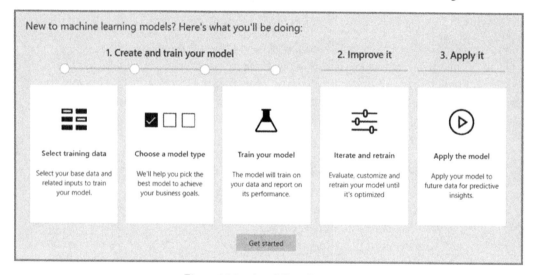

Figure 12.9 – AutoML in PowerBI

In this case, AutoML is integrated with **PowerBI dataflows**, a self-service data preparation tool. As with AutoML on Azure, you can use it to train models, save (register) models, and use models to make predictions that can be saved as new columns in your data. Unlike AutoML on Azure, it only supports regression and classification problems, not forecasting. Another feature that both services have in common is model explainability.

If you're a data analyst who regularly builds data visualization dashboards, AutoML on PowerBI is a great tool to add to your repertoire. You can easily add predictions into your data directly and visualize them with little effort. AutoML on PowerBI is also great for one-off ML jobs. Azure Synapse Analytics is another common service where data analysts use AutoML.

# Using AutoML within Azure Synapse Analytics

**Azure Synapse Analytics** (**ASA**) is Azure's premier data analytics service. It features an SQL data warehouse for big data, Spark-based analytics, and ADF-style ETL pipelines, all in one place. If you have an AMLS workspace and link it to ASA using a linked service similar to ADF, you can also use Azure AutoML directly within Synapse.

In order to use AutoML, you will need to have a Spark cluster and create Spark tables from your data. **Spark** is an open source analytics engine used to quickly process big data through distributing workloads across a cluster of virtual machines. With ASA, you can code Spark solutions with either PySpark (a version of Python), C#, Spark SQL, or Scala. Spark tables are simply data tables made within this framework.

Once you have a Spark table, all you need to do is right-click it, click **Machine Learning**, and then click **Enrich with new model**. You'll then be greeted by a very familiar interface: the AutoML GUI you first used in *Chapter 3, Training Your First AutoML Model*. Since ASA directly uses your AMLS workspace to train models using AutoML, the capabilities and user experience are identical. You can also code an AutoML solution using PySpark within ASA.

It's best to think of Synapse's AutoML capability as a shortcut rather than a separate experience from AMLS. Use it whenever you're already working within ASA and would like to quickly train an ML model using data inside an ASA data warehouse.

# Using AutoML with ML.NET

**.NET Framework** is a software development framework that lets you build applications in C#, F#, and Visual Basic. **ML.NET** lets you add ML capabilities to .NET Framework and AutoML is one of its many capabilities. You can code ML.NET solutions into your application or use the **ML.NET Model Builder** to create AutoML solutions through a guided user interface.

One interesting aspect of the ML.NET Model Builder is that you can use AutoML for a variety of predefined scenarios, including regression, classification, image classification, text classification, and object detection. You are thus not limited to only tabular data but can use automated ML with images too.

Try using AutoML within ML.NET if you are building a .NET application and would like to easily add ML to it. This is the most appropriate use case, and it assumes that you have a great deal of experience developing within .NET Framework. If you are not a .NET developer, you're better off developing your AutoML solutions within AMLS workspaces.

## Using AutoML on SQL Server, HDInsight, and Azure Databricks

AutoML is also available on a variety of other services, including **SQL Server, HDInsight, and Azure Databricks**. SQL Server is Microsoft's well-known **relational database management system** (**RDBMS**), whereas HDInsight is Azure's version of Hadoop for processing big data. Azure Databricks is the premier cloud-based Spark tool on Azure for big data processing and analytics. All three of the services can make use of Azure AutoML through Python.

When working with these tools, you will first need to create an AMLS workspace, install the AzureML-SDK, and connect your AMLS workspace to the other service. Then, you will need to code a solution. With HDInsight and Databricks, you will use Spark, whereas in SQL Server you will need to use a `sp_execute_external_script` stored procedure to run Python code. **Stored procedures** are reusable bits of SQL code that you can save and repeatedly use.

An important difference between these three services and ASA, PowerBI, and ML.NET is that there is no guided user interface option for AutoML. You must create solutions with code. If you are already building an application or data pipeline in SQL Server, HDInsight, or Azure Databricks and would like to include AutoML as part of that solution, feel free to do model training within those services.

Another use case for Azure Databricks specifically is when you would like to train an AutoML model with very large data (100 GB dataframes); it's then appropriate to run AutoML using the Spark distributed framework.

Now that you're familiar with the many different tools in which AutoML is available, you will have a lot more flexibility in building AutoML solutions. Just because you've built a solution, however, doesn't mean that people will use it. To conclude this chapter and the book, the last section will focus on strategies and techniques to gain end user acceptance, the key to realizing business value.

# Realizing business value

Realizing business value ultimately comes down to whether your business partners choose to act on the predictions of your ML models. Without action, the work of data scientists amounts to little more than a science experiment. Your business partners must be motivated and willing to make your predictions a part of their decision-making process. Gaining their trust is paramount.

In order to gain the trust of your company's decision-making leadership, you first have to ascertain what kind of solution you are building with AutoML. Some solutions are rather easily and rapidly adopted, while others are likely to encounter hard resistance.

There are key two factors that determine how readily your AutoML solution is accepted: whether your tool is replacing an existing solution and whether your tool is directly involved in an automated decision process or is assisting human decision makers. *Figure 12.8* shows how difficult it is to gain acceptance based on these factors:

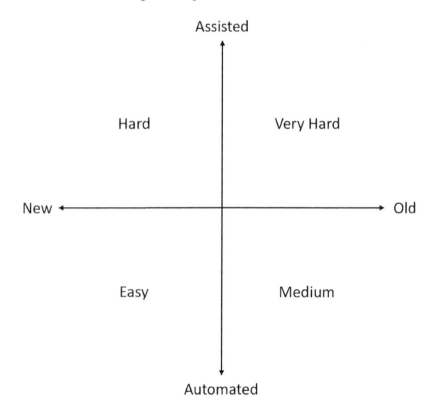

Figure 12.10– Difficulty of gaining traction with business users based on key factors

The more automated your solution is, the easier it is to gain acceptance. Processes that run under the hood, after all, are not subject to human supervision. There is no human manually deciding whether each credit card transaction is fraudulent; this task can only be accomplished by automated processes.

Since there's no human in the loop in the first place, you're not going to encounter resistance when trying to improve automated processes with ML models. In contrast, when you try to augment a human decision maker with AI-generated predictions, you are likely to encounter skepticism and resistance.

Likewise, entirely new solutions are much more easily accepted than tools that replace old solutions. While this is also true for replacing existing automated systems with AI solutions, this is even truer when you are trying to replace existing systems that executives and managers use to make decisions. Many people are slow to embrace change, especially change that they don't fully understand.

In this section, we'll introduce strategies to gain trust and get business users to adopt your AutoML-based solution based on the key factors.

# Getting the business to adopt a new, automated solution

This is easy. Imagine your company is building a new sales portal and they want to create a system that automatically generates product recommendations for online shoppers as they browse items on your website. You propose to build a recommendation system training an ML model using AutoML and scoring the model using a real-time scoring endpoint hosted on AKS.

Very likely, the response to your proposal will be overwhelmingly positive. Your executive leadership will be impressed by your adoption of cutting-edge AI technology. Business management in charge of the project will be happy just to have a high-performing solution. Your IT department will be interested in learning the new technology and will be more than happy to help you implement a new, high-profile project.

If there's any resistance at all, it will be from people who will want to get a better understanding of how your AI solution works. For this reason, it's recommended that you provide model explanations along with a general overview of how ML works and how AutoML works. People are more likely to support your project if they can explain how it works to other people, so work at developing that understanding.

# Getting the business to replace an older, automated process

Replacing an older automated solution with one driven by ML is a bit more difficult than creating an entirely new process. This is usually because business users already understand how the old process works. If you are trying to replace a rules-based system, based on a series of if-then statements, this is even more difficult because the old process was easier for a human being to understand.

In this case, your best strategy is to compare the results of your new AutoML-based solution with the results of the old solution side by side for weeks or months. Do not immediately shut down the old process; you should run both processes simultaneously until your end users are convinced and have faith in the output of your ML model. Only then should you turn off and permanently shut down the old solution.

You may think that explaining how ML and AutoML works would be your best strategy here, but end users used to one system mistakenly assume that AI works similarly to the old solution. Dispelling this notion can be difficult and the extreme difference in approach may make some users lose trust. For this reason, it's best to orient your end users to results first before providing them with deep, detailed explanations. Once they trust your results, they will naturally open up to the process.

# Getting the business to adopt a new, decision-assistance tool

One key thing to realize when providing AI-generated recommendations or predictions to a group of decision makers is that, for the problem at hand, they've been making decisions for years. They may not yet have a tool, but they do have their gut intuition and years of experience. Thus, they're often skeptical of any new tool or technology that proclaims it will help them in their job. Remember that no one ever rose to the top of a company by making bad decisions.

In this case, it's best to try to assuage their fears by assuring them that this is just a tool to provide them with predictions or recommendations. It's advice. It may be AI-generated, but at the end of the day, advice is advice, and the decision ultimately still rests in their hands.

One analogy that's useful is that, in the world of chess, AI may beat grandmasters, but grandmasters assisted by AI can beat AI. Humans ultimately remain in control.

You should also stress the statistical nature of ML-generated predictions. They are not perfect, nor are they infallible. If you forecast market share to fall to 11.3% next month with a 95% confidence interval of plus/minus 0.2% and it actually falls to 11.1%, your model was correct and within the expected range.

If your model tells you a certain basketball player has a 70% chance of doing well on your team and that player fails, then your model was still right, but the 30% chance happened.

> **Important tip**
>
> When making an AI for decision assistance, such as most forecasting models, it's important that your model is as accurate as possible and doesn't show wide swings in accuracy. Nothing loses trust as fast as a widely fluctuating model.

By stressing that you are only providing advice and that the advice is statistical in nature, your model has a higher chance of being used by the business over a long period of time. They won't feel threatened if it's just advice and they won't stop using your model when the statistically less likely thing happens because they understand that it will happen once in a while.

# Getting the business to replace an old decision assistance tool

Perhaps the most difficult type of project regarding gaining acceptance from a business audience is when you replace an old, trusted tool with one driven by ML. In this case, the tool you are replacing may have existed for many years.

Many experienced users are likely to object to a new process or solution, irrespective of how much it improves the current state. This is due to **familiarity bias**, the preference of human beings of the familiar to the unfamiliar.

Overcoming familiarity bias and getting business users to adopt your solution is quite a challenge and needs to be approached systematically. First, like replacing an older, automated process, you should not shut down the old solution; you need to keep it running so you can compare results side by side. If you do not do this, it is likely that experienced users will negatively and unfairly compare your tool to the old solution; they need to see that it is an improvement upon the old solution.

Comparing results side by side is necessary but not sufficient to gaining end user acceptance. Additionally, you need the users to understand your AutoML-generated solution.

One common criticism of AI solutions is that it is difficult to understand how they work. In contrast, the system you are replacing will have had years to teach its users its ins and outs. Thus, you should present explainability slides at the forefront of your solution; you should also explain the architecture and explain exactly how AutoML works, when you plan on retraining models, and how you plan on continually evaluating and monitoring the solution.

A person-by-person approach to gaining trust will also go a long way to your solution's success. Only present your solution to the entire group after you've had a series of one-on-one meetings with all end users individually.

If there are too many end users, identify and meet the most influential people within the group. By addressing their concerns, training them on their solutions, and encouraging them to talk to other end users, you will be able to build a group of people who will champion your solution, increasing its chances of long-term success.

In order of difficulty, from easiest to hardest, to gain end-user trust and guarantee adoption over time, here's the list of solution types: an AutoML solution for a new automated process, an AutoML solution replacing an automated process, an AutoML solution to help human beings make decisions, an AutoML solution to replace an existing decision-assistance tool. The following table provides a summary:

|  | Difficulty of gaining trust | Who is most likely to offer resistance | How to overcome resistance |
|---|---|---|---|
| **Completely new automated process** | Easy as the process is being created with ML in mind | Resistance is unlikely if your ML model performs as expected | Build an ML model that exceeds expectations and works well |
| **Replacing an old, automated process** | Medium as you are replacing an older process | People who built or oversee the output of the older process | Compare results of the old and new process side-by-side |
| **Completely new assisted decision making process** | Hard as many people may not trust AI generated output | People who feel their decision making is threatened by AI | Stress that AI exists as an advisor to enhance their own decisions |
| **Replacing an old, assisted decision making tool** | Extremely difficult as users will fondly recall the old tool | People who cannot understand the tech behind the new tool | Emphasize the explainability of your AutoML-built solution |

Figure 12.11 – How to gain trust based on the type of AutoML solution

As you can see, just because you build a highly performing AutoML solution does not mean it will be adopted by the business. You also need to work just as hard at gaining your end users' trust. By identifying the type of AutoML solution you are building and following the appropriate guidelines, you will be able to gain trust one end user at a time. Once enough people champion your solution, it will be well on its way to becoming a trusted tool set up for long-term success and adoption.

## Summary

Gaining end user acceptance can be difficult, but having the right approach can make it a lot easier. Walking your end users through an architectural diagram, carefully explaining the model's performance to them using the right metrics, and spending time explaining which features the model is using to make predictions are all key to selling your solution to end users. Furthermore, you can tailor your message based on what type of solution you are building to gain end user trust.

You are now at the end of the book and I'd like you to reflect on the journey. You've acquired many technical skills, including the ability to train AutoML models, deploy AutoML models for scoring in batch and real-time scoring, and design, create, and implement full end-to-end AutoML solutions. You also have an approach to sell those solutions to your business partners, gain their trust, and, ultimately, realize value. By crafting powerful solutions with AutoML on Azure, you'll be able to make a lasting impact and advance your career.

Packt.com

Subscribe to our online digital library for full access to over 7,000 books and videos, as well as industry leading tools to help you plan your personal development and advance your career. For more information, please visit our website.

## Why subscribe?

- Spend less time learning and more time coding with practical eBooks and Videos from over 4,000 industry professionals

- Improve your learning with Skill Plans built especially for you

- Get a free eBook or video every month

- Fully searchable for easy access to vital information

- Copy and paste, print, and bookmark content

Did you know that Packt offers eBook versions of every book published, with PDF and ePub files available? You can upgrade to the eBook version at packt.com and as a print book customer, you are entitled to a discount on the eBook copy. Get in touch with us at customercare@packtpub.com for more details.

At www.packt.com, you can also read a collection of free technical articles, sign up for a range of free newsletters, and receive exclusive discounts and offers on Packt books and eBooks.

# Other Books You May Enjoy

If you enjoyed this book, you may be interested in these other books by Packt:

**Automated Machine Learning**

Adnan Masood

ISBN: 978-1-80056-768-9

- Explore AutoML fundamentals, underlying methods, and techniques
- Assess AutoML aspects such as algorithm selection, auto featurization, and hyperparameter tuning in an applied scenario
- Find out the difference between cloud and operations support systems (OSS)
- Implement AutoML in enterprise cloud to deploy ML models and pipelines
- Build explainable AutoML pipelines with transparency

**Learn Amazon SageMaker**

Chaitanya Hazarey, Javier Ramirez

ISBN: 978-1-80020-891-9

- Create and automate end-to-end machine learning workflows on Amazon Web Services (AWS)
- Become well-versed with data annotation and preparation techniques
- Use AutoML features to build and train machine learning models with AutoPilot
- Create models using built-in algorithms and frameworks and your own code
- Train computer vision and NLP models using real-world examples

# Packt is searching for authors like you

If you're interested in becoming an author for Packt, please visit authors.packtpub.com and apply today. We have worked with thousands of developers and tech professionals, just like you, to help them share their insight with the global tech community. You can make a general application, apply for a specific hot topic that we are recruiting an author for, or submit your own idea.

# Leave a review - let other readers know what you think

Please share your thoughts on this book with others by leaving a review on the site that you bought it from. If you purchased the book from Amazon, please leave us an honest review on this book's Amazon page. This is vital so that other potential readers can see and use your unbiased opinion to make purchasing decisions, we can understand what our customers think about our products, and our authors can see your feedback on the title that they have worked with Packt to create. It will only take a few minutes of your time, but is valuable to other potential customers, our authors, and Packt. Thank you!

# Index

Printed in Great Britain
by Amazon

83527134R00194